Elon University

JUL 0 1 2010

NO LONGER THE
PROPERTY OF
ELON UNIVERSITY LIBRARY

D1520061

BEING THERE EVEN WHEN YOU ARE NOT: LEADING THROUGH STRATEGY, STRUCTURES, AND SYSTEMS

MONOGRAPHS IN LEADERSHIP AND MANAGEMENT

Series Editor: James G. (Jerry) Hunt

MONOGRAPHS IN LEADERSHIP AND MANAGEMENT
VOLUME 4

BEING THERE EVEN WHEN YOU ARE NOT: LEADING THROUGH STRATEGY, STRUCTURES, AND SYSTEMS

EDITED BY

ROBERT HOOIJBERG
International Institute for Management Development, Lausanne, Switzerland

JAMES G. (JERRY) HUNT
Rawls College of Business Administration, Lubbock, TX, USA

JOHN ANTONAKIS
Faculty of Management and Economics, University of Lausanne, Switzerland

KIMBERLY B. BOAL
Rawls College of Business Administration, Lubbock, TX, USA

with NANCY LANE
International Institute for Management Development, Lausanne, Switzerland

ELSEVIER
JAI

Amsterdam – Boston – Heidelberg – London – New York – Oxford
Paris – San Diego – San Francisco – Singapore – Sydney – Tokyo
JAI Press is an imprint of Elsevier

JAI Press is an imprint of Elsevier
Linacre House, Jordan Hill, Oxford OX2 8DP, UK
Radarweg 29, PO Box 211, 1000 AE Amsterdam, The Netherlands
525 B Street, Suite 1900, San Diego, CA 92101-4495, USA

First edition 2007

Copyright © 2007 Elsevier Ltd. All rights reserved

No part of this publication may be reproduced, stored in a retrieval system
or transmitted in any form or by any means electronic, mechanical, photocopying,
recording or otherwise without the prior written permission of the publisher

Permissions may be sought directly from Elsevier's Science & Technology Rights
Department in Oxford, UK: phone (+44) (0) 1865 843830; fax (+44) (0) 1865 853333;
email: permissions@elsevier.com. Alternatively you can submit your request online by
visiting the Elsevier web site at http://elsevier.com/locate/permissions, and selecting
Obtaining permission to use Elsevier material

Notice
No responsibility is assumed by the publisher for any injury and/or damage to persons
or property as a matter of products liability, negligence or otherwise, or from any use
or operation of any methods, products, instructions or ideas contained in the material
herein. Because of rapid advances in the medical sciences, in particular, independent
verification of diagnoses and drug dosages should be made

British Library Cataloguing in Publication Data
A catalogue record for this book is available from the British Library

ISBN: 978-0-7623-1332-7
ISSN: 1479-3571 (Series)

For information on all JAI Press publications
visit our website at books.elsevier.com

Transferred to digital printing 2007

Working together to grow
libraries in developing countries

www.elsevier.com | www.bookaid.org | www.sabre.org

ELSEVIER   BOOK AID
International   Sabre Foundation

DEDICATIONS

John Antonakis: To SFA, AFA, AFA, BFA, MFA, RFA and the unnamed bunnies.

Robert Hooijberg: Personally, I thank my wife Brenda Steinberg for her support and encouragement in writing this book and my young daughters Marta and Brianna for asking simple, pointed questions ("What is strategic leadership dad?") that forced me to formulate clear answers.

Nancy: To Pascal and Raphael.

Jerry Hunt: To my wife, Donna, who provided more than moral support.

From Kimberly B. Boal: For my wife Frances.

CONTENTS

LIST OF CONTRIBUTORS

John Antonakis	Faculty of Management and Economics, University of Lausanne, Switzerland
B.R. Baliga	Babcock Graduate School of Management, Wake Forest University, Winston-Salem, NC, USA
Michèle Barnett Berg	IMD – International Institute for Management Development, Lausanne, Switzerland
Corey Billington	IMD – International Institute for Management Development, Lausanne, Switzerland
Kimberly B. Boal	Texas Tech University, Lubbock, TX, USA
Paul V. Broeckx	Corporate Human Resources division, Nestlé, Vevey, Switzerland
Heike Bruch	Institute for Leadership and Human Resources Management of the University of St. Gallen, Switzerland
Mary Sue Coleman	University of Michigan, MI, USA
David V. Day	Lee Kong Chian School of Business, Singapore Management University, Singapore
Galit Eilam-Shamir	Ono College, Israel
Daniel A. Gruber	Stephen M. Ross School of Business, University of Michigan, MI, USA
Robert Hogan	Hogan Assessment Systems, Tulsa, OK, USA
Robert Hooijberg	IMD – International Institute for Management Development, Lausanne, Switzerland

James G. (Jerry) Hunt	Institute for Leadership Research, Texas Tech University, Lubbock, TX, USA
Kazuo Ichijo	IMD – International Institute for Management Development, Lausanne, Switzerland
Robert B. Kaiser	Kaplan DeVries Inc., Greensboro, NC, USA
Tracey Keys	IMD – International Institute for Management Development, Lausanne, Switzerland
Nancy Lane	IMD – International Institute for Management Development, Lausanne, Switzerland
Thomas Malnight	IMD – International Institute for Management Development, Lausanne, Switzerland
Russ Marion	Clemson University, SC, USA
Patricia M.G. O'Connor	Center for Creative Leadership, Singapore
Timo J. Santalainen	STRATNET, Geneva and Helsinki School of Economics, Finland
Boas Shamir	Hebrew University of Jerusalem, Israel
Gretchen M. Spreitzer	Stephen M. Ross School of Business, University of Michigan, MI, USA
Mary Uhl-Bien	Gallup Leadership Institute, University of Nebraska-Lincoln, NE, USA
Ellen Van Velsor	Center for Creative Leadership, Greensboro, NC, USA
Luc Verburgh	Wellant College, The Netherlands

ACKNOWLEDGMENTS

We are very grateful for the financial assistance of (a) the Swiss National Science foundation (Grant 10C012-104433/1), (b) IMD and (c) the Institute of Research in Management, whose generous funding and support made the 2004 Real Leaders (CEO Strategic Leadership) symposium possible. This book is based in part on the papers presented at this symposium. We are also grateful for IMD's additional financial, organizational and intellectual support in the later stages of writing the book. We would also like to thank the IMD Editing Team – Beverley Lennox, Lindsay McTeague and Michelle Perrinjaquet – for their outstanding work.

CHAPTER 1

BEING THERE EVEN WHEN YOU ARE NOT: THE LEADERSHIP *OF* ORGANIZATIONS

Robert Hooijberg, James G. (Jerry) Hunt,
John Antonakis and Kimberly B. Boal

As we write a book about leadership, we should first share our premises. For us leadership means getting performance beyond expectations through people. First, this definition emphasizes that we see performance as the ultimate objective of leadership. Second, the definition highlights that leaders should motivate and enable people to perform beyond what they thought possible. As leaders we need to encourage and enable our people to share their best ideas and efforts. If we do that then we believe that the total of their efforts and ideas will almost always surpass what we could have conceived ourselves.

Most leadership researchers have focused on (a version of) this definition by trying to better understand how leaders influence others to follow them and most of this research has focused on direct ways of influencing (potential) followers. Leaders at the strategic apex of large organizations, however, rarely have the opportunity or the possibility to personally influence all those who work in their organization. The challenge then becomes, as the title of our book indicates: Being there even when you are not. How do strategic leaders reach the members of their organizations to share their vision and values, engage with them, and make them see the world their

Being There Even When You Are Not: Leading Through Strategy, Structures, and Systems
Monographs in Leadership and Management, Volume 4, 1–9
Copyright © 2007 by Elsevier Ltd.
ISSN: 1479-3571/doi:10.1016/S1479-3571(07)04021-7
All rights of reproduction in any form reserved

way? Our subtitle "Leading through strategy, structures, and systems" expresses our view of how you can be there even when you are not. That is, how you can create conditions that enable and encourage people to share their best ideas and efforts. Although we are not the first to raise these questions, they have received relatively little attention in the leadership literature.

Late in the 20th century, the well-known sociologist Robert Dubin (1979) argued strongly that much of the leadership research was misdirected. Instead of focusing on organizational problems, it tended to emphasize interpersonal, face-to-face relations. Although he provided no data, he further contended that the vast majority of leadership activity in organizations was non face-to-face (Dubin, 1979, p. 226) and that the study of individual leadership had not advanced the study of leadership in organizations very much. For him, the findings, though statistically significant, were trivial (p. 227).

To further reinforce his point, he coined the terms leadership *of* organizations and leadership *in* organizations. Leadership *of* referred to the non face-to-face activities emphasized at the top of the organization (now commonly termed "strategic leadership"). In contrast, leadership *in* indicated the interpersonal or face-to-face leadership (often termed "supervisory leadership") emphasized at lower levels in the hierarchy.

Since Dubin's publication, leadership researchers have not really picked up on his challenge to focus more on the leadership *of* organizations. We take up the gauntlet in this book and have reflected the challenge in both the book title and the content. The exception we make to Dubin's distinction is that leadership *in* takes place at all levels of the organization, not just at the lower levels.

The *of* and *in* designations are extremely useful in describing the two kinds of leadership when dealing with organizations, if – as in this book – one wants to reflect them as they really are. Not differentiating them assumes that all leadership is interpersonal or face-to-face. A moment's reflection reveals that this is not so. At the same time, of course, virtually all leaders engage in leadership *in* organizations. The CEOs and their management team and/or immediate subordinates engage in interpersonal, face-to-face leadership. And sometimes, of course, supervisory leadership does not use face-to-face activities. However, by and large, the *of* and *in* labels are highly descriptive of two distinct kinds of leadership. Below we summarize the key activities differentiating them.

DIFFERENTIATING LEADERSHIP *IN* AND *OF* ORGANIZATIONS

A key distinction, mentioned by Dubin (1979, p. 227), is "leadership at a distance." When Dubin was writing, there was little research on this topic. More recently, however, there has been an upsurge in leadership-at-a-distance work. We see a major review by Antonakis and Atwater (2002), following an earlier one by Napier and Ferris (1993), along with work by authors such as Shamir (1995) and Waldman and Yammarino (1999).

Antonakis and Atwater (2002) conceptualized distance in terms of leader–follower physical distance, leader–follower social distance (differences in rank, status, and authority) and degree of leader–follower interaction frequency. How distant the leader is or should be from followers is contingent on the situation. For Antonakis and Atwater, leadership knows no physical barriers – leaders can influence direct and indirect followers, as long as they use the appropriate means to do so. These means include electronic communications; subordinate leaders (who in turn influence others below them); the impression-management techniques of the leader (e.g., symbolic activities, rhetoric), the leader's qualities and characteristics; and the organizational systems and controls.

Along with the importance of leadership at a distance, Dubin argues that leadership must deal with the universal problems of organizational systems – coordination and integration. For him, a key characteristic of leadership is to constantly "evaluate the coordinating functions and mechanisms of an organization and to introduce the necessary changes that will improve their outcomes" (p. 229). Dubin also argues that adaptation is crucial. To paraphrase and then quote him, such adaptation is about changes generated within the organization and the environment where organizations, particularly work organizations, are systems attempting to maintain stability, and stability is at best short-lived or a myth. It is "one of the functions of leadership to recognize the conditions affecting the organization that require adaptation on its part, and then to provide, or at least select and/or approve, the kinds of viable alternatives that will make the adaptations effective" (p. 229).

He also emphasizes the leader's role as being one of dealing with the conflict generated by the differential points of view and differential objectives of those who collectively engage in a complex division of labor (e.g., sales versus production people). This kind of conflict is inherent in the organization's design, in contrast to the various kinds of intra and interpersonal conflict often focused on in interpersonal, face-to-face leadership activities.

Finally, Dubin argues that "the fourth universal organizational problem is to keep the goal(s) of the organization clear for its participants, and where necessary, select and legitimate new goals" (p. 230). These days, researchers refer to this more as the formulation and communication of the vision of the organization. The vision should provide the members of an organization with a sense of the direction of the organization beyond immediate, day-to-day concerns, as well as representing a clear response to existing and anticipated environmental threats and opportunities.

Of course, Dubin is not alone in arguing for these kinds of activities at the organization's strategic apex, or dominant coalition, as it is sometimes called. That work is embedded in studies of differing management/leadership requirements at different organizational levels. We will simply touch on such work to convey its flavor as it relates to leadership *of* and *in* and as it informs the leadership activities emphasized in this book. One of the more informative works here is Katz and Kahn (1978). It is widely cited and conceptually elegant. Its authors argue in terms of three types of leadership occurring in organizational hierarchies:

1. *Origination of structure (origination)* – introduction of structural change or policy formulation.
2. *Interpolation of structure (interpolation)* – piecing together the incompleteness of current organizational structure through implementation of policies to handle immediate problems.
3. *Applying existing structure (administration)* – using current formally established structure to keep effectively operating and moving the organization forward, that is, the routine application of prescribed remedies for predicted problems.

One can see the increasing face-to-face leadership requirements at lower hierarchical levels. In other words, the amount of discretion to originate and substantially operate structure becomes increasingly less as one moves down the hierarchy. This also means, as Katz (1955), Mann (1965), Mintzberg (1980), and others, have argued that different mixes of skills are required at different levels of the organization.

Jaques and his colleagues (e.g., Jacobs & Jaques, 1987; Jaques & Clement, 1991; Jaques, 1989) have argued that as managerial leaders move up the hierarchy, they need themselves to possess increasing levels of cognitive capacity (complexity) built on top of the interpersonal, face-to-face capacity required at lower levels to handle increasingly more demanding critical tasks. At the very top of large-scale organizations the CEO, who is seen as operating in a nearly unbounded world environment, must enact a vision with a time span of 20 years or more. Such a long time span becomes progressively shorter, until it is in the nature of three months or so at the production supervisor level.

In sum, we see a minimum of four key distinctions between leadership *of* and leadership *in* organizations: leadership at a distance, systems focus, leading through the design of the organization, and the formulation and communication of the vision of the organization. We also see that the leadership *of* organizations requires a distinctly different competency set than leadership *in* organizations. While both formulating a vision and – to some extent – leadership at a distance have started to receive attention, leading through systems and processes and organizational design have received little attention as strategic leadership tools. Although formulating a vision has received attention, communicating and cascading it has received much less attention. It is on these topics that we focus in this book.

Let us state upfront that we acknowledge that the interpersonal, face-to-face competencies remain important, and perhaps even increase in importance, as one moves up the organizational hierarchy. In this book, however, we focus especially on the strategic leadership requirements and competencies (i.e., the leadership *of* organizations) because this area traditionally has not received as much attention from leadership researchers as leadership *in* organizations. In doing so, we emphasize the architect role of the strategic leader. Just as an architect designs the layout of a house, the strategic leader designs the layout of his or her organization. The architect role includes, among many others, choosing markets in which to compete, whether to group people functionally or by product, how to develop leaders of the future, how to shape the organizational and environmental views of the organization's stakeholders, and how to not only share a vision but also truly engage people in that vision.

We would like to say one word of caution. We have juxtaposed the words strategic apex and leadership. Furthermore, we often equate the term manager with leader. We want to make it clear that we do not assume that just because someone has reached a top-level position in an organization that he/she has great leadership abilities. We do mean to say that we expect leadership from people in these positions and that the indirect *effective* leadership *of* organizations that we discuss in this book should have a prominent position in their portfolio of leadership skills.

In this book we cannot address all the areas that deserve a strategic leader's architectural attention; we explore six of them. Below we give a preview of each of the book's six parts, which have been designed to address the critical task and competency requirements of the leadership *of* organizations.

THE STRUCTURE OF THE BOOK

The book has six major parts, plus an introduction by the editors and some concluding thoughts. The first chapter in each part provides a short theoretical introduction to the main theme of that part. The following chapter(s) – usually two – highlight the practical application of the theory. The six parts are briefly described below:

1. *Developing leadership capacity.* In this part we focus on the structures, systems and processes that support and encourage the development of leaders in the organization. David Day introduces the theme, exploring the social architecture most conducive to the development of leadership throughout the organization and the role strategic leaders need to play to create such architecture. The next two chapters show how two large organizations have gone about changing their social architecture in order to develop both a broader and a more engaged leadership cadre. Ellen Van Velsor and Patricia O'Connor show how a large US service organization has started to change its social architecture by creatively combining empowerment, learning and performance orientations. Paul Broeckx and Robert Hooijberg show how Nestlé, the Swiss-based global fast-moving consumer goods company, has started to replace the most limiting aspects of the traditional hierarchy to more fully engage the full human capacity of its workforce.

2. *Knowledge management.* Kimberly Boal examines what companies and strategic leaders can do to enhance knowledge acquisition, retention, and dissemination. In doing so, he explores how leaders create environments where people throughout the organization utilize both strong and weak network relationships in the pursuit of finding, exploiting, and protecting new knowledge and ideas. Kazuo Ichijo then hones in on how strategic leaders at electronics manufacturer Sharp Corporation developed processes, systems, and structures that allowed the company to build and exploit its knowledge of and competence in LCD technology.

3. *Managing meaning.* As CEOs now communicate with a wide variety of stakeholders, it has become increasingly difficult to ensure that the

intended meaning of their messages is received. Boas Shamir focuses on how leaders engage in the management of meanings in order to (1) justify their actions and the changes they introduce to the organization; (2) recruit followers and motivate members of the organization to support their actions; and (3) create shared perceptions and interpretations so that members' actions are guided by a common definition of the situation. Heike Bruch, Boas Shamir and Galit Eilam-Shamir show how the leader of a large Swiss-based company actively managed the views, interpretations and energy of more than 100,000 employees through weekly e-mail letters when the company faced grave financial difficulties. Gretchen Spreitzer, Mary Sue Coleman and Daniel Gruber show how an incoming university president dealt with an ongoing lawsuit regarding the university's use of affirmative action in its admissions processes and worked with various stakeholders to firmly establish the university's identity.

4. *Leadership discretion.* Organizational structures, systems and processes can and do limit the discretionary decision-making space of all involved in organizational life. However, high up in organizations leaders have significant discretion in making decisions. Robert Kaiser and Robert Hogan explore the dark side of what might happen if strategic leaders use their discretionary freedom for personal rather than organizational benefit. Timo Santalainen and Ram Baliga present a real example of discretionary leadership gone bad in an NGO that looks quite healthy on the outside. They refer to the phenomenon of a financially successful company with a sick leader as the "healthy-sick organization." We juxtapose this chapter with the one by Corey Billington and Michèle Barnett Berg to show how Duncan Covington at computer products, services, and solutions company IQ used his discretionary freedom for the good of the company. Covington inherited a sick organization and introduced key systems, structures, and processes to bring it back to health.

5. *Cascading vision for real commitment.* Although creating blueprints and structures, systems and processes may be appealing and useful, successful implementation throughout the organization is a major issue. John Antonakis and Robert Hooijberg explore how strategic leaders can cascade their vision throughout their organizations in ways that truly engage leaders at all levels. Tom Malnight and Tracey Keys show how Carlsberg Breweries successfully cascaded the must-win battles identified by its top management team through all of its major regions in the world. Luc Verburgh and Nancy Lane show how the new general director of a group of 16 secondary,

vocationally oriented schools cascaded his strategic vision and teaching philosophy to the directors and then the teachers of these schools.

6. *Leadership in complex environments.* This part aims to push thinking on strategic leadership one step further. In all of the previous parts we follow quite a hierarchical model, in which leaders at the top outline the vision, the strategy, and the key implementation tools. Here, Russ Marion and Mary Uhl-Bien challenge the validity of this view of strategic leadership. They argue that strategic leadership is about interacting effectively within a complex interplay of environmental and organizational forces to enable fit environments and adaptive organizations. For them this means that strategic leaders need to pay significant attention to the interdependence between their organizations and both competitors and other relevant organizations in the niches in which they operate. It also means that they need to develop adaptive leadership capacity far down in the organization and show a willingness to follow those leaders at the lower levels. Marion and Uhl-Bien then argue both that strategic leaders have a more interdependent view of organizations and that they have a greater willingness to act as followers than we see in any of the leadership and/or strategy literature. As this approach to strategic leadership is quite new, we do not have application chapters here.

Together these chapters present a diverse set of ideas as to how senior leaders can use strategies, systems and structures to get performance beyond expectations through people.

REFERENCES

Antonakis, J., & Atwater, L. (2002). Leader distance: A review and a proposed theory. *The Leadership Quarterly, 13*, 673–704.
Dubin, R. (1979). Metaphors of leadership: An overview. In: J. G. Hunt & L. L. Larson (Eds), *Crosscurrents in leadership* (pp. 225–238). Carbondale, IL: Southern Illinois University Press.
Jacobs, T., & Jaques, E. (1987). Leadership in complex systems. In: J. Zeidner (Ed.), *Human productivity enhancement* (pp. 7–65). New York, NY: Praeger.
Jaques, E. (1989). *Requisite organization.* Arlington, VA: Cason Hall.
Jaques, E., & Clement, S. D. (1991). *Executive leadership.* Arlington, VA: Cason Hall.
Katz, D., & Kahn, R. L. (1978). *The social psychology of organizations.* New York, NY: Wiley.
Katz, R. L. (1955). Skills of an effective administrator. *Harvard Business Review, 33*(1), 33–42.
Mann, F. C. (1965). Towards an understanding of the leadership role in formal organization. In: R. Dubin, G. C. Homans, F. C. Mann & D. C. Miller (Eds), *Leadership and productivity.* San Francisco, CA: Chandler.
Mintzberg, H. (1980). *The nature of organizations.* Englewood Cliffs, NJ: Prentice Hall.

Napier, B. J., & Ferris, G. R. (1993). Distance in organizations. *Human Resource Management Review, 3,* 321–357.

Shamir, B. (1995). Social distance and charisma: Theoretical notes and an exploratory study. *Leadership Quarterly, 6,* 19–47.

Waldman, D. A., & Yammarino, F. J. (1999). CEO charismatic leadership: Levels-of-management and levels-of-analysis effects. *Academy of Management Review, 24,* 266–285.

PART I: DEVELOPING LEADERSHIP CAPACITY

In this part we focus on the structures, systems, and processes that support and encourage the development of leaders in the organization. David Day introduces the theme, exploring the social architecture most conducive to the development of leadership throughout the organization and the role strategic leaders need to play to create such architecture. The next two chapters show how two large organizations have gone about changing their social architecture in order to develop both a broader and a more engaged leadership cadre. Ellen Van Velsor and Patricia O'Connor show how a large US service organization has started to change its social architecture by creatively combining empowerment, learning and performance orientations. Paul Broeckx and Robert Hooijberg show how Nestlé, the Swiss-based global fast-moving consumer goods company, has started to replace the most limiting aspects of the traditional hierarchy to more fully engage the full human capacity of its workforce.

CHAPTER 2

STRUCTURING THE ORGANIZATION FOR LEADERSHIP DEVELOPMENT

David V. Day

ABSTRACT

It is proposed that the desirable goal of structuring the organization for leadership development has less to do with formal hierarchical structure than with the informal norms and networks that support organizational systems and processes. In this manner, strategic leaders need to think of themselves as social architects in helping to generate the kinds of normative conditions that facilitate leadership development. In particular, priority concerns for leadership development are issues such as what are the culture and climate for learning and development? and how healthy is the interpersonal context in which the shared work of the organization takes place?

The purpose of leadership development is to enable experiences that contribute to the ongoing growth and development of individual leaders, teams, and entire organizations. To this end, leadership development should "broaden the horizons of participants so that they can see and understand different realities or alternative courses of action" (Vicere & Fulmer, 1998,

Being There Even When You Are Not: Leading Through Strategy, Structures, and Systems
Monographs in Leadership and Management, Volume 4, 13–30
Copyright © 2007 by Elsevier Ltd.
All rights of reproduction in any form reserved
ISSN: 1479-3571/doi:10.1016/S1479-3571(07)04001-1

p. 17). Leadership development should also expand the capacity of individuals and teams to be effective in leadership roles and processes, particularly those related to setting direction, creating alignment, and maintaining commitment (Van Velsor & McCauley, 2004). The central problem for strategic leaders as architects becomes one of how to best design an organization to broaden horizons, enhance perspective taking, and build the capacity to participate in the fundamental leadership tasks of the organization.

A question worth considering is whether it makes any sense to draw a relationship between the structure of an organization – including its systems and processes – and its leadership development processes and outcomes. The short answer is yes (otherwise this would be a very brief chapter); however, a somewhat longer answer is needed to clarify what is thought to be the essence of this relationship. The gist of this connection rests with the role of experience in leadership development. It has been recognized for quite some time that on-the-job experience is perceived by executives as the most potent force for their development (e.g., McCall, Lombardo, & Morrison, 1988). Experts in the field of leadership development have proposed that any experience (work or otherwise) can be made more developmentally potent to the extent that it includes aspects of assessment, challenge, and support (Van Velsor & McCauley, 2004). So if the structure of an organization shapes the experiences of a developing leader by enhancing or impeding levels of assessment, challenge, and support that are embedded in an experience, then there is a likely relationship between that structure and the broader ideal of leadership development. Indeed, both practice and theory suggest that organizational structure can enhance or limit access to assessment data, the kinds of developmental challenges that are faced, and the support that a developing leader receives.

Despite the potential connection, formal organizational structure alone is an inadequate lens through which to approach leadership development. As an example, consider the case of Jack Welch and General Electric (GE) (oh no – not again you say!). Before he became "Saint Jack," Welch was known in the business press as "Neutron Jack" because, like a neutron bomb, he left all the buildings at GE standing but eliminated most of the people. As a result of these actions, he created the opportunity to put in place a relatively lean and flat structure, at least compared with the pre-Welch GE. But this structure by itself was insufficient for creating the kind of developmentally focused organization that he wanted. To help realize this strategic goal, Welch introduced and championed the norm of "boundaryless behavior" in order to get GE employees out of their functional silos and to reach across organizational boundaries to accomplish their work objectives more effectively.

The basic premise of creating a boundaryless organization was to remove all the barriers between different functions and to be open to the best practices and ideas from anywhere. These ideas could be from a colleague, another department, another country, and even another company. According to Welch, boundaryless behavior broadened the company's awareness and enhanced its "intellect" (Byrne, 2003). Thus, it was a revised organizational structure coupled with strong norms for open and non-hierarchical behavior that enhanced development and performance at GE. It is difficult to say whether changes to the formal structure or informal norms associated with the corporate culture in GE explained most of the variance in reaching its development and performance outcomes, or whether it was matching a particular structure with appropriate behavioral norms (i.e., culture). But as will be discussed later in this chapter, intervening on social norms may go a long way toward creating the kind of hospitable space for ongoing learning and development to occur in organizations; furthermore, it is often overlooked as a powerful way of structuring the organization for leadership development.

OF BUREAUCRACIES AND LEADERSIIIP DEVELOPMENT

At the core of this chapter is an argument for a deeper consideration of the distinction between the formal and informal organization and the respective implications for leadership development. At a formal level, organizations tend to be defined by their respective position charts, which specify the reporting relationships between the various job roles. These descriptions are usually dictated in terms such as the *span of control* of management. Other relevant concepts include function (location of the position in the work flow of an organization), *division of labor* (job specialization), and *hierarchy* (fusion of status, power, and material rewards).

All of these are components of classic organization theory, the best known of which is that of bureaucracy (Weber, 1947), which has become – for better or worse – nearly synonymous with large, impersonal, and often ineffective organizations. Despite the pejorative nature of the term bureaucracy in the contemporary organizational literature, the original use was neutral if not somewhat positive (i.e., business as a bureau in which each drawer represents a different office held by a competent individual). From this perspective, organizations are defined by their positions and how these positions are linked in terms of a formal hierarchy. But it is from this perspective that classic organization theory begins to lose its relevance for contemporary organizing in which individuals are more likely than not to hold multiple fluid roles.

At a general level, it is proposed that the greater the extent to which an organization is designed to value specialization of functions and encourage adherence to fixed rules and a hierarchy of authority (i.e., bureaucracy), the less likely it is to have a social climate that facilitates leadership development. Although bureaucracies do have certain strengths such as being predictable and fairly efficient in terms of handling routine matters, they face distinct challenges, especially when it comes to enabling leadership development. Table 1 outlines some of the particular challenges associated with the basic assumptions of bureaucratic organizations and their implications for leadership development.

Bureaucratic structuring tends to impede leadership development because it channels people into functional silos (see assumption 5 in Table 1), provides little discretion for doing things differently from how they have always been done (assumption 2), and limits access to others especially those in higher level positions (assumption 3). In the most extreme examples bureaucracy can lead to the treatment of individual human beings as interchangeable, impersonal objects (assumption 7), which hardly provides the psychological environment to learn and develop. Nonetheless, the shortcomings with regard to bureaucracies may have as much or more to do with the mindset that they tend to inculcate, which is one of a narrow and rigid perspective on how to think and behave (see Merton (1957) for a classic analysis of the unintended consequences of bureaucracies in terms of depersonalization and rigidity of behavior). In particular, there is little motivation or reward for taking on challenging assignments or working on self-development in highly bureaucratic organizations (see assumption 4).

Research and theory from the field of adult learning can help to better understand this assertion. Specifically, Experiential Learning Theory is based on a number of principles that pertain to "making space" for learning, including acting and reflecting, and thinking and feeling (Kolb & Kolb, 2005; Kolb, 1984). Obviously, this does not refer to a physical space so much as a psychological one: Do people feel connected to others as part of a receptive learning environment or do they feel alienated, alone, unrecognized, and devalued? Learning is difficult because it often runs counter to our apparently preferred tendency to operate on a type of cognitive and behavioral autopilot (Macrae & Bodenhausen, 2000; Sherman, Lee, Bessenoff, & Frost, 1998) compounded by myriad factors that hinder effective learning from experience (Feldman, 1986). Learning is made even more difficult if the psychological climate feels unsafe or hostile to learning (see assumption 7).

Table 1. Basic Assumptions of the Bureaucratic Organization and the Implications for Leadership Development.

Assumption*	Description*	Implications for Leadership Development
1. Process specialization of tasks	Efficiency attained by subdividing any operation into its elements. The partial tasks can be taught, proficiency readily achieved, and responsibility for performance fixed	Fragmented perspective on the task and organization, which limits a "big picture" perspective
2. Standardization of role performance	As tasks become subdivided, their performance can be standardized. There is one best way to perform a task and it should be taught and enforced	Overly rigid approach to job functions. Inhibits creativity and innovation (and thus development)
3. Unity of command and centralization of decision making	To maintain coordination of the whole, decisions must be centralized in one command. Bypassing hierarchical chain of command is not allowed. To further this end, there should be a limited span of control so no person at any level has more immediate subordinates than can be controlled	Leadership is centralized at the top of the organization. Little room for leadership to be developed or enacted at lower organization levels, stifling opportunities to learn from leadership experiences. Small span of controls reduces autonomy while enhancing control of subordinates
4. Uniformity of practices	Behavior must be controlled by the specification of uniform institutionalized practices. Identical practices should be followed with respect to all individuals at a given status	No recognition for individual differences in developmental readiness or that practices and experiences need to be tailored to the individual
5. No duplication of function	One part of the organization should not duplicate functions being performed by another. Operations for the whole organization should be centralized	Little opportunity to understand or take part in different organization functions. Increases "silo" thinking around one's function

Table 1. (*Continued*)

Assumption*	Description*	Implications for Leadership Development
6. Rewards for merit	Selection and promotion of personnel should be based on technical proficiency and performance achievement	Succession planning based on past accomplishments rather than leadership potential. Recipe for the "Peter Principle"
7. Depersonalization of office	The office is independent of the particular incumbent, who is responded to not because of any personal attributes but because he or she occupies an official position with limited and prescribed prerogatives	Leadership viewed as a position and not as a process that anyone can contribute to. The values, beliefs, and personal qualities of a leader are ignored

*Adapted from Katz and Kahn (1978).

A second-order implication of these detriments to learning is that leadership development also becomes difficult if the organizational environment is indifferent to learning, and nearly impossible if it is hostile to it. How many times have you heard, "That's not how we do things around here" or "That's not the [insert name of your organization here] way?" Comments such as those are a good indication that there is little hospitable space for learning in that particular organization. A distinct obstacle to learning and development can occur if no one – especially no one in a formal leadership role – takes the initiative to create a regular and hospitable learning space. Without the right conditions for learning to take place, there is not much hope that long-term development will occur, especially leadership development. The role of a strategic leader is important in achieving such ends, but may be more fruitful if focused on designing the right conditions (e.g., systems and processes) in the informal organization rather than trying to construct the ideal formal structure for leadership development.

DESIGNING THE SOCIAL ARCHITECTURE OF AN ORGANIZATION

For the reasons introduced previously, it might be more useful to think about the relationship between organizational structure and leadership development by focusing on social structure rather than physical structure per se.

It is possible to have ongoing leadership development in a strict hierarchical organization if the "right" set of norms is in place; however, without these norms, development will be difficult or impossible even with a lean formal structure. Thus in keeping with the theme of strategic leader as architect, one way to frame this challenge is in terms of the *social architecture* of an organization.

At the core of an organization's social architecture is some understanding of how people interrelate with each other. This involves considering the kinds of factors that are related to how and why people form connections with others. One reason for making connections may be sheer proximity, in that people who are co-located and proximal to each other have more opportunities to interact. Other factors can include things such as functional specialty (e.g., marketing people interact mainly with other people in marketing) or hierarchical power (i.e., leaders tend to interact mainly with other leaders at roughly the same position or status level). Other reasons may be less obvious, such as connections formed in a boundaryless organization in which ideas or practices become the social magnets. In such cases people come together around an innovative idea, work with it, dissolve, and then re-form subsequently around other ideas. Fluid structures such as this might be found in organizations that value idea communities as a way to foster innovation and creativity.

What might leadership look like in these kinds of learning collectives? There is a prevailing leader-centric view in much of the leadership literature that a leader operates as an autonomous unit from which influence and other forms of leadership flow. From this perspective, leaders *act on* followers, and followers gravitate to or organize around a central leader. This perception is overly simplified and limiting for at least a couple of reasons. One is that it ignores a basic organizational reality that leaders live in a broader network of workplace actors than merely with those considered to be subordinates. Likert (1961) introduced the concept of linking pins that connect various "families" or subsets of actors in an organization. Likert's insight in this regard was that organizations are structured as overlapping groups and not as a strict pyramid. Such broader, group-based network forces can shape the thinking and behavior of a leader, which is contrary to many of the basic assumptions of a bureaucracy.

Another reason that a completely leader-centric approach to development may be an oversimplification is that it ignores the dynamic nature of leadership. From the perspective of leadership as process, it is quite possible for people in subordinate positions to lead those in higher-level roles through influence, sense making, or by enhancing commitment and meaning

(Podolny, Khurana, & Hill-Popper, 2005). The role of leader and follower often shifts among people in a collective. We enact both roles in our daily lives and can switch between them in a dynamic fashion. Also, leaders often *act with* others in creating the leadership needed to address challenges to the organization (cf. assumption 3). In this manner it is possible to develop a collective leadership capacity in teams and organizations (Day, Gronn, & Salas, 2004). In such cases, the leadership does not reside with any one person but rather with the connections between people, therefore becoming a systems-level, rather than an individual, property (O'Connor & Quinn, 2004).

Leadership in this collective form develops as an outcome of social structure and process (Salancik, Calder, Rowland, Leblebici, & Conway, 1975) rather than solely as an individual input. Whereas the traditional way of thinking about leadership is of an influence-based force that flows from an individual leader to others, a different way of conceptualizing this force is as a resource that is created through individuals and groups interrelating in constructive ways. In this form, leadership capacity is a resource that teams and organizations can draw on to enhance resilience and adaptability when faced with significant challenges requiring leadership. Put in somewhat different terms, what is an output from a previous cycle of a team performing together becomes an input for some future performance episode (Ilgen, Hollenbeck, Johnson, & Jundt, 2005; Marks, Mathieu, & Zaccaro, 2001).

One question that might arise is why such an aggregate resource is needed at all. The simple answer is because the big bosses no longer hold all the answers – that is, if they ever did. The challenges many organizations face today are too daunting for any single leader to figure out consistently and successfully. Such complex challenges also are not suited to the rigid ways of thinking and acting that are characteristic of classic bureaucracies and those that populate them. As Weick (1993) has noted, if we cannot rely on our leaders to save us, then all we have left is each other. Helping people to engage in dialogue across boundaries, to reflect on those dialogues, and to build a different, more sophisticated understanding of the nature of leadership and how it might be enacted represents an essential element of the development of the leadership capacity of an organization.

Adam Kahane's (2004) book on "solving tough problems" includes some powerful examples of this need for dialogue across boundaries, how it can be facilitated, and how it creates a collective capacity for leadership. One memorable case in point describes helping the South African government and the African National Congress opposition to implement a peaceful transition from authoritarian apartheid to a racially egalitarian democracy. The exact details of how Kahane and his collaborators assisted with this remarkable transition are beyond the scope of the chapter. But suffice it to say that it was not accomplished by any single leader (strategic or otherwise) setting the course of action and then building the commitment to make it happen. Instead, the team worked with members of various constituent stakeholders that were simultaneously engaged in scenario planning exercises designed around the fundamental assumption that there was more than one possible future and that the actions they and others took would determine which future would unfold. Through collectively envisioning a shared future and mapping out how to go about realizing it, Kahane came to recognize that across many different contexts there is a widespread "apartheid syndrome." As he explains:

> By this I mean trying to solve a highly complex problem using a piecemeal, backward-looking, and authoritarian process that is suitable only for solving simple problems. In this syndrome, people at the top of a complex system try to manage its development through a divide-and-conquer strategy: through compartmentalization – the Afrikaans word *apartheid* means "apartness" – and command and control. Because people at the bottom resist these commands, the system either becomes stuck, or ends up becoming unstuck by force. This apartheid syndrome occurs in all kinds of social systems, all over the world: in families, organizations, communities, and countries. (Kahane, 2004, pp. 32–33, italics in original)

Effectively structuring an organization for leadership development can be construed as one way of helping to overcome this apartheid syndrome. When there is a collective capacity for leadership, there is less likelihood of and need for compartmentalization and command-and-control approaches to respond to complex leadership challenges. Having a broad-based leadership capacity helps to resist the tendency to try to solve such complex challenges with methods best designed for simple problems.

But how might organization structure help or hinder leadership development? To help answer this question, it might be worth looking at the kinds of embedded factors that can contribute to developing leadership capacity in organizations. To understand this possible relationship it is first necessary to get beyond the traditional, yet limited, perspective that structured, individual-based programs are the source of leadership development in organizations.

FROM FORMAL POSITIONS TO NETWORKED CONNECTIONS

There is the compelling argument that leadership is a process, not a position. That is, one's position does not inherently make one a leader or ensure that leadership inevitably will occur. Certainly, one's position in an organization can provide some legitimate position power and authority; however, leadership involves more than the mere exercise of that authority. If leadership relied completely on those of a lower rank obeying the orders of those of a higher rank, then all organizations would be structured like an army. But even most first-world armies do not rely completely on their respective formal structures in addressing challenges to their missions (Day & Halpin, 2004). It simply is not enough.

A different approach to understanding leadership in organizations focuses on the informal connections or interactions between organization members. The emphasis is not so much on who reports to whom in a formal sense, but who goes to whom for advice or support. This is termed the social networks approach to organizations (Kilduff & Tsai, 2003; Scott, 2000), which seeks to understand the informal organization through the connections or interpersonal ties between members of a group or organization. The classic, formal organization approach can tell you where in the organizational hierarchy a particular position is located, but the social networks approach can tell you how connected someone is in the informal organization. Although the formal organization can shape or influence the informal (e.g., a boss might be more likely to be consulted for expertise and advice than a subordinate), they are typically not identical. Indeed, the informal organization as reflected in the underlying social networks may have more to do with the ongoing daily leadership of an organization than its formal structure. Social networks reveal a great deal about the day-to-day leadership *in* an organization (Boal & Hooijberg, 2000) by elaborating on the inner workings of how information, influence, and support are distributed within the organization.

Building social networks involves making connections and often reaching across experienced boundaries. Regardless of how bureaucratized the formal structure, an informal social network that connects people across organizational boundaries is likely to build the kind of capacity for adaptive behavior that is needed when significant challenges are faced. As long as the norm is in place that engaging in such boundaryless behavior is acceptable and even encouraged, then it really does not matter what the formal role relationships are. The informal organization is where the real leadership resides within an organization, which is not exclusively in formal position power.

Strategic leaders, however, can do much to encourage and enrich the informal networks of their organizations. An important issue associated with structuring informally for leadership development concerns the "right" norms; that is, the kinds of interpersonal standards and expectations that can either support or impede learning and development. A question arising from this assertion is what are the right norms and how they can be nurtured in organizations?

NORMS FOR LEADERSHIP DEVELOPMENT

The following part of the chapter identifies and briefly reviews what are proposed as three important and interrelated norms for enhancing leadership development in organizations. Such a short list can in no way be exhaustive, but extensive lists of what needs to happen in order for something as complex as development to occur can also be overwhelming and paralyzing. Social architects interested in enhancing leadership development in their organizations are encouraged to focus on just these three important norms, at least initially. Doing so can help in profound ways to create a healthy psychological space for learning in their teams and organizations (Kolb & Kolb, 2005).

Power Distance

It is an unfortunate fact of organizational life that many "leaders" prefer to see only the formal organization and respond mainly to organizational position and formal power. One way to describe these people (and there are less charitable terms) is as holding a core value of *high power distance*. The concept of power distance comes originally from Geert Hofstede's research on organizational and societal cultures (e.g., Hofstede, 2001), which defines the concept in terms of the degree to which organization (or societal) members expect and agree that power should be shared unequally. High power distance thus reflects the core value that power should be distributed unequally among members of a collective, whereas low power distance values more egalitarian expectations regarding power.

Subsequent research sponsored by Project GLOBE (House, Hanges, Javidan, Dorfman, & Gupta, 2004), which sought to identify cross-cultural differences and similarities in leadership, demonstrated the relevance of power distance to leadership. Specifically, it was hypothesized that high power distance cultures might give more credence to formal leadership because they are more likely to endorse the legitimacy of a leader's authority. Conversely, low power distance cultures might be more likely to perceive the value of participative and shared leadership models. Indeed, the House et al. findings supported this distinction in terms of the relationship between type of leadership (authoritarian versus participative) and perceived effectiveness as a function of a culture's orientation toward power distance. The more strategic leaders are willing to allow or foster the empowerment of others, the more opportunities exist for leadership capacity to develop more broadly and deeply in a given organization. The House et al. findings suggest, however, that empowerment of others would be more likely in low power distance cultures than in those cultures valuing high power distance.

At an organizational level, how might one go about changing organizational values so that power distance is lowered? It probably will not happen if strategic leaders are unwilling to let go of some of their formal power and allow more informal, networked bases of leadership capacity to develop. Maintaining a chokehold on power essentially means that others are unlikely to experience the kinds of stretch assignments that are so important for leadership development. As noted previously, it is likely that letting go of power at the top is going to be more difficult in bureaucracies than in less rigid and hierarchical organizations. Resistance to letting go of power also sends strong signals about how much (or little) trust exists, which is relevant to the next norm that will be discussed.

Psychological Safety

The work of Edmondson and colleagues (Edmondson, 1999; Edmondson, Bohmer, & Pisano, 2001) has demonstrated the role of psychological safety in team learning. Specifically, psychological safety refers to how comfortable members of a team are in taking interpersonal risks with each other. Such risks include admitting a mistake or owning up to one's ignorance about an issue of relevance to the team. Learning in an interpersonal context often requires that individuals expose certain vulnerabilities, which is difficult to do in a climate that lacks basic trust. Edmondson's research has shown that psychological safety can facilitate and accelerate team learning. Although she has not examined leadership development directly, it would seem to be a safe bet that leadership capacity is also enhanced or developed more rapidly when there are high levels of psychological safety in the team or broader organization.

One domain in which Edmondson et al. (2001) have studied team learning is that of cardiac surgery. The focal challenge was a difficult new procedure for performing cardiac surgery that required a completely different way of working together as a surgical team. The criterion of interest in the research was how quickly different surgical teams mastered the new procedure. Their findings indicated that:

> Teams whose members felt comfortable making suggestions, trying things that might not work, pointing out potential problems, and admitting mistakes were more successful in learning the new procedure. In contrast, when people felt uneasy acting this way, the learning process was stifled. (p. 131)

Granted, Edmondson and colleagues were focused on team learning with regard to a specific type of technical challenge dealing with cardiac surgery. Nonetheless, the technical challenge also had significant leadership challenges embedded in it. In particular, the teams and especially their formal leaders had to develop ways to manage themselves in order to facilitate becoming team learning units. Building such a capacity for team learning would be expected to transfer to building better leadership capacity as well. Being able to learn the way out of a leadership challenge has been pointed to as the hallmark of adaptive and successful organizations (Dixon, 1993).

There are some specific things recommended by Edmondson et al. (2001) for leaders to help promote psychological safety in their teams. Such prescriptions also apply to strategic leaders who desire the same kind of norm in their organizations. We know that modeling is a powerful force for learning, and modeling these specific norms can help to create the kind of learning space needed for ongoing leadership development. First, be *accessible* and not aloof. Being seen as aloof sends the message that the leader has it all figured out and that others' advice is neither welcomed nor valued. Second, be *proactive* and ask for input. In addition to reinforcing the norm that others' perspectives are valued, it also sets the expectation that others will be explicitly tapped for their thoughts and opinions on a regular basis. If I ask for your input it shows that I am open to learning from you, which models an important norm that can spread across the social networks within an organization. Requesting input can be as straightforward as regularly asking others, "What have we learned?" from a shared experience or situation. Third, serve as a *fallibility model* that fosters a learning environment by admitting one's own mistakes openly. This is an especially difficult behavior to model if one has fallen into the trap of believing in the "leader as savior" perspective. No one has all of the answers needed to solve the kinds of complex leadership challenges facing contemporary organizations (keep in mind Kahane's apartheid syndrome). Admitting one's limits may be just the invitation to broader participation that can lead to developing the leadership capacity required for adaptability and long-term success.

Learning Orientation

There is a robust literature on the effects of different goal orientations in terms of how individuals approach their tasks and challenges. On the one hand, a performance orientation focuses on demonstrating competence in safe (i.e., relatively non-challenging) environments, making as few errors as possible, and demonstrating proficiency in a task with as little effort as possible. On the other hand, a learning orientation focuses more on mastering the nuances of a task, seeking challenges to develop and perfect competencies, which occurs over a possibly extended period of time. From this particular orientation, making mistakes are acceptable as long as it promotes effective learning. Thus, a learning orientation involves not only demonstrating proficiency in terms of committing the fewest possible errors but also reaching a deeper understanding of the nature of the task with the overarching goal of building expertise (Dweck, 1986). Subsequent research has extended this goal orientation framework beyond individuals to include teams as well (Bunderson & Sutcliffe, 2003; Porter, 2005).

The default goal orientation in most individuals, teams, and organizations appears to be toward favoring a performance orientation over a learning orientation. There may be many reasonable explanations for this, the most important of which is that rewards are more often tied to demonstrated performance than to effective learning. This is either mirrored or reinforced in the academic leadership literature. The primary emphasis in the leadership domain is on whether or not various leaders and leadership approaches are associated with measurable performance outcomes (Day & Lord, 1988) rather than focusing on explicit links to learning and development. Among other things, a focus solely on performance also risks perpetuating an "ends justifying the means" kind of thinking.

In practice it would be unrealistic to expect individuals, teams, and organizations to abandon completely a performance orientation in favor of a learning orientation. It probably would also be unhealthy and quite possibly threaten long-term survival. But an emphasis entirely on performance with no attention to learning has its own long-term limitations, especially with regard to leadership development. Thus, it may be more realistic to seek a more equal balance between a performance and a learning goal orientation. Instead of an "either/or" approach it may be better to think in terms of "both/and."

Action learning is a recognized approach to leadership development that attempts to optimize "both/and" in terms of balancing action (i.e., performance) with learning. As noted in Chapter 3 in Van Velsor's and

O'Connor's case study of how action learning was used to build leadership capacity in a large bureaucratic organization, teams of participants focused on designing and completing a project of strategic importance but also took time to reflect (individually and collectively) on how leadership was being enacted in their respective teams. Instead of relying on an individual leader (appointed or emergent) to (1) structure the work, (2) support team members, and (3) build commitment and alignment with the project objectives, all of the teams in the developmental initiative agreed to focus on trying to enact leadership more collectively. The emphasis was not on who in particular emerged as a leader but on recognizing the capacity for leadership embedded in the network of relationships that developed between team members. Doing so requires a different way of thinking about leadership that is a less leader-centric or "postheroic" (Fletcher, 2004) perspective on leadership. If it is true that thinking is for doing (Fiske, 1992), and if the only way that leadership can be thought of is as based on the heroics of individual leaders, then there is little hope that any substantive leadership capacity will emerge beyond the dependency of followers on visible leaders.

Elevating the learning orientation of an individual, team, or organization is especially critical in efforts targeted toward enhancing leadership development. Development of any form in humans is often associated with initial performance losses (Fischer, 1980; Kegan, 1994). Getting out of well-entrenched performance routines and trying different approaches can feel difficult, uncomfortable, and scary (hence the term stretch assignment). Without the necessary support, there is an unfortunate tendency to regress to a previous way of thinking or behaving in order to maintain higher levels of performance at least for the time being as well as to feel more comfortable and in control. A strong performance orientation without a concomitant emphasis on learning can accelerate that tendency. Inculcating a learning goal orientation in an organization while also maintaining a performance orientation could be instrumental in building sustainable support norms to create the kind of learning organization in which leadership development is an ongoing activity.

Summary

The focus in this part of the chapter has been on three particular norm sets that are proposed to enhance the development of leadership capacity in organizations: power distance (especially low power distance), psychological safety, and a learning goal orientation. These are interrelated norms in the sense that building the expectation for more equally shared power (low power distance) would also enhance perceptions of trust and the willingness to take interpersonal risks (psychological safety). Furthermore, an emphasis on learning (learning orientation) is unlikely to take hold if there is a lack of trust about possible repercussions for trying new things and making mistakes. These particular norms subsume some of the others that could also be seen as important to facilitating learning and leadership development. For example, being relatively open rather than closed could be considered to be part of psychological safety as well as a necessary condition for a learning orientation. Being flexible rather than rigid could be construed as part of low power distance. The main point of relevance is that the three specific normative sets proposed here are not the only possibilities, although they do cover a broad swath of territory associated with creating an organizational social architecture that is conducive to developing a broad capacity for leadership within the organization.

CONCLUSION

This chapter examined the role of the strategic leader in structuring the organization for leadership development. The point was made that the desirable goal of structuring for development probably has less to do with the formal hierarchical structure of an organization and more to do with the informal norms and networks that support its systems and processes. In this manner, strategic leaders need to think of themselves as social architects helping to generate the kinds of normative conditions that would facilitate leadership development. Instead of focusing on the formal positions and reporting lines in an official organization chart, it may be a better idea for strategic leaders to think how to go about developing the "white space" in those charts. That is, what is the culture and climate for learning and development? How healthy is the interpersonal context in which the shared work of the organization – including its development – takes place? Addressing these kinds of issues is the primary responsibility of strategic leaders. Sure, it is probably easier to move around the boxes and lines that are found in a formal organizational chart than it is to "muck around" in the informal guts of the place. But in terms of making a long-term impact on the leadership and its development, all signs point to the guts as being where it is at.

REFERENCES

Boal, K., & Hooijberg, R. (2000). Strategic leadership research: Moving on. *Leadership Quarterly*, *11*, 515–549.

Bunderson, J. S., & Sutcliffe, K. M. (2003). Management. Team learning orientation and business unit performance. *Journal of Applied Psychology*, *88*, 552–560.

Byrne, J. A. (2003). *Q&A with Jack*, from http://www.straightfromthegut.com/meet/meet_qa.html, retrieved September 15, 2005.

Day, D. V., Gronn, P., & Salas, E. (2004). Leadership capacity in teams. *Leadership Quarterly*, *5*, 857–880.

Day, D. V., & Halpin, S. M. (2004). Growing leaders for tomorrow: An introduction. In: D. V. Day, S. J. Zaccaro & S. M. Halpin (Eds), *Leader development for transforming organizations: Growing leaders for tomorrow* (pp. 3–22). Mahwah, NJ: Erlbaum.

Day, D. V., & Lord, R. G. (1988). Executive leadership and organizational performance: Suggestions for a new theory and methodology. *Journal of Management*, *14*, 453–464.

Dixon, N. M. (1993). Developing managers for the learning organization. *Human Resource Management Review*, *3*, 243–254.

Dweck, C. S. (1986). Motivational processes affecting learning. *American Psychologist*, *41*, 1040–1048.

Edmondson, A. (1999). Psychological safety and learning behavior in work teams. *Administrative Science Quarterly*, *44*, 350–383.

Edmondson, A., Bohmer, R., & Pisano, G. (2001). Speeding up team learning. *Harvard Business Review*, *79*(9), 125–132.

Feldman, J. (1986). On the difficulty of learning from experience. In: H. P. Sims Jr. & D. A. Gioia (Eds), *The thinking organization: Dynamics of organizational social cognition* (pp. 263–292). San Francisco, CA: Jossey-Bass.

Fischer, K. W. (1980). A theory of cognitive development: The control and construction of hierarchies of skills. *Psychological Review*, *87*, 477–531.

Fiske, S. T. (1992). Thinking is for doing: Portraits of social cognition from daguerreotype to laserphoto. *Journal of Personality and Social Psychology*, *63*, 877–889.

Fletcher, J. K. (2004). The paradox of postheroic leadership: An essay on gender, power, and transformational change. *Leadership Quarterly*, *15*, 647–661.

Hofstede, G. (2001). *Culture's consequences: Comparing values, behaviors, institutions, and organizations across nations* (2nd ed.). Thousand Oaks, CA: Sage.

House, R. J., Hanges, P. J., Javidan, M., Dorfman, P. W., & Gupta, V. (Eds) (2004). *Culture, leadership, and organizations: The GLOBE study of 62 societies*. Thousand Oaks, CA: Sage.

Ilgen, D. R., Hollenbeck, J. R., Johnson, M., & Jundt, J. (2005). Teams in organizations: From I-P-O models to IMOI models. *Annual Review of Psychology*, *56*, 517–543.

Kahane, A. (2004). *Solving tough problems: An open way of talking, listening, and creating new realities*. San Francisco, CA: Berrett-Koehler.

Katz, D., & Kahn, R. L. (1978). *The social psychology of organizations* (2nd ed.). New York: Wiley.

Kegan, R. (1994). *In over our heads: The mental demands of modern life*. Cambridge, MA: Harvard University.

Kilduff, M., & Tsai, W. (2003). *Social networks and organizations*. Thousand Oaks, CA: Sage.

Kolb, A. Y., & Kolb, D. A. (2005). Learning styles and learning spaces: Enhancing experiential learning in higher education. *Academy of Management Learning & Education, 4,* 193–212.

Kolb, D. A. (1984). *Experiential learning: Experience as the source of learning and development.* Englewood Cliffs, NJ: Prentice Hall.

Likert, R. (1961). *New patterns of management.* New York: McGraw-Hill.

Macrae, C. N., & Bodenhausen, G. V. (2000). Social cognition: Thinking categorically about others. *Annual Review of Psychology, 51,* 93–120.

Marks, M. A., Mathieu, J. E., & Zaccaro, S. J. (2001). A temporally based framework and taxonomy of team processes. *Academy of Management Review, 26,* 356–376.

McCall, M. W., Jr., Lombardo, M. M., & Morrison, A. M. (1988). *The lessons of experience: How successful executives develop on the Job.* Lexington, MA: Lexington Books.

Merton, R. K. (1957). *Social theory and social structure* (rev. ed.). New York: Free Press.

O'Connor, P. M. G., & Quinn, L. (2004). Organizational capacity for leadership. In: C. D. McCauley & E. Van Velsor (Eds), *The Center for Creative Leadership handbook of leadership development* (2nd ed., pp. 417–437). San Francisco, CA: Jossey-Bass.

Podolny, J. M., Khurana, R., & Hill-Popper, M. (2005). Revisiting the meaning of leadership. *Research in Organizational Behavior, 26,* 1–36.

Porter, C. O. L. H. (2005). Goal orientation: Effects on backing up behavior, performance, efficacy, and commitment in teams. *Journal of Applied Psychology, 90,* 811–818.

Salancik, G. R., Calder, B. J., Rowland, K. M., Leblebici, H., & Conway, M. (1975). Leadership as an outcome of social structure and process: A multidimensional analysis. In: J. G. Hunt & L. L. Larson (Eds), *Leadership frontiers* (pp. 81–101). Kent, OH: Kent State University.

Scott, J. (2000). *Social network analysis: A handbook* (2nd ed.). Thousand Oaks, CA: Sage.

Sherman, J. W., Lee, A. Y., Bessenoff, G. R., & Frost, L. A. (1998). Stereotype efficiency reconsidered: Encoding flexibility under cognitive load. *Journal of Personality and Social Psychology, 75,* 589–606.

Van Velsor, E., & McCauley, C. D. (2004). Our view of leadership development. In: C. D. McCauley & E. Van Velsor (Eds), *The Center for Creative Leadership handbook of leadership development* (2nd ed., pp. 1–22). San Francisco, CA: Jossey-Bass.

Vicere, A. A., & Fulmer, R. M. (1998). *Leadership by design.* Boston, MA: Harvard Business School.

Weber, M. (1947). In: A. M. Henderson & T. Parsons (Eds), *The theory of social and economic organization* (Trans.). New York: Oxford University.

Weick, K. E. (1993). The collapse of sensemaking in organizations: The Mann Gulch disaster. *Administrative Science Quarterly, 38,* 628–652.

CHAPTER 3

DEVELOPING ORGANIZATIONAL CAPACITY FOR LEADERSHIP

Ellen Van Velsor and Patricia M.G. O'Connor

ABSTRACT

This chapter describes an approach to leadership development that focuses on enhancing an organization's capacity for "connected leadership." The framework is based on the idea that, in the face of complex challenges, three organizational-level leadership tasks must be accomplished: (1) direction must be set not once and for all, but in a way that is recurring and iterative; (2) alignment must be created among aspects of a work flow, among people and groups, and among organizational systems and processes; and (3) commitment must be generated and maintained throughout times of change. We describe four features of our approach and illustrate using examples from an organization in the midst of significant transformation.

This chapter describes an approach to leadership development that focuses not on the development of individual leader capabilities, but on enhancing an organization's capacity for what we will call "connected leadership." This approach recognizes leadership as emerging from an organization's social networks and interdependent work groups, through influence and

Being There Even When You Are Not: Leading Through Strategy, Structures, and Systems
Monographs in Leadership and Management, Volume 4, 31–49
Copyright © 2007 by Elsevier Ltd.
All rights of reproduction in any form reserved
ISSN: 1479-3571/doi:10.1016/S1479-3571(07)04002-3

meaning-making processes and the use of collective or shared leadership practices and belief systems.

The connected leadership framework is based on the idea that, in the face of complex challenges, three organizational level leadership tasks must be accomplished (Van Velsor & McCauley, 2003). Direction must be set not once and for all, but in a way that is recurring and iterative. Alignment must be created among aspects of a work flow, among people and groups, and among organizational systems and processes. And finally, commitment must be generated and maintained throughout times of chaos and change.

Direction, alignment, and commitment – what we refer to as the tasks of leadership – can be accomplished in a limited way by an individual leader working within a framework of supervisory leadership. These tasks can also be accomplished by a group of people working together to enact leadership – by an executive team, a middle management team, a project team, a team of teachers in a public school, or an emergency room team in a hospital setting. But to maximize organizational effectiveness, we believe there are many times when direction needs to emanate from collectively shared sense-making processes, both within and between groups doing interdependent work. In today's fast-paced, global environments, organizational sustainability demands that alignment come from engagement across boundaries, through processes that work to integrate diverse perspectives in order to better collaborate around a complex challenge. And commitment comes from the shared experience in creating group or organization level direction and from the trust built through personal relationships with the collective. These organizational level capabilities and processes are the focus of the connected leadership development approach.

DEVELOPING "CONNECTED LEADERSHIP"

The structure of our approach was informed by leadership, social capital, adult learning, organizational development, and action-learning theory and practice, as well as the Center for Creative Leadership's 30 years of experience in developing individuals, teams, and organizational practices. For our purposes here, we will focus on four key features of this connected leadership development approach:

(1) Discovery: A collaborative and interactive process yielding what we refer to as the organization's "learning agenda," essentially an articulation of the complex challenge(s) facing the organization, and the group/ organizational targets for development.

(2) Stakeholder Development: A process of educating, advising, and preparing senior executives to function effectively in roles as steering committee members and action-learning leadership team sponsors, to legitimize, support, and participate in the development of new connected leadership practices.
(3) Design: A multi-modal process, based on the "critical reflection" school of action learning, which includes storytelling; sense-making, within and across team collaboration experiences; tools to surface assumptions and foster dialogue; just-in-time coaching; and learning-focused presentations. Typically six months long, the design process is customized specifically to develop and enhance both strong and weak ties, distributed intelligence, both single and double loop collective learning, dynamic interaction, and mutual cooperation.
(4) Evaluation: The strategy for assessing the quality and utility of initiatives and the advancement of the organization's learning agenda.

This approach will be illustrated through a case example involving a US-based quasi-governmental service agency. One of the largest employers in the United States, it is wholly operated within the US and is part of the delivery services industry. The primary target of the leadership development initiative was 100 of the agency's senior executives, who reside in the organizational structure two and three levels down from the CEO. Specifically, we will share how we applied the four features of discovery, stakeholder development, design, and evaluation to this leadership initiative.

Discovery

The discovery process clarifies both the complex challenges facing a particular organization and the associated targets for developmental change. Taken together, the articulation of the key complex challenges and the associated targets for change comprise the organization's "learning agenda." This focus on naming a learning agenda as a first step in the overall initiative starts what will be an ongoing focus on learning as an orientation – a focus that will be carried out by both the external facilitators and the internal sponsors for the duration of the work.

As the name implies, "discovery" is an unfolding process designed to draw out the key aspects of the organization that require further examination and development. It is a co-inquiry process that involves the active participation of a cross-section of organizational members. Unlike traditional needs assessment, discovery assumes that expertise for assessing the organization's needs resides *both* within the organization *and* outside the organization, in the form of leadership development specialists. This approach helps the organization not only to take more explicit responsibility for what to develop further, but also to reflect more deeply on the readiness for that development.

The first purpose of discovery is to identify the key complex challenges facing the organization that are limiting its effectiveness in significant ways. These challenges are generally systemic and multidimensional in nature and the organization has not yet arrived at an agreed solution for dealing with them. Clarifying the complex challenges serves to ground the leadership development initiative in a strategically purposeful context, providing the primary reason for change. Beyond simple identification of the collectively recognized challenge, discovery also serves to uncover the root causes and underlying tensions that are producing challenges. For example, competing commitments among various constituent groups often give rise to organizational challenges that are experienced and labeled as challenges with "diversity." In this case, we would expect that the discovery process would enable organizational members to articulate not only what the various commitments are but also the assumptions, values, and worldviews preventing groups from recognizing and understanding the commitments that compete with theirs.

The second purpose of discovery is to identify developmental targets – what the organization needs to develop further in order to more effectively address its complex challenge. Discovery may yield a need for the organization to leverage an existing core capability (keep doing), introduce a new capability (start doing), eradicate a dysfunctional or no longer useful capability (stop doing), or some combination. In terms of leadership development, the capability may relate to individuals' skills and perspectives, the pattern of relationships between those individuals (i.e., social networks), or the leadership practices and belief systems that connect (or divide) parts (groups, systems, or processes) of the organization, or some combination.

In the case example, the discovery process took approximately three months and involved 22 senior executives, four area vice presidents, and eight executive team members, including the CEO. A variety of traditional and action research tools were used to collect data about the organization and its functioning, including:

- Document analysis of its strategy and transformation plan;
- A survey of the social networks of senior executives;

- Structured interview and card-sort exercises focused on challenges and core capabilities;
- Focus groups assessing organizational values; and
- A dialogue session with the top executive team, which involved reviewing and making sense of the discovery findings.

The case organization was in the midst of a significant, 10-year organizational transformation. In order to develop the capacity to address the current and future complex challenges of this transformation, it was determined that four collective leadership practices needed development throughout the executive population:

(1) *Engaging across boundaries*, including hierarchical, functional, and geographic boundaries.
(2) *Leading from an integrated understanding of the organization*, which was a very large, dynamic, and complex system.
(3) *Shifting from a primary focus on internal operations to more continual scanning of the external environment*, which was turbulent due to both competitive and regulatory forces.
(4) *Bringing best of self to the organization*, which underscored the vital importance of executives' self-awareness, regulation, and overall developmental and physical health.

It should be noted that the discovery process in this organization also revealed two forms of existing capability that led the team to focus on connected leadership development. First, the organization demonstrated deep capability in preparing individuals to take on people management positions (i.e., supervisory leadership). Second, as well as possessing a clear, compelling, and thus far successful transformation plan, the organization's executive team had progressively become more strategic in its oversight of the organization's new direction. Thus, the development of deeper capacities for either supervisory or strategic leadership was not recognized as the prioritized target for development.

Stakeholder Development

Stakeholder development is the process we engage in, as external collaborators, to educate, orient, advise, and support the key stakeholders of a connected leadership developmental initiative. The primary purpose of stakeholder development is to develop the buy-in, participation, and support of highly informed and influential organizational members. This process includes members of the formal organizational structure, such as the executive team, the senior human resource development professionals, and the supervisory managers of the target population. It also includes those individuals who may take on specialized roles in the initiative such as steering committee members and sponsors (to be described later in the chapter).

The primary process for stakeholder development is the documentation of and dialogue about the why, what, who, how, and so what of the leadership development initiative. Specifically, time is invested in developing a shared and deepened understanding of the learning agenda, the desired outcomes, and timing of the initiative, key participants, the evaluation strategy, the process design, role descriptions, tips for providing effective support, and other means to help prepare stakeholders and clarify what they may expect – and not expect – from the initiative.

As with any change effort, some stakeholders in our case example were skeptical about introducing new approaches to leadership and leadership development. In this case, the senior human resource executive within the organization played the important role of holding regular 1:1 conversations with these "friendly critics," fielding their questions, listening to their concerns, and sharing periodic updates on the impact of the initiative. The importance of this more personal communication, as part of the overall stakeholder development, cannot be overemphasized, as one of our key goals is to increase stakeholder awareness around new approaches to leadership and the benefits those approaches can yield for their organization.

While more concentrated levels of stakeholder development activity typically occur in the early phases of the initiative (e.g., stakeholder participation in discovery), specific groups are often targeted in the stakeholder development process. In our case example, we worked with five stakeholder groups: (1) the executive team, (2) the steering committee, (3) the employee development group (i.e., human resources), (4) the sponsors, and (5) the target population's managers. We describe two of these groups in greater detail.

The Steering Committee (SC)
This seven-person team consisted of the CEO; two executive team members; two area vice presidents responsible for significant portions of the organization's business; the head of core headquarters function; and a senior human resource specialist. The SC was chartered to provide oversight and be responsible for the outcomes of the leadership development initiative. In

this capacity, the committee collaborated with us on the design and ongoing development of the initiative (including the evaluation strategy); provided overall supervision of the action-learning leadership projects (described in the next section); represented the initiative to their peers; and participated in periodic sense-making sessions as the pilot portion of the initiative got underway. The SC development occurred through a series of readings, meetings, and dialogues. Some aspects of the work were routine for these senior executives, such as reviewing outcomes and making decisions. Other aspects were more outside the norm of their duties, such as dialogue about organizational resistance to changing "the way things are done around here" and the nature of developing leadership practices in the executive population that would move the organization to where it needed to be. In essence, the SC members were highly successful supervisory and strategic leaders with varied experience in connected leadership.

The Sponsors
The action-learning leadership teams received direct support and guidance from senior executives, or sponsors, who were intentionally assigned to projects for which they had no technical expertise, to avoid the possibility of over-influencing the work of the team. They provided strategic perspective on the organization, introduced team members to key people in their own social network, and lent support as needed, whether it be financial resources or feedback on project milestones. Further, sponsors were given the role of representing and championing the initiative with their peers and others who might ask about the work. Because sponsors are typically higher-level executives, working with teams like these can demonstrate a willingness to engage in a way that reduces power distance between levels. It can also increase the probability of teams interacting effectively and acting independently, rather than depending on a higher authority to set direction for the project or create alignment among team members.

In addition to an overall orientation to the initiative, sponsors are offered tips on effective sponsoring as well as things to avoid. For example, sponsors are coached to emphasize learning goals and outcomes as well as (and sometimes instead of) performance goals and outcomes, particularly in the case described here as this was a highly performance-oriented operations culture. The most effective sponsors in our case example demonstrated curiosity about and energy for the team's work, provided timely and honest feedback on project outcomes, frequently inquired about the team's learning, served as a politically savvy sounding board when the team met with organizational resistance, and avoided over-influencing the team's direction.

It should be noted that all SC members, including the CEO, served as sponsors for the first cohort of the initiative. This provided a three-fold benefit: It demonstrably illustrated the SC's commitment to the initiative, it helped the SC members understand the developmental process in more detail, and it gave the participants more experience of working with senior officers.

Design

The connected leadership development approach is based on the "critical reflection" school of action learning (Marsick & O'Neil, 1999). As such, the design of the initiative is intended to maximize participant opportunities to reflect on their actions and experiences, as well as on the assumptions and beliefs that shape their leadership practice. The design is customized specifically to build and enhance both strong and weak ties (Brass, 2001); single and double loop collective learning (Argyris, 1990; Torbert & Cook-Greuter, 2004; Yukl & Lepsinger, 2004); and both distributed intelligence and dynamic interaction (Marion, 1999).

In terms of structure, the initiative consists of two face-to-face "intensives" separated by a period (often six months) of activity in action-learning leadership teams (more about these teams below). Placed at the beginning and near the end of the participant experience, the two intensives provide a means for the teams to come together in multi-team sessions to exchange information and learning within and between teams. Between the two face-to-face intensive sessions, participants work in five-person action-learning leadership teams on projects that deal directly with key complex challenges facing their organization. Throughout the process, teams are assigned an action-learning leadership coach (typically from outside the organization) who meets with them both during the intensives and for face-to-face and teleconference sessions during the six-month period between intensives, when most of the project work gets done.

First Intensive
The first session, typically lasting five days, communicates to all participants the purpose of the initiative and its design; introduces tools for reflection and dialogue; and furthers understanding of the core capabilities on which the initiative will focus. The action-learning leadership teams are formed and choose their projects. Through this first large, multi-team meeting, participants gain perspective on the whole system's nature of the initiative and begin a process of collective learning and network building.

This first session is an important opportunity for senior leaders to interact with participants to set the context for the initiative and to engage in networking. Several members of the senior team (often including the CEO) begin by addressing the group about the organization's complex challenges, its strategy, and the relationship of those to the organizational capabilities that the initiative is designed to develop or enhance. Opportunities for informal networking are built-in throughout, often taking the form of informal meetings over dinner or during planned socials. During the time between the intensives, networking opportunities also abound, given that action-learning teams frequently need to forge new connections both horizontally and vertically in order to move forward on their project work.

Another way that participants interact with senior executives during the first intensive is through storytelling. Stories are powerful because they promote the transfer of knowledge and tacit learning. Senior executives choose particular stories to share because they illustrate situations in which the storyteller played a key role as the organization faced a complex challenge. Storytellers are asked to use the story to illustrate the need for, or use of, the core capabilities on which the initiative is focused. In our case example, stories involved organizational crises where working across boundaries, taking an external perspective, bringing the best of self to the job, or working from an integrated understanding of the organization were critical to facing the challenge successfully. For example, one story dealt with the organization's response to an unexpected environmental threat that affected the employees, their customers, and their community. The participants gained a fuller appreciation not only of the number and diversity of constituents that had to be involved in the response but also of how the individuals involved worked together to create processes and protocols for alignment across those entities. Not surprisingly, the most powerful stories included both successes and mistakes on the way. This level of transparency demonstrated the storyteller's commitment to learning, enhanced the climate of trust and safety within the program, and perhaps also worked to reduce the perceived distance between senior executive storytellers and program participants.

In addition to the interactions with senior leaders, participants are also exposed, during this first intensive, to various tools and modules for surfacing assumptions and engaging in dialogue. One tool we frequently use helps leaders understand the competing commitments that underlie an individual's or an organization's ability to change (Kegan & Lahey, 2001). This experience provides good grounding for the work to come on action-learning projects that challenge current systems, processes, and knowledge bases.

Other tools introduced in the first session support group decision-making, collective sense-making around complex subjects, and team norm-setting.

A key part of the first intensive is the assignment of projects to the action-learning teams. As mentioned above, action learning generally emphasizes learning by doing, is team-based, and focuses on critical organizational issues. Often, the challenges posed to teams are complex challenges, for which there are currently no recognized, widely shared solutions and no agreement about how to move toward resolution – for example, developing viable business strategies for collaborating with the company's competitors, in order to more fully address their customers' needs. Usually, action-learning teams are asked to bring about change or put forward recommendations for change that are formalized in presentations to senior managers (Marquardt, 1999; Conger & Toegel, 2003).

In our work, action-learning *leadership* teams are action-learning teams used for the additional purpose of developing an organization's collective capacity for leadership (O'Connor, 2005). Based on the aforementioned principles of action learning, action-learning leadership teams focus on both the action of getting the projects done and on critical reflection about how leadership is accomplished (how direction, alignment, and commitment are being created, other than from an authority-based hierarchy) in the course of the team's shared project work. The critical reflection is facilitated over time by action-learning coaches – individuals who have been trained to use a set of tools designed to help the group surface and question assumptions, work collaboratively and share leadership, practice dialogue, stop action for reflection, engage across boundaries, and create a greater sense of shared meaning about their work.

A second important feature of these action-learning leadership teams has to do with the way they are put together and matched with action-learning projects. Because a central objective of this connected leadership development approach is to further relationships between individuals and groups (and thereby enhance social networks), a key characteristic of these teams is that they are comprised of individuals who come from diverse parts of the organization – from a variety of functions and diverse geographies. The projects they take on must focus on work in which no team member has special expertise, inside knowledge, or management responsibility. We believe this requirement facilitates exploratory behavior and collective approaches to leadership because no one has a significant degree of expert power or formal authority. It also promotes new interactions between individuals within and outside the team, as well as between and across teams and groups in the wider organization.

The assumption is that this dynamic interaction will foster and speed up distributed intelligence, and afford each group and every individual the opportunity to gain a more integrated understanding of the organization as a whole. We expect it will also increase the probability that novel ideas and solutions will emerge as an inherent part of the process. And finally, this approach requires that individuals cross the boundaries of their established networks, their own functions, and their geographical locations, and that groups cross the boundaries of their newly established teams, not only to seek out new information but also to connect early on with the ultimate stakeholders for their project outcomes.

In addition to being assigned an action-learning coach, each team is assigned an executive sponsor – an internal, senior executive whose role is to provide the team with support and access to organizational resources that might otherwise be outside their reach. The criteria for choosing the executive sponsor are similar to those for team composition and project assignment. That is, the executive sponsor should have no special expertise in or authority over the area of the organization seen as a "stakeholder" in the team's project. For example, if a project has to do with key marketing activities in the organization, the sponsor in addition to the team members should not be connected to the marketing function or have any special expertise in or authority over the marketing area.

Once teams have had time to do initial thinking about how to approach their projects, they are given the opportunity to reconvene as a multi-team group to engage in what we call a "network café." This module is designed to further enhance distributed intelligence and to increase participants' awareness of the value of sharing knowledge and expertise across, as well as within, teams. In this segment, participants develop questions they want to ask of other teams, inquire about the availability of needed resources, or administer surveys to collect pilot data concerning their project. Questions posed range from individual (e.g., Does anyone have personal experience or expertise in....? Any cautions or watch-outs you'd advise us to consider?) to relational (Can anyone introduce us to....?) to organizational (What are some strategies that have been effective in the past that might be relevant to our project?).

A key task for the action-learning leadership teams during this first week is to draft what we call a "done statement" for their project. Generating this statement creates lively dialogue about direction, creates some awareness about the need for "alignment" both within the team and between the team and the wider organization, and builds some "commitment" to the work. This statement is a one-page document that summarizes the focus of the team's work and the task and learning outcomes it will produce. Creating the "done statement" is a powerful exercise in meaning-making and critical reflection, combining team members' divergent and experience- based perspectives with the need to question assumptions and explore understanding of organizational systems, processes, and relationships. While some teams frame their project outcomes as actual changes in an organizational system, process, or policy, others aim to create recommendations as outcomes signifying completion of their work. Table 1 provides a "done statement" exemplar.

Action-Learning Project Work
Following the first intensive, participants return to their home assignments and work on advancing their projects through virtual and face-to-face meetings over the next six months. Typically, this involves meetings or further discussion with key stakeholders, initial or additional data collection, and solidifying of action steps. Often, as teams work to uncover additional information on their planned approach and outcomes, they discover that the scope, direction, or planned outcome of their "done statement" needs adjustment. We typically require teams to have their project sponsor sign off on their done statement within six weeks of the end of intensive one.

An example from our case study may be in order here. In this initiative, five-person project teams were given six months to complete a set of strategic projects. One such project involved coming up with an employee ideas (suggestion) program that worked – that is, a program that all employees were able and willing to use. This was seen as strategically important to foster the enhanced morale and organizational innovation necessary for a successful and sustainable transformation. The team assigned to this project was geographically dispersed, drawn from both headquarters and field locations and included people from corporate law and finance as well as field human resource and operations managers. No one on the team had formal "ownership" of the existing suggestion program, so part of the work of this team was to come up with new perspectives on what would make such a system work and to involve key organizational stakeholders early on. To accomplish this, they had to engage across internal boundaries of function, geography, and level, as well as learning about other best-practice organizations externally.

Over the six months of their project work, the team moved through a process of identifying the problems in the current system (e.g., people do not

Table 1. "Done Statement" Exemplar.

WHO	The Strategic Capabilities Team (*names of team members*)
WHAT	will develop a *portfolio strategy* for the Americas division of (*company name*), that will guide prioritization of services to be developed, offered, and delivered to Priority One Clients. This will be accomplished by:
	(1) Chartering ourselves as a team and laying necessary ground work to work effectively across geographic boundaries
	(2) Reviewing the most current internal and external market studies of demand from this client segment
	(3) Developing a list of criteria to assess services against these demands
	(4) Assessing the current state of the division's portfolio of services against those criteria, identifying strengths, weaknesses, opportunities, and threats
	(5) Developing a plan with specific recommended steps to leverage the identified strengths and opportunities, and minimizing the weaknesses and threats
	(6) Presenting the plan to the Executive Steering Committee and facilitating a discussion thereafter to elicit questions, reactions, and inputs
WITH WHOM	This work will be accomplished in collaboration with the seven unit heads of the Americas division (*names*), subject matter experts within each unit (TBD), an outside industry expert on portfolio development (TBD), and a client focus group
WHEN	We intend to accomplish phases (1) – (4) no later than (*date*) and phases (5) – (6) no later than (*date*). The team's overall goal is to have the project completed one month before the launch of the FY04 system-wide planning process
FOR WHOM	We view the following individuals/groups as key stakeholders, and as such, will seek their assessment of the project's primary contribution, as defined as the relevance, rigor, and operational usefulness of the delivered plan:
	(a) Executive Steering Committee
	(b) Unit Heads
MEASURE OF SUCCESS	We will consider the project a success if:
	(a) We complete each phase on or ahead of schedule
	(b) The plan is accepted for pilot in this fiscal year
	(c) We improve our skill at working on geographically dispersed teams
	(d) We each apply at least one learning from the project experience to the day-to-day management of our regional teams
	(e) We each would choose to work together on a future project, if asked

Table 1. (*Continued*)

CONSTRAINTS	We recognize that the following may represent constraints to our success: (a) Current workloads of team members (although we have brainstormed tactics for managing this) (b) Cultural shift from a single-service mindset to an integrated portfolio approach to servicing our clients (c) Interest and availability of those with whom we intend to collaborate

know about it, people do not have access to computers needed to participate in it, supervisors don't act on employees' suggestions) and targeting the issues they believed would have the most impact if addressed. They pilot-tested ideas for improvement, collected data, and came up with recommendations for change. Examples of recommendations included regional pilot tests of new tools or processes, the adoption of new system-wide policies, and the restructuring of certain reporting relationships.

Second Intensive

During the second whole-group intensive, which follows the six months of focused project work, the action-learning teams are asked to present the outcomes of their projects. Presentations focus on both operational and learning outcomes and are addressed to the executive sponsor group as well as to the other action-learning teams. Following the presentations, sponsor group members participate in a "fishbowl" dialogue[1] to discuss what stood out for them in the presentations, particularly with respect to learning outcomes (the "what?") and the organizational implications of that learning (the "so what?"). This was accomplished in two ways. First, the teams were coached in advance to structure their presentations to address both the "what" and "so what" of their projects. Second, the sponsors themselves were coached to ask clarifying and exploratory questions to assist team members in reflecting on their learning and identifying potential implications for the organization. It is particularly important that the sponsors focus, in their listening and questions, on the learning outcomes of the projects, and the organizational implications of that learning, as this reinforces that action-learning projects are vehicles for organizational learning as much as they are useful for the direct strategic or operational value they may add. In an operations-focused organization such as this one, with a strong performance culture, the need to frequently reinforce the importance of learning outcomes cannot be overemphasized, given the participants' ongoing skepticism as to whether these were truly desired and would be rewarded in balance with the operational or strategic deliverables of their work.

Following this presentation and dialogue session, the sponsors work with the teams on implementation and handover of the work, given that they are, by design, not the final "owner" of the team's work. Rather, the "owners" are those individuals or groups (stakeholders) normally responsible for work in a particular domain. In order for this handover to be effective, of course, those stakeholders likely had to have been involved in some way by the action-learning team throughout the process, and the team will likely need to do some follow-up to help stakeholders take over implementation of recommended system-changes.

Harking back to our earlier example, the team working on the employee ideas system had connected with stakeholders, collected data, and pilot tested ideas for improvements prior to intensive two. In their presentation to senior executive sponsors, they reviewed their recommendations for further data collection and system change. However, the people to whom they needed to turn over the continuation of project work (the additional data collection and system changes) were those in the organization responsible for internal communication and system design. So, it was with the help of their executive sponsor and their action-learning coach that they constructed plans on day two of the second intensive, for further connection with stakeholders and handover of the project plans. Because the team had been working all along with these key organizational partners, and because the initiative had strong senior executive sponsorship, the team was able to organize an implementation session at corporate headquarters right after the close of the program for further planning and implementation. They eventually decided to carry forward additional data collection by extending their initial pilot study, in collaboration with organizational stakeholders, following the end of intensive two.

Evaluation

The evaluation of connected leadership initiatives is not unlike the evaluation of any long-term intervention meant to produce change at multiple levels. The purpose of evaluation is *both* to assess the quality and utility of the initiative features *and* to measure the longer-term outcomes of tangible benefit to the organization. As with other processes described, evaluation is approached in a collaborative manner with the co-crafting of the evaluation strategy with the client organization. As stated earlier, in our case example, the steering committee played an important role in the design of the strategy. In addition, internal evaluators partnered with our external evaluator to craft the detailed evaluation method and items.

The evaluation of the leadership development initiative serves four purposes:

(1) *To improve and refine the initiative.* In our case example, this was accomplished by collecting data about the quality, value, and utility of the various components of the initiative and feeding those data into the ongoing redesign of the process. Components of the initiative included classroom modules, group activities, action-learning projects, coaches, sponsors, and technology used for communication. Primary methods included end-of-program questionnaires to participants, debriefing of sponsors and coaches, and monitoring of each team's online collaboration tool.

(2) *To provide evidence that the initiative is producing the outcomes it was designed to produce.* In our case example, this was accomplished by assessing growth of targeted leadership capabilities in the executive population (i.e., engaging across boundaries; leading from an integrated understanding of the organization; demonstrating a basic shift in focus from internal environment to external environment; bringing the best of oneself to the organization). Specifically, this was done through: (a) ratings of effective use of these four capabilities in action-learning projects submitted by participants, action-learning coaches, and sponsors; (b) participants' descriptions of overall lessons learned; (c) evidence that capabilities are being applied in back-home unit through a customized 360-degree rating submitted by bosses, peers, direct reports, and customers; and (d) an executive connections map submitted by the executives, which captures current social networks between executives.

(3) *To provide evidence that projects produce both meaningful learning and tangible benefits to the organization.* This was done in our case example by collecting data on the outcomes from action-learning projects, such as developing enhanced practices for aligning headquarters and field priorities (meaningful learning) and piloting a new strategy for deploying injured employees into meaningful and profitable work for the organization (tangible benefit). Primary methods used included gleaning data from project presentations and follow-up interviews with sponsors and those affected by the project.

(4) *To provide evidence of how changes in the executive population improve organizational outcomes.* This involved assessing the broader impact of

the initiative on the organization, such as the adoption of the leadership capabilities by populations other than the targeted executive population.

In terms of how the evaluation strategy was pursued in this organization, several general principles were adopted:

- Collect data from multiple perspectives (e.g., participants, sponsors, coaches, participants' back-home units, units involved in action-learning projects).
- Collect data before, during, and after each run of the program.
- Collect organizational-level data before the entire initiative begins and after the entire initiative is complete.
- Report to the steering committee on evaluation data from each run of the program.
- Use evaluation data for ongoing program improvement.
- Tap into existing organizational data when appropriate.

While it is beyond the scope of this chapter to go into great detail on the outcomes of this particular case, we can say that in terms of the program quality and utility, most components were well received with those involving significant executive interaction – either with each other or with internal and external stakeholders – rated most highly (e.g., storytelling by senior executives, network café). The lowest rated components tended to be those aspects that involved more theoretical content and those that required structured reflection. Given the action-oriented, operations-focused culture of this organization, this outcome is not surprising.

In terms of growth of targeted leadership capabilities in this executive population, preliminary data show the most development in the practice of "engaging across boundaries" and the least development in the practice of "demonstrating a shift in focus from internal to external environment." One reason for this may be that while all projects required teams to engage across boundaries, not every project required the development of a more external focus. Further, compared to the other three capabilities, relatively little program time was devoted to external focus. This was a recognized limitation going into the initiative, as trade-offs for time needed to be made between internal and external speakers. It is too early to report permanent changes in the executives' social networks, although project presentations provided some evidence of this growth.

We also have evidence that this kind of initiative has impact, in terms of both meaningful learning and tangible outcomes. For example, follow-up research indicates that the teams most likely to have project recommendations formally considered within the organization and project outcomes formally adopted were the teams whose sponsors stayed actively involved in post-program implementation work. The impact of the initiative on belief systems (i.e., beliefs about how the best work gets done) seems to be particularly strong, as reflected in the "lessons of experience" generated by the teams in our case example at the end of intensive two. These lessons included statements such as "it is critical for our groups to be more customer-focused," "we can all be helped by 'fresh eyes' on our work," "be bold as an organization" and "try stuff" (apply non-traditional approaches to persistent problems), "avoid one-way conversations" (dialogue rather than inform), "engage all stakeholders to understand their needs," "freely express ignorance so we can learn," "work cross-functionally and eliminate stereotypes," and "the organizational value of expanded networks."

In addition to sharing their lessons, participants offered specific actions for applying these lessons. For example, the customer-focus lesson translates into bringing the customer point of view into decision making about new products, the fresh-eyes lesson translates into periodically bringing temporary members onto teams to help teams look at their issues and opportunities in a fresh light, and the try-stuff lesson means resisting the urge to over analyze new ideas – and instead take action by running more small experiments to test those ideas.

Taken together, these lessons not only go beyond the traditional outcomes of most individual-leader development programs but also reflect a focus on collaborative work and learning that holds promise for developing new ways of understanding and practicing leadership as an outcome of shared work.

NOTE

1. A "fishbowl" dialogue is a technique for enhancing learning through careful listening and reflection. A small group of participants (in this case, the senior executive sponsors) are asked to form a circle and talk with each other about the issue at hand. Others (in this case, the action-learning team members) form a second, concentric circle around the outside of the first, smaller circle. The task of those on the outside circle is to listen carefully to the discussion taking place in the inner circle. The participants in the outer ring may make notes but are not allowed to speak. The initial discussion goes on for about 20 or 30 minutes, and then the groups can trade places, with the second group reflecting aloud on what they heard in the conversation of the first group. There are many variations on how this technique can be used, but in any of its forms it is designed to deepen the levels of conversation and of listening, helping a group move from advocacy and conflict to dialogue and learning.

REFERENCES

Argyris, C. (1990). *Overcoming organizational defenses: Facilitating organizational learning.* Boston, MA: Allyn and Bacon.

Brass, D. (2001). Social capital and organizational leadership. In: S. Zaccaro & R. Klimoski (Eds), *The nature of organizational leadership: Understanding the performance imperatives confronting today's leaders.* San Francisco, CA: Jossey-Bass.

Conger, J., & Toegel, G. (2003). Action learning and multi-rater feedback as leadership development interventions: Popular but poorly deployed. *Journal of Change Management, 3*(4), 332–348.

Kegan, R., & Lahey, L. (2001). *How the way we talk can change the way we work.* San Francisco, CA: Jossey-Bass.

Marion, R. (1999). *The edge of organization: Chaos and complexity theories of formal social systems.* Thousand Oaks, CA: Sage.

Marquardt, M. (1999). *Action learning in action: Transforming problems and people for world-class organizational learning.* Palo Alto, CA: Davies-Black Publishing.

Marsick, V., & O'Neil, J. (1999). The many faces of action learning. *Management Learning, 30*(2), 159–176.

O'Connor, P. M. G. (2005). Developing leadership practices: A strategy for developing organizational direction, alignment, and commitment. *Practitioner forum presented at the 20th annual conference of the society for industrial and organizational psychology,* April, Los Angeles, CA.

Torbert, W. R., & Cook-Greuter, S. (2004). *Action inquiry: The secret of timely and transforming leadership.* San Francisco, CA: Berrett-Koehler.

Van Velsor, E., & McCauley, C. (2003). Our view of leadership development. In: C. McCauley & E. Van Velsor (Eds), *The Center for Creative Leadership: Handbook of leadership development* (2nd ed.). San Francisco, CA: Jossey-Bass.

Yukl, G., & Lepsinger, R. (2004). *Flexible leadership: Creating value by balancing multiple challenges and choices.* San Francisco, CA: Jossey-Bass.

CHAPTER 4

NESTLÉ ON THE MOVE: EVOLVING HUMAN RESOURCES APPROACHES FOR COMPANY SUCCESS

Paul V. Broeckx and Robert Hooijberg

ABSTRACT

In this chapter we discuss the "Nestlé on the Move" program. The program focuses especially on the areas of leadership and people development and finding ways to better align people with the organization, gain their insights, engage them cooperatively, and stimulate initiative.

Many companies have operated for years and still operate today according to a s with a top-down approach when it comes to defining objectives and strategies. One could question whether the traditional pyramidal structure is not more of a hindrance than a facilitator when it comes to providing an intrinsically humanistic environment as well as getting the best contributions to company efficiency and effectiveness. Pyramidal hierarchical structures were in reality designed for uneducated, uninformed people who needed supervisors to tell them what to do and how to do it. In today's world, with high levels of education and unlimited access to information for all, at least

Being There Even When You Are Not: Leading Through Strategy, Structures, and Systems
Monographs in Leadership and Management, Volume 4, 51–66
Copyright © 2007 by Elsevier Ltd.
All rights of reproduction in any form reserved
ISSN: 1479-3571/doi:10.1016/S1479-3571(07)04003-5

at the worksite, a pyramidal structure may well inhibit people's contribution. This chapter presents the "Nestlé on the Move" program, which Nestlé initiated since 2002, together with other initiatives for reviewing its functioning, challenging the most limiting aspects of the traditional, pyramidal structure in order to find better ways to align people with the organization, gain their insights, engage them cooperatively, and stimulate initiative.

LIMITATIONS OF THE PYRAMIDAL MODEL

Below we discuss some of the limiting aspects of the more traditional hierarchical models. At no point do we wish to imply that organizations should not have hierarchies, and at no point do we say that in the past employees were not performing or intelligent. Rather, we want to expose some of the negative impacts the hierarchical model has had and still has on the behavior and motivation of those working in them, and on the performance of the organization as a whole. In essence, these impacts that could be described as the "bad cholesterol" of hierarchy can be summarized as follows.

Vertical Career Progression

In order to support the role of hierarchy, the professional-development pattern in companies tends to take a vertical approach. This in turn leads to a focus on vertical career progression as the only model for professional development. Climbing the hierarchical ladder frequently becomes a system in itself, to the extent that corporate management-development plans are still largely based on vertical ascension. Usually, this model is accompanied by status symbols indicating clearly the prevalence of hierarchy over flat structures and it also inspired the remuneration pattern.

Command Communication

The communication style in a hierarchical organization is essentially the command mode: Strategies and objectives are transmitted for execution by a structured framework of managers, with a clear top-down mission. The basis of such an organization starts from the viewpoint that people at lower ranks cannot contribute much to designing strategies and defining objectives.

Company Experience

The pyramidal model attaches great value to experience in general and, more specifically, to experience acquired within the same company. Until recently, experience acquired outside was often considered as of less relevance or at least regarded with distrust or skepticism. Most people spent their entire professional life in one company with the result that little credit needed to be granted to the experience acquired outside the organization – hence giving rise to the well-known not-invented-here syndrome. The longer the experience, the more value it supposedly brought to the company. No wonder that length of experience and seniority were often confused. Logically, experience was frequently the basis for promotion, so people were pushed into leadership roles with the main merit of having been with the company for many years. The cost of such a policy has become unaffordable today.

Internal Competition

In the traditional pyramidal model, people work mostly for only one boss. With strong focus on execution of individual tasks, the managerial principle is to put employees in a competing mode. As a consequence, sharing knowledge and cooperation are generally restricted and even discouraged. Reporting and control mechanisms naturally enhance vertical rather than horizontal communication.

Silo Thinking

Organizations such as those described above automatically create silos: The reporting line to one superior (with some ambiguity where dotted lines interfere with how they should operate) combines with the competitive mode to create strong "allegiance" to the superior. For many years, one of the roles of a manager was centralizing information and being the sole point of communication between his or her team and the hierarchy. These practices have clearly evolved, but they are still embedded in the mentality of many managers.

Obedience Orientation

In the pyramidal model, obedience and discipline in execution are essential. As the quality of execution is defined by the superior, it is more important to conform to his or her expectations than to concentrate on results. Initiative is only welcome as long as it does not go beyond the scope of task delegation decided by the superior, as evidenced by the angry question, "Who authorized you to do that?" As a consequence, an obedient employee has more chances of being considered as a performing employee than someone who really cares for results.

Delegation of Tasks Rather than Authority

Finally, the pyramidal model leads to an interpretation of delegation as delegation of tasks rather than delegation of authority and responsibility. The manager retains decision-making authority and is often the "correcting" manager as well as the only judge to measure the quality of the delivery of performance.

BUILDING ON HUMAN POTENTIAL

We find that the limitations of the pyramidal model – vertical career orientation, command communication, company experience, internal competition, silo thinking, obedience orientation, and delegation of tasks rather than authority – block four key factors modern organizations need from their people in order to take full advantage of the knowledge and skills they bring with them. They inhibit the qualities of alignment, insight, cooperation, and initiative (see Fig. 1 for a summary).

Alignment

For a long time, it was accepted that the command mode was the most efficient way to produce results swiftly: No time is wasted on discussions and orders are executed without delay. If the work is executed properly, the results must be there. The reality, at least today, is quite different: The command mode, by not questioning or discussing what results are to be expected, leads to alignment between the expectations of the superior and the action, and not between the action and the expected results. The alignment mode offers a much better chance of obtaining result orientation than the command mode as one can only align when there is a proper understanding of "what to align to," which is the essence of result orientation.

The alignment mode needs a clear sense of the expected results, as well as more dialogue: Today, people cooperate with others who are not their superiors. Everyone needs to be convinced and to engage rationally and emotionally. The command mode, with its unavoidable "Befehl ist Befehl," does

Pyramidal model	What modern organizations need
• Vertical career	• Alignment
• Command communication	• Insight
• Focus on company experience	• Cooperation
• Internal competition	• Initiative
• Silo thinking	
• Obedience orientation	
• Delegation of task not authority	

Fig. 1. Pyramidal Model vs. What Modern Organizations Need.

not allow such a debate. As a consequence, the alignment mode requires a much higher quality of the decision-making process than the command mode. This also means that the quality of the debate and of the thinking preceding that debate becomes essential.

In fact, not only do people seek alignment on purely managerial issues, but they also want to be able to align with values, and if they do not feel they can do so, they will simply not join an organization that they do not feel comfortable with. In other words, it is no longer only material conditions that prevail in the choice of an employer.

Insight

Promotion and reward based on experience alone can be harmful if experience is confused with seniority. Experience is obviously precious, but it is only useful if it can be transformed into action. Converting experience into action is called insight, and insight is therefore the sublimation of experience. Without this additional dimension, experience can rapidly become a showstopper, a killer of creativity and initiative, as has been seen so many times. In today's world, experience (like knowledge) may rapidly become obsolescent and its relevance should therefore be systematically recalibrated.

If priority is to be given to insight over experience, it requires a different way of assessing people for specific roles. If it is indeed easy to measure experience, judging on insight is more delicate, as it can only be measured by those who have insight themselves! As a consequence, those who have insight are more important than those who have only experience. Many corporations may need to adapt their development model because of this concept, since it requires a different values set, which needs to be communicated and understood by all.

Cooperation

The aggregation of individual performance does not lead to an overall performance, unless it is aligned and convergent. Failing to improve cooperation between well-educated, informed people may be costly, as their knowledge and insight are not brought together and the company misses out on efficiency and result orientation. If one wishes to foster cooperation and encourage people to build on each other's insight and knowledge, then it is essential to eliminate all barriers to cooperation and to invite all to share genuinely everything they have to share. One of these barriers is clearly the classical rating systems or, even more, forced ranking.

Initiative

While the obedience mode may work for a poorly-educated and less-informed workforce, today it is a sheer waste not to raise the level of initiative and not to optimize all the skills and insights that are available in a well-educated workforce. It is this need for initiative that has given rise to the many executive-education programs on leadership and motivation that have become so important in recent years.

In order to harness people's skills and initiative, they need to be motivated and therefore better led. The difference between the contribution of a motivated person and a discouraged one is obvious. Demotivated employees have virtually no power and can do little to reverse bad managerial decisions or to fight inefficiency, but they can lower their contribution in a way that is imperceptible: The cost is immeasurable, but huge.

To raise the level of initiative in companies, another change is necessary. To truly invite initiative, it is necessary to create a working climate where people can feel free and have breathing space.

A real performance culture is one that builds self-confidence. No one can be efficient without a reasonable level of confidence. Most managers, by trying to maintain their superiority, tend to stifle others' self-confidence.

More importantly, those companies that confuse an assessment culture with a performance culture do more to destroy self-confidence than to build it.

When alignment, insight, cooperation, and initiative start to come together, one of the first consequences is the disappearance of silos and the silo mentality. This alone is worth the effort and will unlock additional efficiency and effectiveness. The second consequence is obviously improved alignment with results – everything that companies wish to have today. They want this to happen, but do not do enough to get it. Often, they think that by saying it, they will have it.

In order to get alignment, insight, cooperation, and initiative from people, managers have to become more like "hubs," that is, able to connect people and combine skills. They do not manage through a hierarchy, but through a network. Skill sets are therefore changing dramatically, with clear consequences for the renewed efficiency and effectiveness of a corporation.

NESTLÉ'S ANSWER

Nestlé is a food and beverage company of about 250,000 employees with factories and/or operations in almost every country in the world and about US $70 billion sales. Nestlé has always adapted its ways of operating to the circumstances of time and location, which explains its permanent success for more than 140 years. Over the last years, it has undertaken a series of concrete actions to prepare its future. In terms of human resources management, one of these is "Nestlé on the Move," an HR strategy to respond to the evolution from a pyramidal structure to a vertical organization. This strategy has been approved by the CEO and the executive board and has therefore received the support needed to transform the concept into reality. This strategically clear focus and top management support greatly facilitate the HR action, as everything it does can be explained by the basic concept of "Nestlé on the Move." There are five major parts to "Nestlé on the Move": Implementing flat and flexible structures, inspiring management, long-term development, dynamic compensation, and lifelong learning (see Fig. 2). All elements call for specific programs and key performance indicators (KPIs). However, the most important change is the change in mindset, which cannot be achieved on command. Therefore, much of the effort focused on and continues to focus on communicating the concept of "Nestlé on the Move" during training sessions, management visits, discussions, and conferences. In addition, the action program that is based on it has clear lines of action and most of its results are measurable and have been measured – at least to a certain extent.

1. Flat and flexible structure

2. Inspire management

    a. Nestlé Leadership Program

        i. Start at top level of management

        ii. Make it a self-development program

        iii. Run program with outside organization

        iv. Feature feedback from each manager's colleagues (peers, subordinates and superiors) using an outside organization

    b. Develop People Initiative

        i. Assessment and rating are different – everyone needs to be assessed, no one needs to be rated

        ii. Assessment refers to the concept of development and of the manager's responsibility for developing her or his people

        iii. Correct assessment always refers to both the past and the future

        iv. Developed the Progress and Development Guide with:

            1. Long-term objectives

            2. The leadership framework

            3. The assessment of the role of the employee and his or her possible development

            4. The Development Plan

        v. Development plan is separate from compensation

3. Long-term development

    a. Destroy silos and build a management development plan that embraced all functions, regions, and stand-alone businesses.

    b. Build a talent pool in line with the Nestlé's development needs.

    c. Have a complete view of succession planning to improve its quality and link it to the talent pool.

4. Dynamic compensation – change from hierarchical to horizontal compensation models so that employees can earn more even without promotion.

5. Lifelong learning

Fig. 2.   The Five Parts of "Nestlé on the Move".

Implementing Flat and Flexible Structures

A network organization requires considerably fewer hierarchical levels than a pyramidal one, so the number of levels has to be reduced.

In 2002, Nestlé undertook a worldwide effort to review its organization, with the purpose of building an agile and flexible organizational structure allowing the company to continue to grow and develop, leveraging its size and its complexity. Also, Nestlé's unique GLOBE program (see page 65), which started in 2001, is part of this permanent effort to prepare Nestlé for the future.

There was an in-depth examination of the role of the corporate head-quarters and the definition of the roles of businesses, functional and all other units at corporate level. This project, undertaken at the corporate level, considerably helped the concept of "Nestlé on the Move" to advance, allowing the HR action to concentrate on its objectives.

Inspiring Management

One of the most challenging parts of "Nestlé on the Move" consists of changing the way managers seek out contributions from their staff. It is clear that, if Nestlé wanted more alignment, insight, cooperation, and initiative from its staff, it would need to start with a change in the way managers led their people. Two programs were developed to address this issue: The Nestlé Leadership Program and the Develop People Initiative.

Nestlé Leadership Program

Nestlé needs *both* managers *and* leaders, not leaders instead of managers. Leadership is not an end in itself, it is a means to improve alignment, gain insights, get cooperation, and stimulate initiative. The Nestlé model makes this clear by referring to the concept of inspiring management, which could only be achieved if the leadership skills at Nestlé were improved. Many companies run leadership programs, but not many start at the top. At Nestlé it was felt that if in a typically hierarchical organization leadership had to be enhanced, such a program should cover the top line first.

A second consideration was that leadership skills could only be improved if the individual accepted that she or he could do better. This meant that the program had to be conceived as a self-development program and not as an assessment tool. Any direct management involvement was therefore to be banned. Any link with compensation was also to be eliminated. Indeed, an essential requirement for improving leadership skills is to make the managers admit that they can improve and that the recognition of possible weaknesses as revealed by the program will not work against them in terms of reward. Therefore, such a program could only be run with an outside organization. This was the third requirement.

The fourth requirement was that the program should be based on actual feedback from each manager's colleagues (peers, superiors, and subordinates).

This feedback, collected by the outside organization, would make up the individual (and most important) part of the program. Because such feedback is delicate, it was felt that it should be communicated to the manager concerned, by a professional coach. The company (through the line manager or HR) would neither receive nor have access to any of the individual feedback.

The first program was run in 2003 and was an immediate success. It was attended by some 25 participants, including two executive board members, and ran for four days. The evening before it began, the skepticism was at its height. After day four, it had been so successful that all the executives requested that their top team could also attend the program. The principle of a follow-up program was confirmed at the same time. The success was certainly due to the excellent work of the outside organization, in this case London Business School, which ran the entire program.

The program went on so well that about 450 executives attended it between 2003 and 2006. The CEO himself took the leadership survey. Furthermore, HR was asked to extend the program and roll it out to another 4,000 middle managers. This decentralized program started its rollout (having run two pilots) in early 2006 and was organized with the support of the same organization and its international network through three centers: Singapore, Miami, and London. In 2006 alone some 1,200 participants attended the decentralized program. Great care was taken to ensure that the decentralized program presented the same characteristics as the top line program and that it was of the same quality. The cost of the decentralized programs amounted to about $25 million.

Due to the feedback (43 questions answered by about 10 colleagues) the information on Nestlé's management style became undeniable and substantiated. It was Nestlé management talking about Nestlé management. The characteristics of the Nestlé culture were also better understood. In addition, because – through the database of the outside organization – Nestlé's leadership could be benchmarked with the leadership of other companies, it was possible to get a better assessment of the management style and the improvements needed therein.

By the end of 2006, both the top line and decentralized programs were considered to have been highly successful. Follow-up programs are continuously requested and these will probably be organized at the local level, so that the whole concept of the program moves progressively from a central approach (top-line program), through a regional program (decentralized program) to monitoring at a local level. The program has undoubtedly improved the Nestlé management style, and in terms of individual behavior, the results are both visible and demonstrated by the evolution of the feedback between the initial program and the follow-up taking place between 12 and 18 months later.

It is already clear that the Leadership Program, in one form or another, cannot be stopped and will continue to evolve with the same objective in mind: To enhance inspiring management and make better use of available resources.

The Develop People Initiative
The need to enhance personal development and also to share knowledge and cooperation was the starting point for a fresh view on how people should be assessed.

The first consideration is that assessment and rating are two different things. To put it bluntly: everyone needs to be assessed, no one needs to be rated. The Nestlé view of assessment refers first to the concept of cooperation, whereby people are required to share everything. Whereas in school, sharing knowledge during an examination is generally considered to be cheating and therefore undesirable, in companies the opposite is true.

Second, assessment, according to Nestlé, refers to the concept of development and of the manager's responsibility for developing her or his people. Everyone agrees that assessment is required, but it is the role of development that has not received sufficient attention. In our view, assessment always refers to both the past and the future, whereas traditional rating refers exclusively to the past. As a consequence, the Nestlé Develop People Initiative was launched with the purpose of making managers responsible for the development of their people and reversing their role from that of a "passive judge" to a "committed developer." A document was developed, called the "Progress and Development Guide," consisting of four chapters:

- Long-term objectives;
- The leadership framework;
- The assessment of the role of the employee and his/her possible development; and
- The development plan

The main and essential characteristic of the Develop People Initiative is that the discussion of the development plan is totally separate from any consideration of reward, so that the discussion between manager and employee is free from any thoughts of compensation. This is essential. For managers, this disconnect is a great help, as they are now able to enter into a discussion entirely turned to the future and specific needs. Many, if not most of the managers felt uncomfortable about ranking their people, as the ranking frequently became a source of tension.

Some managers have found it difficult to cope with this new model, as the traditional rating model is an intrinsic part of a pyramidal model and is convenient. Many of them still believe that rating is a performance driver, whereas it drives only submissiveness and obedience – if not flattery.

It took more or less two years to break through with the new approach, which is now generally accepted and valued. The implementation of the "Progress and Development Guide" already covers 70% to 80% of the management population and the 100% target achievement is now within reach – a good result in a strongly decentralized organization.

As one can imagine, the communication process has been crucial and it was necessary to launch a vast campaign and to visit the affiliates with detailed presentations. The fact that the "Progress and Development Guide" operates on a Web-based platform has facilitated its implementation. However, it is the quality of the dialogue that is the most crucial.

Summary

With the Leadership Program and the Develop People Initiative, Nestlé is transforming its management practices and enhancing the role of the inspiring manager. This also plays a crucial role in the implementation of flat and flexible structures. The implementation of flat and flexible structures frequently leads to having more direct reports, which have to act more independently and thus require a different management approach (one does not manage three direct reports in the same way as 15). We believe that an inspiring management approach forms an essential complement to the flatter flexible structures.

Long-Term Development

The third part of "Nestlé on the Move," also to be implemented simultaneously, was the Long-Term Development. Nestlé has a long-standing tradition of international development. It invests heavily in training, uses internal promotion to a large extent, and has a very low staff turnover rate – about 4% worldwide. The pyramidal model had introduced a silo approach to development, so that most careers were managed within one region or within one function.

Interregional and interdisciplinary moves were reduced, whereas the best way to a top-level general management position was via a marketing career. Many took this route, even if their profile did not exactly correspond to the requirements of a marketing career and, sometimes, still less to those of a general manager.

With the introduction of a network organization with flat and flexible structures, the situation has changed dramatically:

- The number of hierarchical levels has been reduced and fewer promotion levels are available.
- Interregional and interfunctional moves have therefore been enhanced to stimulate both personal development and organizational learning.
- New types of roles have been created that cut across the traditional career paths – for example, specific project work, supply chain management, GLOBE (a worldwide program to implement integrated data and common systems across the Nestlé Group), and so on. These new functions have to tap into all the available resources as much as the more traditional units. As a consequence, the management development model needs to be entirely reviewed.

The first requirement was to destroy the silos and to build a management development plan embracing all the functions and regions, as well as the stand-alone businesses. The second was to build a talent pool in line with the development needs of the company; thus far, the talent pool was incomplete and much talent was not registered, sometimes even deliberately so. The third was to have a complete view of the succession planning, to improve its quality and link it with the talent pool. The fourth was to link training attendance with the talent pool and to development plans.

It took three years to get the long-term development program off the ground. The reason for this was not so much the technical aspects, but mostly management's lack of willingness to share the talent pool and ensure that it encompassed all regions, businesses, and functions. The bad habit of hiding resources is now progressively fading away.

By the end of 2006, the talent pool included 2,200 names and the link with succession planning is now clearly established. Twice a year, the list of "Group Assets" and "Group High Potentials"[1] are discussed in the executive board, as is succession planning, with a clear view of the situation of the 1,200 key positions. This global approach to management development is now fully accepted and allows Nestlé to dynamically drive the professional development of the total resources of the company.

Dynamic Compensation

The pyramidal mode almost naturally imposes an inflexible compensation model, with insufficient room for expanding remuneration horizontally.

At Nestle, the flattening of the pyramidal model changed not only career paths but also the remuneration model. Thus, it became necessary to develop horizontal remuneration models, allowing employees to expand their remuneration even without promotion. This means that the strength of the correlation between promotion and reward had to be reduced.

The concrete measures resulting from this new situation are manifold:

- The variable part of remuneration, being geared exclusively to past achievement, was decoupled from the other elements of remuneration. It needs to be kept in mind that short-term variable remuneration has little to do with motivation. It intends, in the first place, to inspire entrepreneurship by making a stronger link between results and rewards. Believing that the leverage of short-term variable pay produces motivation would mean that our managers' motivation is for sale. Fifty years ago, managers did not have any variable remuneration and were just as motivated as our managers today.
- The other elements of remuneration (base salary, long-term incentives) are geared essentially to the future and have little to do with rewarding past performance. Companies grant salary raises and stock as an engagement for the future with the purpose of retaining their best people.
- Nestlé considers that, in general, short-term bonuses should not exceed 50% of base salary. Many companies believing that high variable remuneration would stimulate performance, intended to build a performance culture. In fact, they were building a gambling culture.
- Introduction of a long-term incentive plan based on stock.

These measures have allowed Nestlé to increase competitiveness and attractiveness, as the increase in the number of spontaneous applications it receives from all over the world proves: 41,000 candidates in the Internet-recruitment site at headquarters alone. However, Nestlé has refused to push the level of variable remuneration out of proportion and considers that the base salary should remain the main component.

Lifelong Learning

The evolution in the level of education and information of the workforce has played and continues to play a major role in the creation and running of "Nestlé on the Move." The combined effect of the rapid obsolescence of science and the increase in life expectancy has generated a need for continuous education, way beyond previous levels. Whereas before, learning and working were kept quite separate, every day it becomes increasingly clear that there is no working without learning and vice versa.

These trends confirm the need for Nestlé to maintain and develop its strong belief in the need for continuous learning. This is probably an area in which Nestlé has only to continue its present practices without major changes. People who do not accept the need to learn are not welcome at Nestlé, which also explains why Nestlé does not have a star system. Learners are generally humble.

Nestlé is a co-founder of IMD and has its own International Training Center in Switzerland. This Nestlé Training Center welcomes about 1,500 participants annually from all the countries in which Nestlé operates. Whereas participation in programs from IMD and other training institutions is viewed as an eye opener and an opportunity for exchange with participants from other companies, as well as exposure to state-of-the-art business models and theories, the International Training Center teaches the Nestlé way. It is also the place where the Nestlé values are broadcast and discussed. Because of its proximity (3 km) to the international headquarters in Vevey, the CEO and executive board members are able to attend many sessions – a very important feature for a training center.

RESULTS AND CHALLENGES FOR THE FUTURE

The HR strategy focuses, in the first instance, on company results and the company's sustainable development in terms of long-term growth by stimulating alignment, insight, cooperation, and initiative. Nestlé has an overall development model, which has shown its validity, and "Nestlé on the Move" is an integral part of it.

"Nestlé on the Move" has already made an important contribution to company results in terms of drive and excitement. It comes over as a positive message on how the company should manage its people, and demonstrates – in a concrete manner – that the people are the most important asset of an enterprise. The importance of the worldwide Leadership Program is recognized and the follow-up program has shown an improvement in individual scores.

The evolution of the compensation model has improved Nestlé's competitiveness at all levels. The combination of this competitiveness and the long-term development strategy of people allows the company to maintain a low turnover rate in a world where changes are becoming increasingly numerous. Change may be necessary, but stability is also an asset as many staff changes are costly. Companies developing a long-term relationship with their people will therefore always be more profitable in the long term and their development more sustainable – the results of the Nestlé Group demonstrate this clearly.

With the Develop People Initiative, the company has taken a lead in how an emancipated workforce should be managed in the future. However, there is still room for development in aligning company practices with the evolution of "Nestlé on the Move":

- Horizontal career development is to be developed further. Professional satisfaction will be derived more from development of job content than from climbing the corporate ladder, which loses a few rungs every day.
- The importance of collective contribution will drive more team-based rewards rather than purely individual ones.
- Nestlé had to change some of its key HR systems, structures, and processes to build a working environment where the "whys" were addressed before the "whats" were fixed and the "hows" determined. Without that, "Nestlé on the Move" could not have evolved and an emancipated, well-educated and well-informed workforce would then unavoidably have turned its back on the company.

The move toward a more humanistic working environment and an engaged workforce is Nestlé's challenge today, and it is well on its way to reaching that goal, while achieving new heights of performance.

NOTE

1. These categories refer to different levels of readiness for holding high-level executive positions.

PART II: KNOWLEDGE MANAGEMENT

Kimberly B. Boal examines what companies and strategic leaders can do to enhance knowledge acquisition, retention, and dissemination. In doing so, he explores how leaders create environments where people throughout the organization utilize both strong and weak network relationships in the pursuit of finding, exploiting, and protecting new knowledge and ideas. Kazuo Ichijo then hones in on how strategic leaders at electronics manufacturer Sharp Corporation developed processes, systems, and structures that allowed the company to build and exploit its knowledge of and competence in LCD technology.

CHAPTER 5

STRATEGIC LEADERSHIP, ORGANIZATIONAL LEARNING, AND NETWORK TIES

Kimberly B. Boal

ABSTRACT

First and second order learning lie at the center of an organization's ability to exploit its core competencies or explore for new opportunities. Strategic leadership lies at the center of this learning process. Strategic leaders enable organizations to learn by telling stories about what the organization is, what the organization does, and what the organization can become. They also enable competence carriers to come together to solve current and future problems by networking. These processes are explored.

History matters. It matters not just because we can learn from the past, but because the present and the future are connected to the past by the continuity of a society's institutions.

Douglas C. North (1991, p. vii)

In the life trajectory of any organization, there are important strategic inflection points (SIPs) (Burgelman & Grove, 1996). These SIPs are caused by changes in fundamental industry dynamics, technologies, and strategies that

Being There Even When You Are Not: Leading Through Strategy, Structures, and Systems
Monographs in Leadership and Management, Volume 4, 69–86
Copyright © 2007 by Elsevier Ltd.
All rights of reproduction in any form reserved
ISSN: 1479-3571/doi:10.1016/S1479-3571(07)04004-7

create opportunities for strategic leaders to develop new visions, create new strategies, and move their organizations in new directions as they traverse through the turbulence and uncertainty. Developing the organization's capacity to learn from its past, adapt to its present, and envision and create the future will become increasingly important. Since a firm's competitive advantage lies in its ability to create, re/combine, and transfer knowledge efficiently within the context of its competitive environment, collective knowledge offers the most competitive advantage due to the difficultly of imitation by other firms. At the same time, it is the most difficult to learn (Kogut & Zander, 1992; Zhao, Anand, & Mitchell, 2004). The very complexity, non-codifiability, and tacitness of collective knowledge require opportunities for frequent interaction, dialogue, and feedback. Senge (1990) argues that if strategic leaders are going to take on the roles of designers, stewards, and teachers, they must value learning and become experts at learning in the context of their organization.

This paper focuses on the impact of strategic leadership and the leader's role in the development of intra- and inter-organizational network ties on the organization's ability to learn and adapt. Strategic leadership is differentially important in the past, the present, and the future of the organization both directly and indirectly through their impact on single-loop, double-loop learning and the development and use of network ties.

Strategic leadership lies at the heart of organizational learning and adaptation. This is shown in Fig. 1.

To appreciate the ways in which strategic leadership impacts organizations, it is useful to discuss organizations as complex social learning systems. This and the nature of organizational learning are discussed before proceeding to a discussion of leadership and organizational network ties. This paper concludes with a series of summary statements.

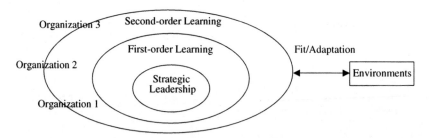

Fig. 1. Strategic Leadership and Organizational Learning and Adaptation.

ORGANIZATIONS AS COMPLEX KNOWLEDGE AND LEARNING SYSTEMS

Organizations are social learning systems. "In a social learning system, competence is historically and socially defined ... Knowing, therefore, is a matter of displaying competencies defined in social communities ... Socially defined competence is always in interplay with our experience. It is in this interplay that learning takes place" (Wenger, 2003, p. 77). These competencies allow actors to modify their ways of thinking or acting when dealing with changing environments. Take for example, Ken Chenalut, CEO of American Express. His capacity to learn enabled him to handle the crisis of September 11, 2001, in which he moved 3,000 people from AE's headquarters at Ground Zero to New Jersey.

Organizational knowledge consists of the organization's stock of skills and beliefs (Spender & Grant, 1996). It is useful to differentiate between four distinguishable, but co-equal forms of knowledge: individual level versus group level knowledge and explicit versus non-codifiable tacit knowledge (Cook & Brown, 1999). Implicit knowledge at the group level is the firm's collective knowledge (Zhao et al., 2004).

Knowledge and learning are distributed throughout the organization in a nexus of networks. Within this nexus of networks, strategic leaders, serve as network brokers (Burt, 1992). Strategic leaders have a unique ability to change or reinforce existing action patterns. Strategic leaders must be responsible for bringing competence carriers together within and across the firm's domain. In doing so, they provide the mechanisms by which organizations encourage, support, and sustain innovation and knowledge creation. Ken Lewis, Chairman and CEO of Bank of America, says that one of the ways talent is developed is through communication and dialogue. He says, "We meet on a quarterly basis as a group to identify the specific need at the various levels, to talk about success stories and failures, and to talk about the process for change where change is necessary" (Lewis, 2002).

By interacting with a wide range of networks, inside and outside the boundaries of the firm, competence carriers are encouraged to bring new solutions to old problems as well as discover new problems to which known or knowable solutions can be applied. This increases not only the store of knowledge and procedural memory, but transactive memory as well. Procedural memory refers to an understanding and mastery of the organization's rules/routines. Transactive memory refers to an awareness of the range of knowledge available and who possesses it. The availability and access to divergent information is crucial to solving complex problems. Organizational creativity is related to the leader's personal networking behavior or the encouragement of subordinates' networking (Amabile, Schatzel, Moneta, & Kramer St., 2004; Shalley & Gilson, 2004). As Heinrich von Pierer, CEO of Siemens AG says, "Having a global workforce of well-trained, highly skilled people obviously isn't enough: The workforce must be efficiently networked and leveraged to maximize benefits across the company" (von Pierer, 2002).

A major problem in the transfer of knowledge or learning, be it intra-organizational or inter-organizational, is the stickiness of knowledge. Some attribute the stickiness of knowledge to its characteristics, e.g., its codifiability and its complexity (e.g., Kogut & Zander, 1992). I assume the difficulties in transferring learning are a function of the processes and situation, as much as they are the characteristics of the knowledge to be transferred. In other words, it is not necessarily the characteristics of the knowledge to be learned that makes it sticky, it is the context in which it is embedded (Rerup, 2004). A second major problem lies in creating and enlarging the organization's procedural and transactive memories. The greater the number of people in an organization that share both procedural and transactive memories, the more the organization can be said to know.

Four problems emerge in the transfer of knowledge:

(1) People who need information do not know who possesses it, and those who possess it do not know who needs it. This is a problem of structural holes where there are no direct or indirect links connecting the nodes within the organization's network, thus inhibiting the development of the organization's transactive memory.
(2) Owing to lack of incentives, there is no motivation to share on the part of the possessor or motivation to learn on the part of the acquirer. This occurs when incentives are split or when internal capital markets are organized as tournaments with the winner taking all. Both cases promote competition and conflict, which undermines the sharing of information, reduces performance (Johnson & Johnson, 1989), and also inhibits the development of transactive memory.
(3) There is an incorrect understanding about the sources of cause and effect and thus poor transfer, which leads to the development of incorrect procedural memory.
(4) Either there is an incorrect understanding about the cause and effect relationship by the target, or there is a desire by the target to modify and imprint their identity on the solution. This results in poor replication of

the organization's procedural memory. Thus, strategic leaders must recognize that learning and knowledge transfer involves both the capacity and the desire of people to do things. Steve Kerr, former chief information officer for General Electric (GE) illustrates this point in his interview with Larry Greiner. "If, for example, at GE you want to cross-market, and the commission is going to be $110,000, who gets it? Well, is it 80/20% or 70/30%? or 50/50%? The result is fighting, and bickering. I remember Welch saying, "Here's what we're going to do. If the commission is $110,000, if two departments or two people share it, they each get $110,000. In one swoop you get a tremendous incentive to cross-market" (Greiner, 2002, p. 347).

In addition, strategic leaders must recognize that the transfer of knowledge involves standing on the shoulders of giants because those who worked hard generally made many mistakes and suffered, but learned from these mistakes. Thus to successfully learn from others takes a degree of humility and discipline. For example, Great Harvest forces its franchisees to sign an agreement to follow everything to the tiniest letter for a year, and when Intel reproduces a semiconductor factory, it forces the engineers to replicate every single detail even to the extent of putting in doors that lead nowhere (Rerup, 2004).

One important role the strategic leader can play in the development of the organization's procedural and transactive memories as well as the facilitation of creative problem solving is that of providing access to and encouraging the sharing of knowledge and information: Knowledge about our history, knowledge about issues confronting the organization in real time, and knowledge about possible futures. Under Jack Welch, the Crotonville training facility of GE grew in its offerings and had, over the course of a year, more than 10,000 managers and customers attending sessions. Jack Welch himself taught a course on Leadership and Values seven times a year to high-potential middle managers. In addition, courses were taught by the vice-chairman and the CFO. In fact, corporate leaders taught 60% of the senior-level courses, with Welch often standing in front of the group. Before Welch retired, GE had created a Crotonville-Europe and a Crotonville-Asia (Greiner, 2002). In the same way, Celestica has courses "in which our top 200 to 300 leaders across the company spend time with the top four executives, including me [Polistuk, Chairman and CEO], engaged in strategic brainstorming not unlike Jack Welch's bear pits" (Polistuk, 2002).

Learning depends upon actual and potential connections between knowledge elements. Knowledge is embedded in an interconnected network of other pieces of knowledge. Changes in parts of the knowledge structure trigger changes in other related or similar parts. Learning thus depends upon establishing connections between prior knowledge and new knowledge (March, Schulz, & Zhou, 2000). Below, we will elaborate on organizational learning and change in general and the role strategic leadership and organizational ties play in addressing the specific issues outlined above.

ORGANIZATIONAL LEARNING

It has long been held that change is necessary and beneficial if organizations are to remain effective (Child, 1972; Fox-Wolfgramm, Boal, & Hunt, 1998; Hannan & Freeman, 1977; Meyer, Brooks, & Goes, 1990; Meyer, Goes, & Brooks,1994). This is based upon the assumption that organizational growth and survival is dependent upon maintaining a "fit" between the organization and its environment (Summer et al., 1990). Thus, survival, learning, and change go hand in hand. This perspective emphasizes the benefits of adaptability and flexibility. But survival and effectiveness also require maintaining a balance between flexibility and stability (Brown & Eisenhardt, 1998). Without stability, a firm would not be able to accumulate knowledge, and would be in a constant state of flux never being able to move any distance from a random state because improvement would vaporize at every new fad.

Learning and change are based upon either exploitation of core competencies or exploration for new opportunities (March, 1991). It is in the exploitation of core competencies that firms maintain their trajectory and identity thus achieving stability in the mists of change (Fox-Wolfgramm et al., 1998). It is in the exploration for new opportunities that firms overcome the related problems of competency traps, core rigidities, or the Icarus Paradox (Levitt & March, 1988; Leonard-Barton, 1992; Miller, 1990). Recall how the initial success of Icarus led him, in his hubris, to fly higher and higher towards the sun until his wax wings melted and he plunged to his doom. Exploitation without exploration can lead to specialization and excess, to confidence and contentment, to dogma and ritual, to death. The ability of a firm to avoid the seduction of success and change, while maintaining performance, is a function of both its capacity to change and its ability to learn (Black & Boal, 1996; Boal & Hooijberg, 2000). Learning is the focus here.

The organizational learning cycle can be described as a four-stage closed loop in which individual beliefs lead to individual action, which results in organizational action followed by environmental responses. Feedback from these environmental responses influences individual beliefs and aspirations, which trigger future action (Schulz, 2002). The philosopher Santana is often quoted as saying that those who fail to learn the lessons of history are doomed to repeat its errors. While it is traditionally assumed that learning is intentionally adaptive, under conditions of ambiguity, experience can be misleading and interpretations are problematic (March & Olsen, 1975). Prior learning, especially those lessons encoded in rules or routines often prevent new learning or the learning of the wrong things making improvement problematic (Schulz, 2002; Wooten & James, 2004). In Chapter 6, Ichijo points out that Sony could not let go of its cathode ray tube (CRT) technology in making televisions, while Sharp, Samsung, and LG Electronics forged ahead producing liquid crystal display (LCD) televisions. Innovations usually come from marginal players in an industry due to the industry leaders' inability to unlearn (Leblebici, Salancik, Copay, & King, 1991).

Beliefs, trust, and perceptions, and not detached data and analysis, determine what happens under conditions of ambiguity (March & Olsen, 1975). Often, to avoid crises, organizations must first unlearn the lessons of history lest they apply them when they are no longer appropriate (Nystrom & Starbuck, 1984). For example, even during the oil embargo, American automobile manufactures first needed to unlearn the lesson that American's would only buy big cars and that there was no profit potential in trying to sell small cars. Volkswagen, Nissan, and Toyota taught the Americans that there was a large, profitable market in smaller cars. Or consider Wal-Mart's misadventure in Germany where it failed to understand the differences between the US and German suppliers, customers, and regulators. More recently, Ford Motor, which like GM, had a difficult time in transitioning from large, rear-wheel drive cars, to smaller, front-wheel drive cars, has again demonstrated myopic vision. For the past 10 years, they have been fighting the notion of global warming. As a result, they did not aggressively pursue hybrid technologies. With the recent rise in the cost of petroleum, they have been forced to purchase the technology from Toyota in order to enter the hybrid automotive market.

The organizational ability to identify, assimilate, and exploit knowledge from external sources reflects the organization's "absorptive capacity" (Cohen & Levinthal, 1990). The ability to learn involves not only the capacity to recognize new information, assimilate it, and apply it toward new ends but that it involves processes used offensively and defensively to improve the fit between the organization and its environments. It is a continuous genesis of creation and recreation where gestalts and logical structures are added or deleted from memory (Piaget, 1968). However, sometimes, these processes only require adjustments within an existing behavioral repertoire. Occasionally, they may require modifications of the interpretative system and the development of new combinations of responses. At other times, they may require the restructuring of the meta-level system that selects and interprets stimuli within a Weltanschauung that provides the worldview in which the situation is defined (Boal & Hooijberg, 2000). Learning can result in organizational *changes in purpose* (*know-why*), *changes in meaning* (*know-what*), and *changes in methods* (*know-how*) (Garud, 1997). Such changes in world views can be seen in IBM's actions to reinvent itself from a PC maker into a seller of business solutions, or Erickson's decision to become the end-to-end wireless solution provider, not just the provider of handsets.

Since knowledge and learning are distributed throughout the organization, absorptive capacity occurs at both the individual and organizational level. A key aspect of absorptive capacity is the procession and development of procedural and transactive memories (Wegner, 1987; Liang, Moreland, & Argote, 1995). Strategic leaders can enhance collective learning and the development and use of the organization's procedural and transactive memories by promoting intra- and extra-organizational dialogue. "Knowledge management depends upon social interaction not computerized information systems" (Greiner, 2002, p. 349). People are "docile." That is, they have a tendency to depend upon suggestions, recommendations, persuasion, and information obtained through social channels (Simon, 1993). Docility contributes to the effectiveness of individuals because the information received is typically better than the information individuals could gather independently. Dialogue aids in surfacing one's own and other's thoughts and assumptions and helps create new ideas and initiate collective action. As Jeff Pfeffer (2002) of the Stanford Graduate School of Business says, "Knowledge management is not about intranets and Lotus notes and all the stuff around technology. It's about having an organization in which people are both encouraged and have the time to talk to each other".

Because strategic leaders are central in the cognitive networks of organizations, they will have the most influence on promoting and interpreting the exchange of information and advice. The giving and receiving of information and advice from one's social network forces the individual to think about the issues they are facing in ways that they would not if the information and advice was not offered (Augier & Sarasvathy, 2004). For example, at one of his sessions at Crotonville, the class told Jack Welch that his favorite mantra of "first or second in market share, or fix, sell, or close" was now dysfunctional because the closer you get to 100%, the lower the upside. As a result of this dialogue, Welch changed his approach and at strategy meetings, he started asking people to answer the question, "Imagine your market share is less than 5%. Describe your market" (Greiner, 2002, p. 345).

Learning occurs whenever an organization achieves what it intended or when a mismatch between intentions and outcomes are identified and corrected. When performance falls short of aspirations, behavioral adjustment intensifies, and it subsides when performance exceeds aspirations. Single-loop learning occurs whenever an error is detected and corrected without questioning or altering the underlying values of the system. Double-loop learning occurs when mismatches are corrected by examining and altering first the preferred states that organizations seek to satisfy and then the actions (Argyris & Schön, 1978). Single-loop learning tends to result in organizational convergence, while double-loop learning tends to result in organizational reorientation. Most organizational learning and change is based upon single-loop learning. However, processes that initiate single-loop learning can also result in double-loop learning (Lant & Mezias, 1992). Organizations learn not only from their own experience but also from the experience of other organizations (Huber, 1991; Levitt & March, 1988). Thus, organizations learn from both their intra- and inter-organizational networks. Learning occurs by connecting people, problems, and/or solutions. Communication, interdependence, knowledge sharing routines, and complementary resources or capabilities all affect knowledge transfer (Lane, Koka, & Pathak, 2002). Moving or modifying people, technology, or structure are alternative mechanisms by which organizations learn and knowledge is transferred (Argote, 1999). However, learning requires stability in relationships (Argote, 2005). ABB learned how difficult it was to transform itself into a transnational organization. Capital One Financial Corporation, on the other hand, now uses social network analysis to maintain links between people with similar jobs after it went through reorganization along product lines. Solvay, the Belgian pharmaceutical and chemical company, uses maps derived from network analysis to help with leadership transitions. Such network analysis helps spark ideas when people go outside their traditional networks. Seeing where the lines of collaboration are missing can help managers find opportunities for growth or help identify key players you do not want to lose post merger.

Problems trigger learning (Cyert & March, 1963). When organizations encounter problems, they initiate a search for solutions, adopt solutions that solve the problem, and retain good solutions for future use.

Repeated encounters with similar problems provide motivation for the organization to develop standardized responses. These standardized responses are often encoded in the form of organizational routines or rules (Levitt & March, 1988; March et al., 2000). Over time, rule/routine makers become more competent at recognizing problems and developing rules/routines to respond to them. At the same time, rule/routine users become more competent at using the rules/routines. Thus, there results an interconnected web of rules/routines. In this way, the organization's procedural memory is developed. In stable environments, this enhances the ability of the organization to exploit its core competencies. Nevertheless, in unstable environments, the dominance of rules/routines can inhibit double-loop learning and exploration (March et al., 2000). Rules/routines capture explicit knowledge about know-who and know-how. However, because routines and rules appeared as disembodied imprints of history, they are not sufficient for understanding. They fail to capture the know-why. It is stories that make history available and help organizations learn from their past. Stories capture informal learning, and as such, are the "soft" repositories of knowledge (Brown & Duguid, 1991). A powerful way of making outsiders feel like insiders and imparting tacit knowledge or its emotional component is through the telling of stories. Stories help link the past to the present and the present to the future. Stories help participants to see continuity in the face of change and make the radical seem more doable.

Gregory Berry (2001) notes, "Stories are a fundamental way through which we understand the world ... By understanding the stories of organizations, we can claim partial understanding of the reasons behind visible behavior" (p. 59). As such, the exchange of stories, rather than merely routines, results in a social learning system that allows participants to develop a new "collective story." Stories are thus an important part of organizational learning. Routines and rules capture only a limited part of explicit knowledge. They do not capture the past and how the organization got there, and they do not capture tacit knowledge or the emotional component of knowledge.

The power of stories can be seen in the experience of the Australasian firm Amcor. In one year, five "new" changes were simultaneously implemented. The changes ranged from work flow and safety changes to new gain share incentive programs to new adding a new shift and changing from a 5-day, 8-hour shift, 3-shift arrangement to a 12-hour, 4-day-on/4-day-off shift system. Joline Francoueur and Darl Kolb, the consultants on the change projects, on the second day of a two-day experiential-learning-based organizational development program, asked the longest serving worker to describe what Amcor was like upon first joining the company. Next, the second longest serving worker was asked the same question. This went on until all of the 30 + participants had told their story. The stories were full of humor and laughter and very few were bitter or full of complaint. The upshot of telling their stories was to connect older workers with younger ones, and the discovery that the "new" was, in fact not "new" at all. Participants discovered that while the proposed changes were not identical to previous ones, they were no more radical than ones the organization and many of those present had successfully lived through. In fact, the telling of stories enhanced the status of senior participants relative to that of their junior managers because they had literally "been there, done that." The result was that by telling their stories, the participants gained a perspective about the proposed changes and this reduced their resistance to change (Kolb, 2003). As Jan Bouwen and Bert Overlaet say, in their retelling of the takeover of a Belgian multinational pharmaceutical company, "There is no continuity without an appreciation of the past. People will experience continuity when they can recognize the past in their present actions and intentions for the future" (Bouwen & Overlaet, 2001, p. 34).

ORGANIZATIONAL NETWORKS

Collective learning is influenced by distributed initiative and cooperation. Collective learning requires constant experimentation and *heedful* interrelating (Weick, 1965; Weick & Roberts, 1993). However, while everybody wants to learn, nobody wants to fail. Thus, collective learning requires a willingness to encourage the tolerance of small failures (Sitkin, 1992). Collective learning occurs when leaders encourage plausible judgment, active listening, information exchange, and working consensus (Weick, Sutcliffe, & Obstfeld, 1999). Collective learning also requires discipline, stretch, trust, and support. Strategic leaders do this by setting clear performance standards, providing fast feedback, promoting open communications, shared ambition, collective identity, and by linking the individual's work and the organization's priorities thus giving meaning to the individual's work (Ghoshal & Barlett, 1994). In studying work teams at Johnson and Johnson, Black and Boal (1996) found that teams that were high in discipline, stretch, trust, and support were able to change work systems and technology while maintaining a high level of performance while teams that were not could not.

Strategic leaders are responsible for creating the context within which collective learning can occur. Because strategic leaders are in unique positions to act to enhance employees' access to knowledge, resources, networks, and learning strategies, strategic leaders play a pivotal role in the creation and use of intra- and inter-organizational network ties. Learning and the transfer of knowledge about the know-what, the know-how, and the know-why of organizational life requires interaction among network ties. The type of ties in a network of firms plays a major role in promoting single-loop and double-loop organizational learning. Four types of network ties have been identified: cohesive, bridging, strong, and weak (Gulati, Dialdin, & Wang, 2002). Cohesive ties connect a focal firm with another firm that is also connected with at least one other partner of the focal firm. Bridging ties connect a focal firm with another firm that is not connected with a partner of the focal firm. Strong ties connect the focal firm and another firm with which the focal firm has intensive interactions. Finally, weak ties consist of the focal firm and another firm with which the focal firm only has very few interactions. While strong ties tend to be cohesive and weak ties tend to be bridging, that is not necessarily always the case (Burt, 1992; McEvily & Zaheer, 1999).

Cohesive ties reduce transaction and coordination costs through social norms and sanctions that facilitate trust and cooperative exchange. In cohesive ties, trust emerges from the firm's embeddedness in a social network beyond the dyad. To the extent that people only act on information they trust, cohesive ties promote action, and thus learning by doing. However, cohesive ties may prevent firms from obtaining new non-redundant information. Thus, cohesive ties promote single-loop and exploitative learning.

Bridging ties connect the focal firm and the bridging partner and thus two disparate networks and two unrelated sets of information. Bridging ties provide information and control benefits for the focal firm in the form of access, timing, and referral to information and learning opportunities (Gulati & Singh, 1998). Thus, bridging ties promote double-loop learning and exploration. However, firms often worry about technology leakage, especially with the use of outside suppliers, thus they may choose to produce important technologies in house. When they do so, co-location of related technologies and production systems can serve as the source of new ideas and dialogue necessary for learning (see Chapter 6).

Strong ties promote trust and reciprocity and facilitate the transfer of private information and critical resources. Trust emerges from the intensive interaction with the dyad (Gulati et al., 2002). The intensive interaction in strong ties facilitates the acquisition and interpretation of tacit knowledge (Hansen, 1999). To the extent that repetition promotes retention in long-term memory, strong ties enhance procedural and transactive memory.

Strong ties also promote the transfer of tacit knowledge (Zhao et al., 2004). However, a firm with many strong ties and few weak ties trades with a confined set of partners and may seal itself off from the market. As a consequence, it will receive less new information about opportunities in the market. This results in single-loop learning and inhibits exploration.

Weak ties provide new information from sources with whom the focal firm does not frequently interact. However, weak ties are best at facilitating explicit knowledge (Hansen, 1999). Weak ties reveal opportunities in the market and may also reduce resource dependence on strong partners, thus promoting exploration.

The importance of bridging and weak ties can be seen in the story of GE's adoption of Six Sigma. Many people now associate Six Sigma with GE just as they do Workout and Best Practices. Collectively these programs focus on efficiency, knowledge, and quality. What most people do not know is that initially Welch was hesitant to implement Six Sigma because he felt it was just not GE. However, on the day the decision was to be made at Crotonville, Welch was absent. In his place, Larry Bossidy (then CEO of Allied Signal) spoke at Crotonville about Six Sigma. According to Steve Kerr, Chief Learning Officer at GE, Bossidy got everyone so excited that by the time Welch returned, he could not stop it. On the other hand, Workout resulted from Welch's conversations with Jim Baughman from Harvard, and demand-flow technology resulted from Welch's contact with customers (Greiner, 2002).

STRATEGIC LEADERSHIP, NETWORKS, AND LEARNING

Boal (2004) has described strategic leadership as:

> ... a series of decisions and activities, both process-oriented and substantive in nature, through which, over time, the past, the present, and the future of the organization coalesce.

In the past tense, strategic leaders should focus on developing strong and cohesive ties to reinforce existing values, identities, and belief systems. The result is single-loop learning that seeks to exploit and build on its history.

In the present tense, under conditions of stability, strategic leadership should focus on developing strong and cohesive ties for organizational members to promote procedural and transactive memories. This will reinforce single-loop and exploitative learning. However, at the same time, strategic leaders should seek to promote weak and bridging ties to raise aspiration levels and to encourage double-loop and exploration learning.

Under crises, strategic leaders need to act. However, since past behavior is self-reinforcing, search behavior is likely to be localized during crises. The result is to reinforce single-loop and exploitative learning. During a crisis, the presence of strong ties may also seal off the organization from new sources of information, again reinforcing single-loop learning. While the crisis may abate, what is often needed is double-loop learning and explorations. Therefore, in these cases, strategic leadership needs to challenge existing causal maps and strategies, as well as develop and promote weak and bridging ties to provide new information to encourage double-loop learning and exploration. Katsuhiko Machida's decision in 1998 to upgrade all televisions sold by Sharp in the domestic market to flat-screen LCD technology by 2005 forced Sharp to rethink and reinvent the technologies, systems, and processes involved in producing televisions (see Chapter 6).

The future tense also requires the strategic leader to build and promote both weak and bridging ties. By doing so, the strategic leader raises the aspiration level of the organization, and encourages the use of new sources of information. But the future tense requires a strategic leader who can envision an unknown future. As by Citing George Bernard Shaw, Edward Kennedy eulogized his brother Robert Kennedy. "Some men see things as they are and say, why; I dream things that never were and say, why not" (Kennedy, 1968, p. 53). In the future tense, the strategic leader is aided by both weak and bridging ties aid. The vision of the leader raises the aspiration level of the organization, and weak and bridging ties serve as sources of new information. As such, the possibility for double-loop learning and exploration is greatest.

CONCLUSION

By focusing on the organization, strategic leaders are constantly faced with reaffirming *who we are*, deciding on *what we do* and envisioning *where do we want to go*. Doing so requires strategic leaders to articulate the organization's values, beliefs, and identity, as well as strike a balance among the organization's core competencies to exploit the present while at the same time encouraging organizational learning to explore both knowable and unknown futures. Thus, strategic leadership is concerned with connecting the past, the present, and the future of the organization to ensure continuity in the face of competition and evolution. In doing so, strategic leaders can influence the organization directly through their charismatic and transformational behavior, or indirectly by encouraging the creation, orchestrating, and/or serving as the hub of intra- and extra-organizational networks through which organizations learn and transfer knowledge.

ACKNOWLEDGMENTS

I wish to thank John Antonakis, Linda Argote, Andre Delbecq, Jerry Hunt, Richard Osborn, and Robert Hooijberg for their comments on earlier drafts of this chapter.

REFERENCES

Amabile, T. M., Schatzel, E. A., Moneta, G. B., & Kramer, J., St. (2004). Leader behaviors and the work environment for creativity: Perceived leader support. *Leadership Quarterly, 15*, 5–32.

Argote, L. (1999). *Organizational learning.* Boston, MA: Kluwer Academic Publishers.

Argote, L. (2005). Reflections on two views of managing learning. *Journal of Management Inquiry, 14*, 43–48.

Argyris, C., & Schön, D. (1978). *Organizational learning.* Reading, MA: Addison-Wesley.

Augier, M., & Sarasvathy, S. D. (2004). Integrating evolution, cognition and design: Extending Simonian perspectives to strategic organization. *Strategic Organization, 2*, 169–204.

Berry, G. R. (2001). Telling stories: Making sense of the environmental behavior of chemical firms. *Journal of Management Inquiry, 10*, 58–73.

Black, J. A., & Boal, K. B. (1996). Assessing the organizational capacity to change. In: A. Heene & R. Sanchez (Eds), *Competence-based strategic management* (pp. 151–168). Chichester, UK: Wiley.

Boal, K. B. (2004). Strategic leadership. In: G. R. Goethals, G. J. Sorenson & J. M. Burns (Eds), *Encyclopedia of Leadership* (pp. 1497–1504). Thousand Oaks, CA: Sage.

Boal, K. B., & Hooijberg, R. (2000). Strategic leadership research: Moving on. *The Leadership Quarterly, 11*, 515–550.

Bouwen, J., & Overlaet, B. (2001). Managing continuing in a period of takeover. *Journal of Management Inquiry, 10*, 27–38.

Brown, J. S., & Duguid, P. (1991). Organizational learning and communities of practice: Toward a unified view of working, learning, and innovation. *Organization Science, 2*, 40–57.

Brown, S., & Eisenhardt, K. (1998). *Competing on the edge: Strategy as structured chaos.* Boston, MA: Harvard Business School Press.

Burgelman, R. A., & Grove, A. S. (1996). Strategic dissonance. *California Management Review, 38*(2), 8–28.

Burt, R. (1992). *Structural holes: The social structure of competition.* Cambridge, MA: Harvard University Press.

Child, J. (1972). Organization structure, environment and performance: The role of strategic choice. *Sociology, 6*, 1–22.

Cohen, W. M., & Levinthal, D. A. (1990). Absorptive capacity: A new perspective on learning and innovation. *Administrative Science Quarterly, 35*, 128–152.

Cook, S. D. N., & Brown, J. S. (1999). Bridging espistemologies: The generative dance between organizational knowledge and organizational learning. *Organization Science, 10*(4), 381–400.

Cyert, R., & March, J. G. (1963). *A behavioral theory of the firm.* Englewood Cliffs, NJ: Prentice Hall.

Fox-Wolfgramm, S. J., Boal, K. B., & Hunt, J. G. (1998). Organizational adaptation to institutional change: A comparative study of first-order change in prospector and defender banks. *Administrative Science Quarterly, 43*, 87–126.

Garud, R. (1997). On the distinction between know-how, know-why, and know-what. In: J. P. Walsh & A. S. Huff (Eds), *Advances in strategic management* (Vol. 14, pp. 81–101). Greenwich, CT: JAI Press.

Ghoshal, S., & Barlett, C. A. (1994). Linking organizational context and managerial action: The dimension of quality of management. *Strategic Management Journal, 15*, 91–112.

Greiner, L. (2002). Steve Kerr and his years with Jack Welch at GE. *Journal of Management Inquiry, 11*, 343–350.

Gulati, R., Dialdin, D. A., & Wang, L. (2002). Organizational networks. In: J. C. Baum (Ed.), *Companion to organizations* (pp. 281–303). Oxford: Blackwell.

Gulati, R., & Singh, H. (1998). The architecture of cooperation: Managing coordination costs and appropriation concerns in strategic alliances. *Administrative Science Quarterly, 43*, 781–814.

Hannan, M. T., & Freeman, J. H. (1977). The population ecology of organizations. *American Journal of Sociology, 82*, 929–964.

Hansen, M. (1999). The search transfer problem: The role of weak ties in sharing knowledge across organization subunits. *Administrative Science Quarterly, 44*, 82–111.

Huber, G. P. (1991). Organizational learning: The contributing processes and the literatures. *Organization Science, 2*, 88–115.

Johnson, D. W., & Johnson, R. T. (1989). *Cooperation and competition: Theory and research.* Edina, MN: Interaction Book Company.

Kennedy, E. (1968). Eulogy for Robert F. Kennedy. *New York Times, 9*(June), 53.

Kogut, B., & Zander, U. (1992). Knowledge of the firm, combinative capabilities, and the replication of technology. *Organization Science, 3*, 381–397.

Kolb, D. G. (2003). Seeking continuity amidst organizational change: A storytelling approach. *Journal of Management Inquiry, 10*, 180–183.

Lane, P. J., Koka, B., & Pathak, S. (2002). A thematic analysis and critical assessment of absorptive capacity research. *Proceedings, BPS M1–M5*, Academy of Management, Denver.

Lant, T., & Mezias, S. (1992). An organizational learning model of convergence and reorientation. *Organization Science, 3*, 47–71.

Leblebici, H., Salancik, G. R., Copay, A., & King, T. (1991). Institutional change and the transformation of interorganizational fields – an organizational history of the United States radio broadcasting industry. *Administrative Science Quarterly, 36*(3), 333–363.

Leonard-Barton, D. (1992). Core capabilities and core rigidities: A paradox in managing new product development. *Strategic Management Journal, 13*, 111–126.

Levitt, B., & March, J. G. (1988). Organization learning. *Annual Review of Sociology, 14*, 185–319.

Lewis, K. D. (2002). Leadership by a holistic approach. In: M. D. Ashby & S. A. Miles (Eds), *Leaders talk leadership: Top executives speak their minds* (pp. 65–71). Oxford, UK: Oxford University Press.

Liang, D. W., Moreland, R., & Argote, L. (1995). Group versus individual training and group performance: The mediating role of transactive memory. *Personality and Social Psychology Bulletin, 21*, 384–393.

March, J. G. (1991). Exploration and exploitation in organizational learning. *Organization Science, 2*, 71–87.

March, J. G., & Olsen, J. P. (1975). Organizational learning and the ambiguity of the past. In: J. G. March & J. P. Olsen (Eds), *Ambiguity and choice in organizations* (pp. 54–68). Bergen: Unversitetsforlager.

March, J. G., Schulz, M., & Zhou, X. (2000). *The dynamics of rules: Change in written organizational codes*. Stanford, CA: Stanford University Press.

McEvily, B., & Zaheer, A. (1999). Bridging ties: A source of firm heterogeneity in competitive capabilities. *Strategic Management Journal, 20*, 1113–1156.

Meyer, A. D., Brooks, G. R., & Goes, J. B. (1990). Environmental jolts and industry revolutions: Organizational responses to discontinuous change. *Strategic Management Journal, 11*, 93–110.

Meyer, A. D., Goes, J. B., & Brooks, G. R. (1994). Organizations reacting to hyperturbulence. In: G. P. Huber & W. H. Glick (Eds), *Organizational change and redesign: Ideas and insights for improving performance* (pp. 66–111). New York: Oxford University Press.

Miller, D. (1990). *The Icarus Paradox*. New York: Harper Business.

North, D. C. (1991). *Institutions, institutional change and economic performance*. Cambridge, MA: Cambridge University Press.

Nystrom, P. C., & Starbuck, W. H. (1984). To avoid organizational crises, unlearn. *Organizational Dynamics, 12*(4), 53–65.

Pfeffer, J. (2002). Leadership by creating and supporting leaders. In: M. D. Ashby & S. A. Miles (Eds), *Leaders talk leadership: Top executives speak their minds* (pp. 95–100). Oxford, UK: Oxford University Press.

Piaget, J. (1968). *Le Stucturalisme*. Paris: Presses University de France.

Polistuk, E. V. (2002). Leadership by creating the right environment. In: M. D. Ashby & S. A. Miles (Eds), *Leaders talk leadership: Top executives speak their minds* (pp. 72–75). Oxford, UK: Oxford University Press.

Rerup, C. (2004). Imperfection, transfer failure, and the replication of knowledge: An interview with Gabriel Szulanski. *Journal of Management Inquiry, 13*, 141–150.

Schulz, M. (2002). Organizational learning. In: J. A. C. Baum (Ed.), *The Blackwell companion to organizations* (pp. 415–441). Oxford: Blackwell Publishers Ltd.

Senge, P. M. (1990). *The fifth discipline*. New York: Doubleday Currency.

Shalley, C. E., & Gilson, L. L. (2004). What leaders need to know: A review of social and contextual factors that can foster or hinder creativity. *Leadership Quarterly, 15*, 33–53.

Simon, H. A. (1993). Strategy and organizational evolution. *Strategic Management Journal, 14*, 131–142.

Sitkin, S. (1992). Learning through failure: The strategy of small losses. In: B. M. Staw & L. L. Cummings (Eds), *Research in organizational behavior* (Vol. 14, pp. 231–266). Greenwich, CT: JAI Press.

Spender, J. C., & Grant, R. M. (1996). Making knowledge the basis of a dynamic theory of the firm. *Strategic Management Journal, 17*(Winter), 5–9.

Summer, C. E., Bettis, R. A., Duhaime, I. H., Grant, J. H., Hambrick, D. C., Snow, C. C., & Zeithaml, C. P. (1990). Doctoral education in the field of business policy and strategy. *Journal of Management, 16*, 361–398.

von Pierer, H. (2002). Leadership by continuing education and networking knowledge. In: M. D. Ashby & S. A. Miles (Eds), *Leaders talk leadership: Top executives speak their minds* (pp. 93–95). Oxford, UK: Oxford University Press.

Wegner, D. M. (1987). Transactive memory: A contemporary analysis of the group mind. In: B. Mullen & G. R. Goethals (Eds), *Theories of group behavior* (pp. 185–208). New York: Springer-Verlag.

Weick, K. E. (1965). Laboratory experimentation with organizations. In: J. G. March (Ed.), *Handbook of organizations* (pp. 194–260). Chicago: Rand McNally.

Weick, K. E., & Roberts, K. H. (1993). Collective mind in organizations: Heedful interrelating on flight decks. *Administrative Science Quarterly, 38*, 357–381.

Weick, K. E., Sutcliffe, M. & Obstfeld, D. (1999). Organizing for high-reliability: Processes for collective mindfulness. In: B. M. Staw & R. I. Sutton (Eds), *Research in organizational behavior* (Vol. 21, pp. 81–123). Greenwich, CT: JAI Press.

Wenger, E. (2003). Communities of practice and social learning systems. In: D. Nicolini, S. Gherardi & D. Yanow (Eds), *Knowing in organizations: A practice-based approach* (pp. 176–199). New York: M. E. Sharpe, Inc.

Wooten, L. P., & James, E. H. (2004). When firms fail to learn: The perpetuation of discrimination in the workplace. *Journal of Management Inquiry, 13*, 23–34.

Zhao, Z., Anand, J., & Mitchell, W. (2004). Transferring collective knowledge: Teaching and learning in the Chinese auto industry. *Strategic Organization, 2*, 133–167.

CHAPTER 6

CREATING, GROWING AND PROTECTING KNOWLEDGE-BASED COMPETENCE: THE CASE OF SHARP'S LCD BUSINESS

Kazuo Ichijo

ABSTRACT

Sharp Corporation, established in 1912, has always tried to identify unique niches that its competitors do not enter, while at the same time continuing to pursue innovation and knowledge creation in those niches. The liquid crystal display (LCD) business is a typical example of Sharp's strategy and innovation. Sharp developed the first successful LCD product – a pocket calculator with a small black and white LCD in 1973 – and since then the company has released a series of unique products with LCDs, including PDAs and camcorders. In 1998, in the face of increasing competition in the traditional cathode-ray tube (CRT) TV market, Katsuhiko Machida, the company's new president and strategic leader, announced his vision of upgrading all bulky CRT televisions sold in the domestic market to flat screen LCD sets by 2005. This vision was bold, since Sharp was the first producer of color CRT TVs and its business was still profitable at the time. However, Machida as strategic leader, predicted tough price competition in the CRT business in the future and began to mobilize Sharp's employees to gain and sustain competitive advantage in the new market.

Being There Even When You Are Not: Leading Through Strategy, Structures, and Systems
Monographs in Leadership and Management, Volume 4, 87–102
Copyright © 2007 by Elsevier Ltd.
All rights of reproduction in any form reserved
ISSN: 1479-3571/doi:10.1016/S1479-3571(07)04005-9

In the current knowledge-based economy, individual and organizational knowledge as well as brainpower have replaced physical assets as critical resources in the corporate world (Drucker, 1993). Therefore, the success of a company in the new 21st century will be determined by the extent to which leaders can develop their intellectual capabilities through knowledge creation and sharing. In the current knowledge-based economy, knowledge constitutes a competitive advantage of corporations (Eisenhardt & Santos, 2001). Companies should hire, develop, and retain excellent managers who accumulate precious knowledge assets. Attracting smart, talented people and raising their level of intellectual capabilities will be a core competence in this new millennium. At the same time, companies should encourage such proficient managers to share the knowledge they develop across geographical and functional business boundaries in an effective, efficient, and fast manner. In other words, to win in the current competitive environment, leaders need to be able to manage knowledge strategically. Leadership for managing knowledge should also constitute a core competence. This is especially the case for companies doing business beyond national borders. However, despite various efforts, few firms succeeded in their initiative to increase their knowledge assets.

In this age of stiff global competition and rapid technological changes, the way firms manage their knowledge assets drives key competing factors. In the most advanced industrial areas such as liquid crystal display (LCD), where technological changes are constant, manufacturers not only need to develop new technologies, they must also focus on protecting their original expertise from competitors (Doz, Santos, & Williamson, 2001). Furthermore, when a manufacturer becomes a leader in introducing new technologies, there is a risk of facing destructive technologies that aim to damage the leader's advantage (Christensen, 1997). Managers nowadays have to relentlessly pursue activities to prevent their original technologies from becoming obsolete. Decision-making issues concerning knowledge-based competence of a corporation are becoming broader and more diverse.

In this chapter, I would like to highlight the importance of the holistic and strategic management of the knowledge-based competence of a corporation by its leaders. It includes creation, sharing and utilization, protection, and discarding of knowledge. In addition, these activities do not occur without a sufficient infrastructure to consistently enable them in organizations (Von Krogh, Ichijo, & Nonaka, 2000). All these activities for the strategic management of knowledge-based competence of a corporation should be planned and executed by leaders (see Fig. 1).

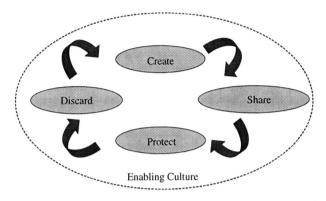

Fig. 1. Strategic Management of Knowledge-Based Competence of a Firm.

This viewpoint is necessary to truly make use of the knowledge-based competence of a corporation in a strategic context. In this paper, I present the case study of Sharp Corporation in order to outline leadership for managing the knowledge-based competence of a firm by analyzing Sharp's outstanding success.

NEW STRATEGY FOR GAINING AND SUSTAINING COMPETITIVE ADVANTAGE

Head-to-Head Competition in the LCD Business in Asia

Corporate leaders facing stiff competition should develop holistic views of knowledge management. Case in point: Sharp Corporation and their "black box" of knowledge assets. Here, the "black box" of knowledge assets refers to a strategy to make a company's unique knowledge difficult to imitate by a combination of factors such as product customization, complexity, and intellectual property protection, as described in more depth later in this chapter. Competing against Samsung and LG Electronics in the fast growing business of LCD devices, Sharp Corporation viewed its black box approach to its knowledge assets as the most important corporate strategy.

Sharp is currently one of the best performing electronics manufacturers in Japan. In 2004, consolidated sales reached 2.53 trillion yen or approximately $21 billion (112.1% of previous year's sales), an operating profit of 150 billion yen or approximately $1.3 billion (123.3% of previous year's sales) and a net income of 75,000 million yen or approximately $639 million

(123.5% of previous year's sales). While other Japanese electronics manufacturers have been struggling with a sales downfall, Sharp's performance has been outstanding. This exceptional success was mainly brought about by LCD devices and related products. For example, Sharp was the first manufacturer to introduce cellular phones with cameras in 2002. The new market creation was enabled by Sharp's original devices such as the complementary metal oxide semiconductor (CMOS) camera module and signalprocessing large-scale integrated circuits (LSI) with the high-performance mobile-sized LCDs using a continuous grain (CG) silicon.

Sharp has become a leading global electronics manufacturer by cultivating a new business frontier using such LCD technologies and Asia has become the leader in a fast-growing LCD industry. Initially, LCD technology was brought into being by RCA in 1963, which also created the very first LCD device in 1968. However, due to manufacturing difficulties, RCA and other US companies gave up the commercialization of LCD technology. Sharp, on the other hand, identified important growth opportunities in the LCD business and took the lead in exploiting LCD technologies for innovative products. Their strategy was to create groundbreaking electronics in which LCD devices were employed. By continuously and relentlessly pursuing this approach, Sharp aimed to improve the LCD technology and cultivate new LCD product markets; as a result, becoming the industrial leader. The first successful LCD product was a small calculator with a small black and white LCD, followed by many other innovative LCD devices such as camcorders and PDAs. These novel products ensured Sharp's leading position in the sector.

Developing larger LCD panels posed a technological challenge. In 1988, Sharp finally succeeded in building up a 14.4-inch LCD panel for PCs. Then, in the 1990s, LCDs gradually began to replace cathode ray tube (CRT) monitors for PCs, and as a result, Taiwanese LCD manufacturers emerged as strong competitors. Since a growing number of US PC makers outsourced PC manufacturing to companies in Taiwan, Taiwanese firms such as Unipac were established to produce LCDs for PC displays and they immediately embarked on a fast-growth track. Their competitive advantage lay in collaboration with leading PC makers such as IBM. It could produce appropriate LCD PC monitors with a faster turnaround time and at a much lower cost. Productionwise, they simply purchased the same LCD-making machines that were sold to Sharp and other Japanese LCD manufacturers. It was especially competitive in producing smaller sized LCD panels for PC displays whereas Japanese firms were more interested in producing bigger LCD panels so that they could produce LCD monitors more efficiently. Leading Taiwanese LCD manufacturers Unipac and Acer Display Technology (ADT) merged in 2001 and became AU Optronics (AUO). Currently, it is the third largest manufacturer of large-size TFT-LCD panels in the world, with a market share of approximately 13.6%, based on units shipped in September 2004.[1]

Sharp has also faced strong Korean competitors such as Samsung and LG Electronics. Samsung is a particularly challenging competitor. The company has been left with a huge debt following the 1997 Korean financial crisis, a crash in memory-chip prices, and a $700 million write-off after a takeover of AST Technologies, a US maker of PCs. A new CEO, Yun Jong, and his superior, Samsung Group Chairman Lee Kun Hee, started a radical transformation. They found a turnaround opportunity in the electronics industry's shift from analog to digital. Speed and intelligence would be key success factors in the new digitized electronics industry. Samsung decided to rationalize its business in response to its loss in profit. Yun cut 24,000 jobs and sold $2 billion of non-core businesses to streamline Samsung. In addition to this management reconstruction, the company revised its strategic focus on its core business to gain more profit. It focused its business exclusively on the fast growing digital products and devices such as LCDs, plasma displays, cell phones, digital cameras, and flash memories. It sought to compete through new product development, manufacturing launches and economies of scale in these hot business segments. Samsung has become a fast mover in the LCD business. In the past, Samsung always lagged behind Sharp in LCD panel launches. However, Samsung surprised the public by bringing the fifth generation[2] of LCD panels to the market well ahead of Sharp (Edwards, Moon Ihlwan, & Engardio, 2003).

Sharp's Strategy for the LCD Business

Although it faced tougher competition with companies such as AUO, Samsung, and LG electronics, Sharp has not changed its strategy: always being a technological leader. In 2002, Sharp succeeded in developing the continuous grain (CG) silicon. It was the first unique technology to control and create crystal particles that could be made into thin layers and attached to glass. With this newly discovered technology, a simple glass board could be transformed into a personal computer with an LCD panel or LCD television capable of memorizing TV programs by operating semiconductor memories inside. The CG silicon has an advantage of clearer display in comparison to other LCDs. Another benefit achieved from its design flexibility is that one can arrange the display and interrelated devices on the same glass board. Each product can be conveniently customized according to its needs.[3]

Surprisingly, the development of the CG silicon had not been openly shared, even inside the corporation, before its release to the market. Until the development was completed, the information about this new LCD technology was strictly confidential among people involved in the development.[4] In addition, Sharp has filed for only a small number of patents related to the CG silicon. This strategy for a newly developed technology, which is applicable not only for the CG silicon but also for other LCD technologies, was different from the usual practice in the industry. For a long time, Sharp had been famous for filing the largest number of patents in the LCD business. The reason for this shift in strategy (in other words its knowledge-related strategy) was that filing patents meant revealing the essence of Sharp's technologies to competitors. Similar technologies could soon be developed and introduced to the market, allowing the corporation to savor the triumph for only a short period. Interestingly, this is how Japanese manufacturers forced Intel out of the DRAM market in the early 1980s and how they were forced to withdraw from the competition 20 years later.

Nowadays, the risk of spillage and imitation of technologies has become even higher. Sharp has decided to introduce a black box strategy to its know-how and technologies to maintain its competitiveness instead of filing for patents and announcing their strengths publicly. By filing the patents, companies disclose the source of competitive advantages to some degree. Competitors might be able to identify it by means of backward engineering. One key outcome of such a decision was creating equipment for manufacturing CG silicones inside the company; thus, Sharp could prevent the leaking of technologies by not outsourcing the equipment production to other manufacturers. With this move, the stickiness of knowledge concerning the technology was expected to improve (Von Hippel, 1998). In cases where some equipment was purchased from outside, Sharp customized it beyond recognition[5] so that the unique high performance level could be achieved without imitation.

What we have seen so far can be perceived as a simple strategic proposal. However, the black box of knowledge strategy requires continuous leadership efforts toward its internal knowledge. Sharp faced the following complicated chain of decisions:

(1) Whether or not to develop the CG silicon as a result of knowledge creation.
(2) How to customize the final product (i.e., to avoid the imitation of a product by potential competitors).

(3) Accelerated structuring of the production process.
(4) How to develop the managerial techniques and skills for mass production within the organization.

The third and fourth initiatives were aimed at delaying a potential catch-up by competitors.[6] These four steps were effective for Sharp in gaining and sustaining a competitive advantage in the head-to-head competition with strong players in Asia. Only with the implementation and continuation of these tightly related strategic plans could Sharp expect to remain the leader in the mobile-sized LCD market.

Sharp's strategic positioning enabled such strategic initiatives. In the 1990s, Sharp saw the importance of the niche market – mobile-sized LCDs in addition to large-sized LCDs – when all other electronics manufacturers focused only on investing in the latter. Sharp's choice may have been a result of a unique corporate strategy of "achieving the top in a one-of-a-kind industry." Adding to such niche positioning, the fact that mobile LCDs were often customized for various uses helped prevent the company's products from being commoditized. Uniqueness of knowledge is one of the effective factors that prevent technology imitations (Chakravarthy, McEvily, Doz, & Rau, 2003). This extra layer of competitive shield, attained through the niche positioning and customizability, provided Samsung with competitive advantages. The combination of strategic positioning and strategic management of the knowledge-based competence of the firm is crucially important for Sharp to gain and sustain their competitive advantage in the LCD industry. Sharp has found a niche where its competitors do not enter, and it continues to pursue innovation or knowledge creation in that niche. By doing so, Sharp can gain a competitive advantage. However, in order to sustain such a competitive advantage, Sharp should first utilize the new knowledge created to develop new innovative products and protect them effectively. Without this strategic management of knowledge, it is difficult for Sharp to sustain its competitive advantage. Only the combination of strategic positioning and strategic management of knowledge will allow Sharp to continue to gain and sustain competitive advantage.

The CG silicon of Sharp shows that layers of interrelated knowledge-based activities protect the corporate knowledge assets. Sharp is now trying to change the rules of competition in the large LCD market by applying the same line of attack. In the following section, I will look at the case of LCD televisions in more detail in order to come up with a valid hypothesis concerning knowledge-based management.

CASE STUDY: SHARP – DEVELOPMENT OF THE LCD TELEVISION[7]

Innovation in the Television Market

Sharp Corporation is known for pioneering the revolutionary LCD televisions. In the Japanese domestic television market, the sales volume of LCD televisions expanded by 50% in the first half of 2003. This growth was due to Sharp's replacement of the CRT TV set with a thin LCD. In July 2003, Sharp's AQUOS brand LCD TVs dominated the market with a 61.8% market share, whereas Sony had 15.9% and Panasonic only 12.7%.[8] Sharp has become one of the leading players in the most prestigious electronics market, the television market, with about a 33.8% global share in 2004.[9]

Knowledge Vision

It was in 1998 that Sharp Corporation first decided to enter a new market. Katsuhiko Machida, Sharp's new president, announced his vision of upgrading all bulky tube televisions sold in the domestic market to flat-screen LCD sets by 2005. This novel corporate vision was announced only two months after he assumed the helm of Sharp. Machida had always been concerned about the future of Sharp's televisions. At the time, aggressive Korean competitors had already begun to sway the market.[10] Although Sharp had started the production of its 14-inch CRT TV sets as early as 1953, original equipment manufacturers (OEMs) supplied CRT monitors for Sharp. The launch of low-priced competitive products could only damage Sharp, since it strongly relied on outside resources in this business. Machida, having several years of experience as a general manager of television products, could foresee the approaching loss of corporate negotiation power if TVs, the most prestigious electronics product line, started to plunge. Losing the grip on TVs could be fatal. Sharp was famous for its unique products, but current problems could mean never reaching the top position in the consumer electronics industry. Thus, the new vision was aimed at gaining and sustaining Sharp's competitive advantage in the global electronics industry. For that purpose, Machida was willing to discard the knowledge that Sharp had accumulated about producing CRT TV sets. Although Sharp did not produce CRT monitors in-house and bought them from their competitors, they did develop knowledge about producing CRT TV sets effectively and efficiently. Therefore, discarding the CRT TV business was a bold decision. On the other hand, given Sharp's long-term commitment in developing LCD technologies, the new concept of the LCD television was significant. It was literally Sharp's "knowledge vision" (Von Krogh et al., 2000) since it had been active in the development of LCDs for nearly 30 years,[11] hence always pursuing innovation in this industry.

Nevertheless, the new vision statement was a surprise. At that time, everyone in the industry believed that the CRT TV sets would stay mainstream for quite a while. Technically, it was not easy to expand the size of the LCD; therefore, the new vision was perceived as a risky bet. In response, Sony, Sharp's strongest competitor in the TV manufacturing industry, was not willing to discard its knowledge of producing traditional CRT monitors, and so Sony stuck with the Trinitron TV monitors. In this respect, Machida's knowledge-based vision statement was neither a mere forecast nor an outlook, but rather a bold bet on the future. Shigemitsu Mizushima, the former development manager of the LCD television project at Sharp was also astounded by the announcement. Now the general manager of Sharp's display technology development group, Mizushima did not know anything about this knowledge vision until it became public. At that time, he did not have enough confidence in making LCD panels through 100% internal production. Later, he was surprised to find that he was assigned to lead the product development team for new LCD televisions – the product that could be the leader of the next television standard.

The organization soon took the necessary steps to carry out the knowledge vision. When making decisions or troubled with obstacles, everyone refers to Machida's statement of "Replacing all televisions sold with LCD televisions by 2005." Mizushima praised the simple but rigid effect of the knowledge vision. It strongly outlined how they should act. The development group began working toward producing a suitable LCD for TV sets. While previous products with LCDs were designed exclusively for viewing from the front, televisions required a broader view angle. This special prerequisite made the team develop a customized LCD, the advanced super view (ASV), even though the team had planned on using the LCD panels from personal computers. Another hot issue was the development of an advanced color display. A joint project team of the LCD group, which held the knowledge of high resolution color display, and the television development group with expertise in the television screen color control was formed. Engineers from the television development group in Tochigi, located in the eastern part of Japan, were requested to join the LCD development group based in Tenri, located in the western part of Japan. This way, Sharp's initiative for developing LCD TVs involved Sharp employees belonging to different business units and functions, and this initiative was seen as the most important corporate project by all the Sharp employees.

It is amazing to see this kind of cross-divisional activity occurring so smoothly at Sharp. In general, companies have strong functional and divisional boundaries that make cross-functional and cross-divisional activities difficult. In contrast, for Sharp, such cross-functional and cross-divisional coordination was not new or difficult; it had experience since 1977 setting up "Urgent Project Team,"[12] – cross-functional task forces for strategically important products. The organization believed it was natural to work across different divisions. Such a tacit culture has been deeply rooted in the corporation and was not easy to duplicate for competitiors (Reber, 1993). Machida has always praised the advantage of this tacit culture. He believed that the rapid process of development and production was due to this "Urgent Project Team" tradition. The strength of an organization was built upon the tacit knowledge brought about by historical organizational activities (Winter, 1987). Of course, people try to make this tacit knowledge explicit so that a wider range of people can share it. But despite this effort, a certain element of tacitness of corporate important remains.

Spiral Process and "Black Box" of Knowledge

Working toward the knowledge vision led the organization to further success. Sharp improved its market share in televisions from 11.5% in 1998 and to 20% in 2003. In 2002, the market volume of LCD televisions, in terms of sales, surpassed that of CRT televisions. Sharp was without a doubt the leader of this historical paradigm shift.

Furthermore, Sharp has started a new bold initiative in the LCD business. A big plant with the latest equipment, built in Kameyama city in Mie prefecture, started its operation in January 2004. Sharp invested 100 billion yen or approximately $85 billion in the plant. All the processes from the production of LCD panels to the assemblies of LCD TVs were gathered. The so-called "sixth generation" LCD panels were produced there. The size of one panel was $1,500 \times 1,800$ mm, from which one could produce eight wide LCD TVs (type 30). According to the estimate, the plant would produce some 100,000 30-inch wide TVs. The machine used for the panel production was so large that, at first, it seemed impossible to find a road that could be used to transport it to the plant.

The Kameyama plant is a strategic initiative for Sharp to change the rules of the LCD business. Until then, the size of panels had been the key factor and companies had been focusing on enlarging them. Instead, Sharp took the lead in terms of efficiency through the Kameyama plant project. What Sharp was aiming at was the optimization of devices and products. Starting the Kameyama venture was a big challenge for Sharp because just before they had been engaged in producing the fourth generation LCD panel and Samsung surprised them with the release of the fifth generation of LCD panels. This meant that Sharp had to skip one product generation and jump to the sixth generation LCD panels. Project members reviewed technologies and processes and changed them radically. They were in desperate need of innovation. The Kameyama plant was the answer because it was producing mother glass and assembling TVs simultaneously. Combining the two would enable both high speed and cost effectiveness. This is called the "spiral effect" of LCD panel production and LCD TV set making. Although the circuits in LCD panels and TVs differ from each other, concentrating the production site enhanced successful integration. The Kameyama plant physically created the context of "Ba" – or context – of innovation or knowledge creation, where organizational members shared tacit and explicit knowledge with each other through dialogue (Von Krogh et al., 2000), thus facilitating cross-divisional and cross-functional coordination. In the past, the department of LCD technology development and the department of TV development were geographically distant from each other. However, the top management of Sharp thought that the collaboration of the two departments would be crucially important in developing a new generation of LCD TVs faster, more effectively, and more efficiently. Therefore, it was decided that they should be co-located. In other words, a new context for knowledge creation in which two different departments work together to pursue innovation was implemented. As stated before, this kind of context already existed at Sharp on an ad hoc basis, as the case of "Urgent Project Teams" indicates. However, in Kameyama, "Ba" is created permanently because cross-divisional and cross-functional coordination is crucially important in developing state-of-the-art LCD panels effectively, efficiently, and fast.

In this context, engineers of the two departments exchange more frequent communication with each other and develop a shared understanding of the market and the challenges facing them, guided by the vision of Sharp's LCD business. One engineer belonging to the LCD technology development department said, "It is so exciting to see the process of LCD TV development just on the spot. I am so happy to see new LCDs I had developed are being assembled in the TV set just in front of me."[13] As this quote shows, the social relationship among engineers belonging to the two departments is improved and the good social relationship is an important aspect of "Ba" as well as a key enabler for knowledge creation. An innovative mix of novel LCD development and manufacturing technology with TV production technology also created an important barrier of complexity. This protects technology from being imitated. As the "value chain" premise indicates, the more different activities are chained, the higher the value that can be created (Simon, 1962).

When the plans of the Kameyama project were announced in 2002, the production process was expected to start in May 2004. However, seeing the rapid growing LCD television market resulted in accelerated actions and Sharp began production in January 2004. A year before, in June 2003, Sharp launched a third plant in Mie, where it tested various activities. Consequently, it used these experiences while building an enormous plant in Kameyama ($300 \times 280\,\mathrm{m}^2$). In this way, Sharp concentrated its knowledge and experience at the Kameyama plant, now called the "integrated knowledge building."

THEORETICAL AND MANAGEMENT IMPLICATIONS FROM THE SHARP CASE

In the final part of this chapter, I would like to use the Sharp example in order to summarize the activities that can help enhance the use of the knowledge asset in an organization. From this example, I would like to demonstrate how leadership initiatives could contribute to gaining and sustaining competitive advantage in the currently volatile environment. In the past, discussions about the strategic management of the knowledge assets of a corporation have tended to focus on the creation and sharing of knowledge assets. However, the Sharp case suggests the necessity for a more holistic view. Holistic knowledge management consists of four main activities: creating, sharing, protecting, and discarding. Leaders should plan and execute these four activities to gain and sustain competitive advantages in industry:

(1) Companies should be knowledge creating, trying to generate new knowledge well ahead of competitors (Nonaka & Takeuchi, 1995). Sharp, a knowledge-creating company, has always taken the lead in innovation in the global LCD business.
(2) After successfully creating new knowledge within a company, this knowledge has to be shared among organizational members across regions, businesses, and functions. Sharp shows excellence at cross-functional

and cross-divisional knowledge sharing. Without active knowledge sharing, Sharp would not have outranked competitors and become the number one player in the new emerging LCD television business.

(3) Protection is literally about protecting knowledge assets from competitors. Sharp has made a tremendous effort to make the imitation of its LCD TV sets time-consuming and difficult for other players. Various initiatives being executed at the Kameyama plant are aimed at increasing complexities of knowledge in order to make imitation extremely difficult.

(4) Companies should reflect on whether or not their knowledge is outdated. In some cases, it may be necessary to discard the existing knowledge and promote new knowledge creation. Sharp discarded various kinds of knowledge about producing CRT TV sets (e.g., manufacturing technologies, color coordination technologies) to create new knowledge about producing LCD TVs because, without discarding old knowledge, the creation of new knowledge is difficult to initiate. Therefore, a time may come when LCD technologies become obsolete. In such a scenario, Sharp should not be afraid to discard its outdated knowledge. Having stuck to Trinitron CRT monitor technology, Sony may be able to learn the importance of discarding obsolete knowledge from Sharp. As a result of not discarding its outdated knowledge, Sony lost its competitive advantage in the global TV market. Therefore, to prepare for a situation such as LCD technology becoming obsolete, Sharp should be ready to discard its knowledge about LCD technology to avoid the "innovator's dilemma" (Christensen, 1997). It may be hard for Sharp to discard their knowledge about LCD technology because it has been the industry leader in this field. It might be much easier for Sharp to discard its knowledge about CRT TV because Sharp was not an industrial leader in this business; Sony was the leader.

So as not to be stuck with obsolete knowledge, Sharp should also pursue research on new technology that could replace LCDs in the future and it has indeed begun to develop new technologies such as electro luminescence (EL) technologies. These inventions could result in making LCD technologies obsolete in certain product categories in the near future. By beginning to develop alternative technologies that may replace LCDs, Sharp could prevent the organization from being beaten by competitors in the case of substitution of the main (LCD) technology by another technology.

Preventing knowledge from being imitated is all about activities that increase "complexity," "tacitness," and "specialty." Leaders should also keep in mind that the maintenance of enabling conditions is indispensable for facilitating these activities. Sharing a mission and vision throughout an organization, a unique strategy to attain them, and an organizational culture that promotes knowledge creation and sharing, are all considered necessary enabling conditions. The activities that are the building blocks of knowledge management should not just co-exist; they should also be linked with each other. In short, it is important to make them influence one another to allow knowledge assets to reach their full potential.

CONCLUSION

In order to cultivate a new business frontier, companies should gain and maintain competitive advantage. To gain competitive advantage, it is critically important to take the lead in developing new technologies and producing innovative products and services using these technologies. In other words, knowledge creation does matter. Leaders should recognize the strategic importance of the knowledge-based competence of a corporation and execute leadership for managing this competence. In order to sustain a technological advantage, companies should be good at utilizing new technology for various business opportunities as well as protecting them from imitation. Therefore, internal knowledge sharing and protection are of importance in sustaining competitive advantage. Yet any technology will become obsolete in the end. Companies that have been leading the industry by developing core technologies, tend to be especially late in developing and using new technologies that may replace the existing technologies. Therefore, in order to accomplish sustainable growth, thus avoiding the innovator's dilemma, leaders should not be afraid to discard the obsolete knowledge of previous core technologies.

To catch new business opportunities before any other competitor, and to keep that advantage for long, it is indispensable to protect and defend knowledge that leads to innovation. Asserting knowledge ownership by acquiring patents is not enough. Management of knowledge assets has to go further than simple technology management. The time has come to recognize holistic "knowledge-based management." Those leaders who intend on gaining and sustaining competitive advantage in the rapidly moving environment must pay more attention to the importance of creating, sharing, protecting, and discarding knowledge and they must execute these activities consistently.

NOTES

1. Source: AU Optronics Corporation (AUO) website. < http://www.auo.com/auoDEV > (accessed October 16, 2006).

2. The generation of panels means the size of an LCD panel. In the LCD industry, terminology for a new generation is used to refer to a new size of LCD panel. The fifth generation of LCD panel, $1,100 \times 1,250$ mm, was the largest at the time.

3. The description on CG silicones is based on interviews with Mr. Shigemitsu Mizushima director of display development section (2003/5/19) and *Nikkei Business*, January 6, 2003.

4. This handy CG silicon is now being used in Sharp's own PDA"ZAURUS" and also in other companies' cellular phones with cameras.

5. From interviews with Mr. Shigemitsu Mizushima director of display development section (2003/5/19).

6. Sharp has incorporated a secrecy device on the CG silicon production line that was made in 2002 with a huge budget of 46 billion. This production line was built inside Sharp's Tenri factory which has a product line especially for "TFTs" built in 1991.

7. Case studies on Sharp are based on interviews with President Machida on May 16, 2003, and director of display development, Shigemitsu Mizushima, on May 19, 2003.

8. *Nikkei Business*, August 25, 2003.

9. Below is Sharp's share in the LCD televisions market in 2004: Domestic 49 9% (1,200,000 units sold), overseas 26.9% (1,500,000 units sold) total 33.8% (2,700,000 units sold) (Data provided by Sharp).

10. The current leader in this market is Samsung, which overtook Sony in large size TVs using LCDs and plasma displays costing over $3,000 and keeps the No. 1 share as of 2003 (Source: *BusinessWeek*, June 16, 2003, p. 47).

11. The first LCD calculator < EL-805 > was sold in 1973.

12. Sharp has developed many hit products via the Urgent Project Team, by assigning firm-wide key issues that needed immediate and cross-sectional efforts.

13. Interview, done by the author at Kameyama plant on January 15, 2004.

REFERENCES

Chakravarthy, B., McEvily, S., Doz, Y., & Rau, D. (2003). Knowledge management and competitive advantage. In: M. Easterby-Smith & M. A. Lyles (Eds), *The Blackwell handbook of organizational learning and knowledge management* (pp. 205–323). Oxford: Blackwell Publishing.

Christensen, C. (1997). *Innovator's dilemma: When new technologies cause great firms to fail.* Boston, MA: Harvard Business School Press.

Doz, Y. L., Santos, J. F. P., & Williamson, P. J. (2001). *From global to metanational: How companies win in the knowledge economy.* Boston, MA: Harvard Business School Press.

Drucker, P. F. (1993). *Post-capitalist society.* New York: Harper Collins.

Edwards, C., Moon Ihlwan, N. J., & Engardio, P. (2003). The Samsung way. *Business Week*, June 16, 46–53.

Eisenhardt, K. M., & Santos, J. F. (2001). Knowledge-based view: A new theory of strategy. In:
   A. M. Pettigrew, T. Howard & R. Whitington (Eds), *Handbook of strategy and man-
   agement*. London: Sage Publications.
Nonaka, I., & Takeuchi, H. (1995). *The knowledge-creating company: How Japanese companies
   create the dynamics of innovation*. New York: Oxford University Press.
Reber, A. S. (1993). *Implicit learning and tacit knowledge: An essay on the cognitive unconscious*.
   New York: Oxford University Press.
Simon, H. A. (1962). The architecture of complexity. *Proceedings of the American Philosophical
   Society, 106*(December), 467–482.
Von Hippel, E. (1998). *Sources of innovation*. New York: Oxford University Press.
Von Krogh, G., Ichijo, K., & Nonaka, I. (2000). *Enabling knowledge creation: How to unlock the
   mystery of tacit knowledge and release the power of innovation*. New York: Oxford Uni-
   versity Press.
Winter, S. G. (1987). Knowledge and competence as strategic assets. In: D. Teece (Ed.), *The
   competitive challenge: Strategies for industrial innovation and renewal*. New York: Harper
   and Row.

PART III: MANAGING MEANING

As CEOs now communicate with a wide variety of stakeholders, it has become increasingly difficult to ensure that the intended meaning of their messages is received. Boas Shamir focuses on how leaders engage in the management of meanings in order to (1) justify their actions and the changes they introduce to the organization; (2) recruit followers and motivate members of the organization to support their actions; and (3) create shared perceptions and interpretations so that members' actions are guided by a common definition of the situation. Heike Bruch, Boas Shamir, and Galit Eilam-Shamir show how the leader of a large Swiss-based company actively managed the views, interpretations and energy of more than 100,000 employees through weekly e-mail letters when the company faced grave financial difficulties. Gretchen Spreitzer, Mary Sue Coleman, and Daniel Gruber show how an incoming university president dealt with an ongoing lawsuit regarding the university's use of affirmative action in its admissions processes and worked with various stakeholders to firmly establish the university's identity.

CHAPTER 7

STRATEGIC LEADERSHIP AS MANAGEMENT OF MEANINGS

Boas Shamir

ABSTRACT

Most of the literature on strategic management portrays the strategic leader as a planner, decision formulator, and implementer of structure and processes. Theories of strategic management have not paid much attention to the essence of all leadership roles, namely the role of influencing others, and have not been much informed by leadership theories in this regard. In this chapter, I argue that the existing gap between the field of leadership and the field of strategic management can be bridged by paying closer attention to the fundamentally social and interpretative nature of the strategy formation and implementation, and in particular to the role of strategic leaders as managers of meanings. The chapter presents the idea of leadership as the management of meanings, applies this idea to the role of strategic leaders, offers a set of meanings to focus on when we consider strategic leaders as managers of meanings, discusses the link between meaning making and organizational performance, and attends to some potential dangers involved in viewing leaders as managers of meanings.

Most of the literature on strategic management portrays the strategic leader as a planner, decision formulator, and implementer of structure and

---

Being There Even When You Are Not: Leading Through Strategy, Structures, and Systems
Monographs in Leadership and Management, Volume 4, 105–125
Copyright © 2007 by Elsevier Ltd.
All rights of reproduction in any form reserved
ISSN: 1479-3571/doi:10.1016/S1479-3571(07)04006-0

processes. Indeed, Chapter 2 of this book refers to "structuring the organization." In other words, the literature portrays the strategic leader as a manager more than as a leader. As noted by others (e.g., Cannella & Monroe, 1997; Hambrick, 2001), there is a gap between leadership theory and the field of strategic management. In recent years, there have been several attempts to apply charismatic and transformational leadership theories to the level of strategic organizational leadership (e.g., Sosik, Jung, Berson, Dionne, & Jaussi, 2004; Vera & Crossan, 2004; Waldman, Javidan, & Varella, 2004). However, notwithstanding such exceptions, theories of strategic management have not paid much attention to the essence of all leadership roles, namely the role of influencing others, and have not been much informed by leadership theories in this regard.

  The purpose of this chapter is to suggest that the existing gap between the field of strategic management and the field of leadership studies may be bridged by paying closer attention to a very important aspect of leadership, which is particularly relevant to strategic leadership, namely the role of leaders as managers of meanings. The chapter contains six sections. The first section presents the idea of leadership as the management of meanings and its origins. The second applies this idea to the role of strategic leaders and includes the suggestion that strategy itself may be viewed as primarily a meaning-making device. In the next section, I offer a set of meanings to focus on when we consider strategic leaders as managers of meanings. The fourth section discusses the link, implied in the first three sections, between meaning making and organizational performance, in view of recent claims that meaning making is worthy of interest regardless of its relationship with performance. In the fifth section, I briefly discuss some of the potential dangers involved in viewing leaders as managers of meanings; and in the final section, I offer some concluding remarks about the need to make the management of meanings a high-priority item in the research agenda of leadership scholars.

LEADERSHIP AS THE MANAGEMENT OF MEANINGS

The idea that leadership includes the management of meanings was implied in the work of prominent organization theories such as Weick's (1979) view of managerial work as the management of myths, symbols, and images and Pfeffer's (1981) perspective on management as symbolic action. Both Weick and Pfeffer did not refer to leaders or leadership explicitly. While Bennis

(1984) listed and briefly referred to the management of meaning as one of four necessary competencies of leadership, it was Smircich and her colleagues (Smircich & Morgan, 1982; Smircich & Stubbart, 1985) who explicitly and intensively introduced the notion that leadership is the management of meanings to the organizational literature.

According to this view, organizational leaders exercise their influence on organization members by influencing the meanings that members attach to various events and circumstances, as well as to their own roles within the organization. Leaders engage in the management of meanings in order to justify their actions and the changes they introduce to the organization, recruit followers and motivate members of the organization to support their actions, and create shared perceptions and interpretations so that members' actions are guided by a common definition of the situation. For instance, according to Smircich and Morgan (1982) "certain individuals ... emerge as leaders because of their role in framing experience in a way that provides viable bases for action, e.g., by mobilizing meaning, articulating and defining what has previously remained implicit or unsaid, by inventing images and meanings that provide a focus for new attention, and by consolidating, confronting, or changing prevailing wisdom ... In so doing, leaders enact a system of shared meanings that provides a basis for organized action" (p. 258).

There are several assumptions behind this view

(1) Action stems from the way people define and interpret their situation.
(2) Organized action requires a common definition of the organizational reality, which is shared by organization members.
(3) Organizations are, to a large extent, systems of shared meanings. The organizational structure, for instance, is of very little consequence unless it is backed by a shared meaning regarding organizational positions, lines of authority, division of responsibilities, etc., and by patterns of behavior that emanate from these shared meanings.
(4) The definition and meaning of organizational reality is not given. Members are exposed to many experiences, events, changes, and other stimuli that have to be interpreted in order to make sense of the situation and guide members' actions within that situation.
(5) The definition of the organizational reality is therefore, at least in part, the outcome of processes of social construction.
(6) Organization members expect the organization's leadership to provide them with interpretation, explanation, justification, and direction.
(7) Owing to their position, salience, and action possibilities, as well as members' expectations, leaders can influence the social construction of

reality by organizational members, and in so doing exert influence on organized action.

Bennis and Nanus (1997, p. 37) report that the first and most important generalization they drew from interviews with about 80 organizational leaders is that all organizations depend on the existence of shared meanings and interpretations of reality, which facilitate coordinated action, and therefore an essential factor in leadership is the capacity to influence and organize meanings for members of the organization. Some authors have taken this view even further by suggesting that leadership should be defined on the basis of its meaning-making aspect. For instance, "leadership is realized in the process whereby one or more individuals succeed in attempting to frame and define the reality for others" (Smircich & Morgan, 1982, p. 158), and leadership is "the guidance and facilitation of the social construction of a reality that enables the group to achieve its goals" (Maier, 2002, p. 186).

Such definitions imply that leadership effectiveness should also be evaluated from the management of meanings perspective. For instance, "the effectiveness of a leader lies in his [or her] ability to make activity meaningful for those in his [or her] role set" (Pondy, 1978, p. 94), and "effective leadership depends upon the extent to which the leader's definition of the situation ... serves as a basis for action by others ... In this sense ... effective leadership rests heavily on the framing of the experience of others, so that action can be guided by common conceptions of what should occur." (Smircich & Morgan, 1982, p. 262). While defining leadership and leadership effectiveness only on the basis of the management of meanings may be seen by some readers as too narrow, one potential advantage of such definitions is that they draw a clear distinction between leadership and other forms of social influence, such as influence by virtue of a legitimate social position, coercion, or the use of rewards.

However, there is no need to fully equate leadership with influence over meanings to acknowledge the centrality and importance of this aspect of leadership as evidenced in other parts of the leadership literature. The literature on organizational culture and leadership (e.g., Schein, 1992; Trice & Beyer, 1993) suggests that leaders use various verbal and symbolic means to influence organizational culture, namely members' shared assumptions, values, beliefs, and perceptions. Leadership communication studies have drawn attention to leader behaviors that attempt to frame or re-frame events and circumstances for followers in order to achieve alignment between the values, priorities and interpretations of the leader and those of the followers (e.g., Fairhurst & Saar, 1996). Finally, the literature on charismatic and transformational leadership (e.g., Bass, 1985; Conger & Kanungo, 1998; Shamir, House, & Arthur, 1993), which emphasizes the leader's vision, inspiration, and intellectual stimulation, also implies that leaders influence organization members by changing the meanings they attach to the organization's identity, mission, and goals as well as to their roles in the organization.

Despite the explicit or implicit centrality of the meaning-making aspect of leadership in several prominent leadership theories, there has not been much research on this aspect of organizational leadership beyond a few studies of vision articulation and communication (e.g., Berson, Shamir, Avolio, & Popper, 2001; Dvir, Kass, & Shamir, 2004) and several studies of leaders' speeches (e.g., Emrich, Brower, Feldman, & Garland, 2001). Furthermore, only recently have students of strategic management started to focus on the meaning-making roles of strategy and strategic leaders in their theorizing or research.

Strategic Leaders as Managers of Meanings

One of the reasons for this state of affairs is that in one important respect, most theories of strategic leadership have not focused on leadership. They have focused on characteristics of strategic leaders (e.g., Hambrick & Mason, 1984), the choices that strategic leaders make (e.g., Fiol & O'Connor, 2003) or the requirements of the role (e.g., Boal & Hooijberg, 2001), but have not paid much attention to the existence of followers and the central leadership role of influencing others.

This separation between field of leadership studies and the study of strategic leaders, as reflected, for instance, in a recent interview given by Hambrick (2001), is artificial and unfortunate. Most authorities on strategic management agree that the success of a strategy depends not only on its content, but also on its implementation. Implementation entails not only efforts to align the organization structures and processes with the strategy and with each other so that they match the strategy and serve its implementation but also aligning people – managers and workers – with the strategy and with the structures and processes that are built to support its implementation. Alignment of people requires the development of shared mental models among organizational members. When members share the perceptions, beliefs, and priorities of the leader, their activities are more likely to be aligned with each other and with the leaders' strategy, and thus promote the strategy's implementation. It follows that influencing the perceptions, beliefs, and priorities of organizational members is an important component of strategic leadership and an important key to the leader's success.

In this regard, Pfeffer (1981) suggests that the meaning-making role of the manager is probably the most important one in contexts in which assessment is difficult, members' involvement is segmented and incomplete, and technology or the connections between actions and results are ambiguous. Under such conditions of ambiguity, meanings are less "given" or agreed upon, and the input of management to the construction of reality is likely to be especially important and consequential. He further suggests that the importance of management-of-meaning activities under such conditions stems from their real consequences for the motivation and mobilization of support, the diversion or satisfaction of stakeholders' demands, and the implementation of change in the organization. Needless to say, these are exactly the conditions faced by more and more organizations and strategists in a globalized, boundary-less, and changing world. Following such claims, Gahmberg (1989, p. 726) asserted that the majority of many excellent managers' time and effort goes into management of meaning activities.

In fact, a recent trend in the strategic management literature suggests that strategy itself is a tool in the management of meanings, and the strategic process largely involves the social construction of a shared organizational reality. Some researchers (e.g., Gioia & Chittepedi, 1991) have looked at strategic management in terms of "sense-giving" activities, defined as managers' attempts to influence organizational members' interpretations by presenting their own construction of environmental circumstances and organizational events. Others (Eccles & Nohria, 1993) have gone even further to suggest that strategy itself is a rhetorical tool that is used by organizational leaders to justify and provide meaning to various organizational actions. In a similar vein, Barry and Elmes (1997) have claimed that strategy is always something that is constructed to persuade others toward certain understandings and actions.

Such claims apply whether we view strategy as a product of a controlled planning process by top management or as emerging or evolving from inside the organization and involving a continuous pattern of management activities at all levels (Gahmberg, 1989; Greiner, 1983). Thus the organizational strategy as a product of controlled planning processes by top management can be viewed as a symbol, which serves as a tool in the management of meanings because its text incorporates explanations of the organization's current situation, assessments of the organization's environment, justifications of required actions, etc. In other words, a formal strategy may appear as neutral and objective, but can be viewed as a text designed to create shared mental models among organization members. In addition, many strategic leaders also continuously engage in management-of-meaning activities around the formal strategy and in addition to it. They label specific organizational actions as "strategic," to highlight, juxtapose, and link them in certain ways, and try to convince others that things have happened in a certain way, and that this account should be the template from which new actions should be considered (Barry & Elmes, 1997). Hence the role of strategic leadership does not include only formulating an appropriate strategy for the organization and designing structures and processes to serve its implementation. "Strategic leadership, in effect, involves providing a conception and direction for organizational process that goes above and beyond what is embedded in the fabric of organization as a structure, i.e., a reified and somewhat static pattern of meaning" (Smircich & Morgan, 1982, p. 260).

Such claims indicate a change of emphasis in the dominant view of the strategic leader's job. If, as Smircich and Stubbart (1985) suggest, to lead means to define the experience of others, the strategist's job shifts from being a decision formulator, implementer of structure, and controller of events to providing interpretations and meaning to the stream of events and experiences that occur in the organization and around it. A primary role of the strategist, according to this view (e.g., Gahmberg, 1989) is to create connections and patterns to account for events, objects, and situations so that they become meaningful for members of the organization and by doing so, to construct the basis on which other people interpret their own specific experiences, decide what is happening, and judge whether they are engaged in worthwhile activities.

This view of strategic leadership and the role of strategic managers is gaining increasing acceptance. For instance, in Chapter 5, which deals with strategic leadership and organizational learning, Kimberly Boal explicitly lists the management of meanings among the roles and activities of strategic leaders, and further highlights this aspect by frequently using terms like "framing," "construction of reality," "stories," "causal maps," "perspective making," "perspective shaping," and "interpretative schemes." Following this theoretical perspective, a growing number of studies within the strategic management literature view strategy making, implementation, and change as discursive activities that involve the use of language, rhetoric, narrative, and other symbolic means to constitute a new reality in the minds of organizational members (e.g., Dunford & Jones, 2000; Hardy, Palmer, & Phillips, 2000).

THE MAIN MEANINGS MANAGED BY STRATEGIC LEADERS

Despite the growing recognition of the potential value in viewing leadership as management of meanings, there is as yet no theory that focuses on leadership in general and strategic leadership in particular as management of meanings and includes propositions about the ways by which leaders influence meanings and about the effects of these meanings on individual and organizational action. Developing such a theory is beyond the scope of this chapter. However, as a first step, we suggest a set of meanings on which a theory of strategic leadership as management of meanings could focus.

There are an infinite number of objects, circumstances, and events that may be relevant to organizational functioning and therefore an infinite number of meanings that an organizational leader may influence or try to influence. However, drawing on the literature on strategic management and leadership, a more limited set of meanings can be identified that seem to be particularly relevant to the production, acceptance, and implementation of organizational strategies and changes. Below, we present a list of these meanings to provide a focus for further discussion and research. The listed meanings may seem obvious to most readers. However, making such a list is a necessary first step in any attempt to understand how strategic leaders manage meanings and draw practical implications from this understanding.

Our departure point for making this list is the assumption that from a management of meaning perspective, a key leadership challenge of strategic management is to create and maintain systems of shared meanings that facilitate organized actions toward the achievement of desirable organizational ends (Smircich & Stubbart, 1985), noting, however, that what is defined as a desirable end is also a meaning that has to be managed. To meet this challenge, strategic leaders have to provide organization members with answers to some basic questions: Where are we? Why are we here? Where are we going? Why are we going there? What are we doing to get there? What are our chances of arriving at our destination? The following list of meanings is built to capture the answers to these questions. For analytic purposes, we list the following five meanings – environment, performance, goals, means, and efficacy – as discrete categories despite the fact that in reality, the boundaries between these categories are fuzzy and they are interrelated in many ways.

The Meaning of the Environment

This aspect of meaning making, which has received considerable attention in the strategic management literature, concerns the interpretation of environmental circumstances and events such as market trends, competitors' actions, technological innovations, regulation and deregulation decisions by the government, and political developments. Many writers on organizational management (e.g., Weick, 1995) present the view that environments are not entirely objective but rather "enacted." In other words, there is considerable room for interpretation of environmental circumstances and events, and therefore the perception of the environment is partially achieved through social construction and interaction processes among organization members. For instance, in a highly influential paper, Dutton and Jackson (1987) suggested that strategic issues in the organizational environment might be labeled by organizational decision makers as either threats or opportunities, with different consequences for the organization. While Dutton and Jackson and following studies (e.g., Thomas, Clark, & Gioia, 1993; Chattopadhyay et al., 2001) have focused mainly on the impact of these labels on the actions undertaken by the strategic actors themselves to address the issues, it is reasonable to expect that such labeling may influence other members' perceptions of the environment as well. For instance, former Intel CEO, Andrew Grove, stated that "only paranoids survive" (Grove, 1999), and tried to frame the environment primarily in terms of potential threats to the existence and success of the organization in order to prevent complacency on the part of organizational members and ensure constant vigilance of the organization's environment. As this example demonstrates, the interpretation of the environment is not limited to the current situation but often includes predictions of environmental trends and of the implications of environmental events and trends for the organization. This is also reflected, for instance, in Kotter's (1996) prescriptive model of leading organizational change in which the first step is "creating a sense of urgency," which is often done by emphasizing the threats involved in the continuance of existing practices in view of changes in the organizational environment. It should be emphasized, however, that managing the meaning of the environment does not only involve the highlighting of threats. It may focus, in contrast, on an attempt to frame environmental events and circumstances as potentially beneficial for the organization. For instance, according to Conger (1991, p. 31), a leader must not only be able to detect opportunities in the environment but be able to describe them in ways that maximize their significance.

The Meaning of Performance

Related to interpretations of the environment are interpretations of organizational performance. The meaning of performance includes, first of all, the answers to questions such as: How are we doing? Are we deteriorating or making progress? Some attention has been given to strategic leaders' portrayal of organizational performance to outsiders such as investors, analysts, and the media. Much less attention has been given to managing the meaning of performance as a leadership act directed toward members of the organization. Like the meaning of the environment, the meaning of performance is not entirely objective. Multiple performance indicators are often available to organization members, but in many situations, their meaning is not fully clear, and there is considerable space for different interpretations. Strategic leaders often engage in selecting, highlighting, and arranging performance data in order to convey a message, not only to outsiders but also to insiders, about how the organization is doing. Sometimes, strategic leaders may have an interest in arranging, presenting, and interpreting performance indicators to portray an unfavorable picture of the organizational situation, for instance, when they want to justify and motivate change. In extreme cases, they may want organization members to define the situation as a "crisis" or at least as intolerable. At other times, they may wish to portray a favorable picture of performance, for instance, after they have introduced a change and want to convey the impression that the organization is on the right track and is making progress toward achieving the aims of the change. Managing the meaning of performance includes not only providing an understanding of the organization's situation but also providing explanations for the situation. Organization members need an explanation to make sense of the current situation of the organization (Meindl, Ehrlich, & Dukerich, 1985), and leaders are often interested in having their own explanation accepted by others. In some cases, the leader's interest is personal, for instance, when the leader wants to divert blame for deterioration in performance from himself or herself and influence members to attribute the reasons for the deterioration to the actions of previous leaders or to unpredictable changes in the environment, or when the leader wishes to take credit for improving performance. In other cases, the interest is less personal, for instance, when the leader wishes to justify a proposed change by tying it to the reasons for poor current performance.

The Meaning of Goals

We refer here to goals in the broadest sense of this term, which includes the organization's mission and vision, as well as more specific targets. Strategic leaders' efforts to define the organizations' mission and values and to articulate and communicate a vision for the organization can be seen as efforts to manage the meaning of goals. Leaders' attempts to justify a certain order of priorities, as well as specific targets and changes in terms of the organization's mission, vision, and values can also be viewed as falling into this category of meaning making. Achieving consensus on goals is, of course, an important pre-condition for voluntary organized action and a major challenge for all managers. However, from a management of meaning perspective, consensus on goals implies more than the acceptance of goals as appropriate and legitimate on rational grounds. It also implies a shared acceptance of the importance of the goals, which is based on linkages between the organizational goals and members' identities, values, and long-term personal goals. These linkages are the basis of members' commitment to the organizational goals and their willingness to transcend their immediate personal interests, invest efforts, and cooperate with others toward the achievement of the organization's goals even in the absence of short-term personal rewards. Forming such linkages is therefore a major management of meanings challenge for strategic leaders.

The Meaning of Means

This category refers to the various ways by which organizational actions of various kinds become meaningful because they are viewed as means for achieving meaningful organizational goals. Three classes of such actions seem to be particularly important in this regard. First, both the strategy itself and the structures and processes designed and established as part of its implementation have to be infused with meaning by linking them to the previous meanings discussed above, namely the meaning of the environment, the meaning of organizational performance, and the meaning of organizational goals. Second, management decisions and actions of various kinds, such as personnel changes in managerial positions, decisions to acquire a new technology, or downsizing and cost cutting moves have to be justified by linking them to a shared perception of the environment and the organization's performance and to meaningful goals. Third, members' roles and tasks and the actions required of them have to be infused with meaning. For members to cooperate with proposed strategies and changes they need to see their roles, tasks, and actions as meaningful in terms of the larger picture. This requires more than an explanation. It often requires what Alvesson and Svenington (2003) have called "the extraodinarization of the mundane," namely getting organization members to be excited about their roles and tasks by convincing them of the importance of their individual contributions in terms of transcendent goals and values.

The Meaning of Efficacy

This category refers to organization members' beliefs about their own abilities and the organization's ability to achieve its goals. For members to act in support of a strategy and related changes advocated by the leader, it is not sufficient that they share the leader's definition of the organizational reality and view the vision and goals set by the leader as meaningful. It is not even sufficient that they share the same view about cause-effect relationships and more specific beliefs about the appropriateness of the means described in the preceding section. They also need to believe the organization has the human, social, and material resources to overcome current difficulties, improve its performance, and make progress toward the achievement of meaningful goals. Managing the meanings of efficacy therefore implies attempts to influence members' perceptions of the adequacy of the organization's technologies, financial resources, people's knowledge and skills, management competence, customer relations, etc. In addition, it involves attempts to influence members' beliefs in their own agency as individuals, groups, and organization, namely their beliefs that their actions will make a difference and have an impact on the organization's performance and success (Thomas & Velthouse, 1990; Spreitzer, 1995). While the management of meanings by strategic leaders may include attempts to raise organization members' self-efficacy beliefs, of particular importance are their collective efficacy beliefs: "If people are to act collectively they must believe that such action would be efficacious, i.e., that change is possible but it will not happen automatically, without collective action" (Snow, Rochford, Worden, & Benrod, 1986, p. 470).

In sum, we suggest that the management of meanings by strategic leaders primarily involves their attempt to influence organization members' perceptions and interpretations regarding the organization's environment, the state of the organization and its performance, the vision and goals of the organization, the appropriateness of various means, decisions, and actions employed by the organization to achieve its goals, and the ability of the organization to make progress toward meaningful goals. Any such list of meanings is arbitrary, of course, and in itself represents an attempt to impose meaning on a much more complex set of perceptions, interpretations, and beliefs. The list of meanings described above is not exhaustive. Furthermore, as mentioned, the listed meanings are interrelated in many ways. For instance, efficacy beliefs are closely related to perceptions of the environment, the organization's situation, and the appropriateness of the means employed by the organization's leadership to address the organization's situation. However, we maintain that both attempts to develop a theory of strategic leadership as management of meanings and attempts to study the phenomenon empirically would benefit from focusing on a set of relevant meanings rather than on meanings in general. Furthermore, the practical implications of the understanding to be gained from such research are also likely to be clearer if such understanding is tied to specific meanings to which most managers can relate rather than to more general or abstract meanings.

IS MEANING MAKING AN END IN ITSELF?

So far, we have justified the importance of the meaning management function of strategic leadership on instrumental grounds. We have mainly emphasized the relationship between meaning and action and the importance of shared perceptions, interpretations, and mental models for concerted action toward strategy implementation. This was the logic behind the set of meanings discussed in the previous section. It was implied in our arguments that leadership as the management of meanings can impact on organizational performance. Our explicit and implicit arguments have followed an instrumental logic that justifies action on the basis of means-ends calculations, which Weber (1946) referred to as "formal rationality" and March (1996) has called "the logic of consequence."

However, the importance of leadership in general and strategic leadership in particular as management of meaning may also be justified on non-instrumental grounds, which Weber (1946) referred to as "substantive rationality" and March (1996) has called the logic of appropriateness. According to this logic, action, such as leadership, is justified not on the basis of its relationship with some desired end such as performance, but on the basis of expressing important end values and identities. It has recently been claimed (Podolny, Khurana, & Hill-Popper, 2005) that the tendency to justify scholarly and practical interest in organizational leadership on the basis of its linkage with economic performance is a relatively modern phenomenon, and the concept of leadership in the organizational literature was originally couched in terms of its significance for meaning making.

According to this claim, earlier organizational scholars such as Weber (1946), Barnard (1968), and Selznick (1984) were not concerned with leadership because of the concept's ability to explain economic performance, but rather because of its capacity to infuse meaning into the lives of individuals.

For Podolny et al. (2005) infusing meaning into the lives of individuals is sufficient to justify leadership and scholarly interest in leadership. "Even if we find ultimately that meaning creation does not have a significant impact on economic performance, we maintain that greater attention should be given to it as an outcome that is worthy of explanation ... Indeed, we can think of no other phenomenon that is more worthy of explanation" (p. 31). For Podolny et al. (2005), action is meaningful when its undertaking (1) supports some ultimate end that the individual personally values and (2) affirms the individual's connection to the community of which he or she is a part. It follows that leadership as meaning creation concerns leader's actions and attributes that link members' actions, as individuals and as a collectivity, to cherished values and a sense of community and close relationships.

Both aspects of meaningfulness emphasized by Podolny et al. (2005) may be seen as components of a more general argument, namely that action is meaningful when it is related to the actor's self-concept because both values and social identities may be seen as components of the self-concept (Shamir, 1991). In this regard, Shamir et al. (1993) have offered a leadership theory, which explains the charismatic effect of leaders on the basis of their ability to infuse action with meaning, namely link both the organizational mission and various roles and tasks within the organization with members' self-concepts, in particular with their values and identities. The difference between Podolny et al. (2005) and Shamir et al. (1993) is that according to the latter, infusing action with meaning in the sense of linking it to organization members' self-concepts is not viewed only as an end in itself, but also as a means for increasing members' commitment, motivation, cooperation, and ultimately their performance as individuals and as an organized unit.

It is also implied in the work of Shamir et al. (1993) that infusing action with meaning in the sense of linking it to members' self-concepts has, in addition to its hypothesized effects on performance via increasing members' motivation, commitment, and cooperation, another potential and indirect effect on performance. They imply that a leader who can infuse action with meaning becomes more charismatic in the eyes of his or her followers, namely, that respect for the leader, attraction to the leader, trust in the leader, emotional bonds with the leader, and voluntary willingness to follow the leader may increase as a result of his or her ability to provide meaning.

In other words, infusing action with meaning is one of the important bases on which leaders may build their ability to influence followers.

This ability may serve leaders to influence followers in ways that extend beyond the meanings discussed above. It may help them influence other meanings, for instance the meaning of various actions by the leader and the meaning of proposed changes. This, in turn, may affect the intensity and direction of followers' efforts, their level of cooperation with the leader's strategy, and eventually the adaptation and performance of the organization. Therefore, at least in theory, the instrumental and non-instrumental logics for management of meanings may be linked. Making organizational and individual actions meaningful for organizational members by linking them to members' values, collective identities and other aspects of their self-concepts may increase the leader's ability to influence the set of meanings discussed in the previous section, which seems more directly essential for organized action, and ultimately organizational adaptation and performance.

THE DARK SIDE OF MANAGING MEANINGS

It is possible to view leadership as the management of meanings as brainwashing or mind control. From a critical perspective, the management of meaning implies attempts by powerful actors to manipulate and control the behavior of others by imposing on the latter a definition of reality that maintains and increases the power, resources, status, and benefits of the former. Critical management thinkers (e.g., Shenhav, 2000) have shown that even seemingly neutral concepts and theories of management and organization may define the organizational reality in ways that lead to the exploitation of the vast majority of organizational members for the benefit of a small number of owners and managers.

Potentially, the management of meanings has a dark side. Some of the most undesirable consequences of leadership in history, including crimes against humanity and mass suicides, resulted from followers letting leaders define the reality for them. These dangers, which have been discussed widely in regard to specific cases and charismatic leadership in general (e.g., Conger, 1990; Howell & Shamir, 2005), cannot be overlooked. However, in organizations, there are many more cases in which leaders' attempts to manage meanings are met with only partial success, if any success at all. In this regard, the terms "management of meaning" and "meaning making" used throughout this chapter may be misleading. Most organized situations are characterized by the existence of rival interpretations and the meanings that organizational members attach to events, circumstances, and actions are derived not only from the organizational leadership but also from other sources, such as their colleagues, informal leaders, the media, and their own prior experiences. Strategic leaders are therefore not really meaning makers who can manipulate symbols, images, and stories to implant their favored definition of reality in the minds of organization members. Rather, they are players in an arena saturated with multiple meanings and multiple sources of influence. Indeed, organization members often react against, reject, or change the definition of reality provided by the leader (Smircich & Morgan, 1982, p. 259).

In view of the potential dangers entailed by leadership as the management of meanings on the one hand, and the limitations on meaning making by leaders on the other, a balanced approach to this issue seems justified. On the one hand, leaders, organization members, and students of organization and management should be constantly aware of the potential dangers of meaning management by leaders. On the other hand, this does not mean that leaders should refrain from any attempt to influence meanings in the organization or that management scholars should focus on only the ma-nipulative aspects of such attempts. To lead implies to play a dispropor-tionately influential role in the construction of reality in the organization. Refraining from doing so implies an abandonment of the leadership role. If we accept leadership as a fact of life and a potentially beneficial source of influence in organizations, we must also accept the role of leadership as the management of meanings, and at the same time remain constantly vigilant that this role is not performed in a way that it serves illegitimate ends such as the manipulation and control of others for personal purposes.

To achieve a balanced view that takes into consideration both the inev-itability of leaders attempts to influence meanings and the dangers entailed by such attempts, perhaps we should replace the terms meaning making and management of meanings with the term "frame alignment" suggested by Snow et al. (1986) in a seminal work on social movements. Frame alignment refers to the creation of linkages between members and leaders interpreta-tive orientations, such that some of the members' interests, values, and beliefs and the organization's activities, mission, ideology, and goals are congruent and complementary. Organized action requires frame alignment. However, frame alignment does not imply a total acceptance of the leader's perceptions, beliefs, and goals by organization members. Rather, as defined by Snow et al. (1986), it refers to "frame resonance" namely alignment between *some* aspects of members' and leaders' interpretative schemes. Since many of the dangers involved in acceptance of leaders' frames stem from a total acceptance of such frames, the term frame alignment together with a narrower focus only on a set of meanings particularly relevant to organized action, as suggested in a previous section of this chapter, may be more appropriate. In addition, in comparison with terms like management of meanings, meaning making, sense giving, or framing, the concept of frame alignment is less unidirectional. It connotes the possibility that leaders' frames or schemata of interpretation may also be aligned to match those of the organization's members.

CONCLUSION

This chapter has argued that the existing gap between the field of leadership and the field of strategic management originates primarily in both fields' inattention to the fundamentally social and interpretative nature of the strategy formation and implementation processes. This gap can be closed by paying more attention to the role of strategic leaders as managers of meanings. In this chapter, we have not examined the means by which leaders influence the meanings held by organization members. This should be the next step in theory development and research. "A focus on the way meaning in organized settings is created, sustained, and changed provides a powerful means of understanding the fundamental nature of leadership as a social process. In understanding the way leadership actions attempt to shape and interpret situations to guide organizational members into a common interpretation of reality, we are able to understand how leadership works to create an important foundation for organized activity" (Smircich & Morgan, 1982, p. 261). Unfortunately, this statement, made over 20 years ago, has not received sufficient attention from management and organizations scholars.

The task is formidable. Let us consider briefly two major challenges. First, an understanding of "the way leadership actions attempt to shape and interpret situations to guide organizational members into a common interpretation of reality" cannot be based only on leaders' public statements, such as vision statements or speeches, or officially orchestrated ceremonies or rituals. In principle, all the leader's communication and interactive activities are potential vehicles for transmitting meanings. As suggested by several authors (e.g., Greiner, 1983; Schein, 1992), the leader's own behavior may carry symbolic meaning because the actions and utterances of leaders draw attention to particular aspects of the overall flow of experience.

"Senior executives, whether they like it or not, are 'on stage,' with a sur-
rounding cast of subordinates and an audience of hundreds, often thousands, of employees. Every action taken by the senior executive, verbal or
non-verbal, carries cues with 'symbolic meaning' to the cast and audience.
They are looking for signs that indicate what is important to the senior
executive, what will be rewarded, where they are going, and if they want to
invest their efforts in expressing the specific behaviors that seem to be valued
by top management" (Greiner, 1983, p. 15). Studying leadership as management of meanings therefore requires the development of conceptual
frameworks and observational methods that would enable us to capture
the meanings that are conveyed by leaders' ongoing behaviors and
communications.

Second, leaders' communications as acts of meaning management or
frame alignment are often much more complex than, for instance, the mere
labeling of events as threats or opportunities or the labeling of certain actions as leadership actions rather than management actions. As suggested by
several writers (e.g., Gabriel, 2000; Gardner, 1995), meanings are often
"packaged" in more elaborate forms of communication such as personal
and organizational narratives. Indeed, some writers advocate storytelling as
the most effective means of conveying meanings. For instance, when Weick
(1995) answers the question, what is necessary for sense making? He says:
"The answer is, something that preserves plausibility and coherence, something that is reasonable and memorable, something that embodies past
experiences and expectations, something that resonates with other people,
something that can be constructed retrospectively but can also be used
prospectively, something that captures both feeling and thought, something
that allows for embellishments to fit current oddities, something that is fun
to construct. In short, what is necessary in sense-making is a good story"
(pp. 60–61). Understanding leadership as management of meanings, therefore, requires an understanding of how complex narratives are constructed,
how they are being told, what meanings are conveyed by them, and what are
their effects.

Perhaps because of the magnitude of such challenges, the topic of leadership as management of meanings has not received the attention it deserves
in the 25 years that have passed since Smircich and Morgan (1982) introduction of this topic to the organizational literature. The field of leadership
has mainly paid attention to other aspects of leader behavior, and while the
field of strategic management has paid some attention to the way strategists
make sense of their situation it has not paid much attention to how they
transmit this sense to others in the organization. This state of affairs is

unfortunate not only from a theoretical perspective, but also because of its practical implications. As a result of our limited understanding of strategic leadership as management of meanings, we tend to ignore this crucial aspect of leadership in our leadership training and development programs. If we do not make the management of meanings issue a central item in our research agenda, we will continue to hold, and convey to others a limited picture of what leadership is all about.

REFERENCES

Alvesson, M., & Svenington, S. (2003). Managers doing leadership: The extra-ordinarization of the mundane. *Human Relations, 56,* 1435–1459.

Barnard, C. I. (1968). *The functions of the executive.* Cambridge, MA: Harvard University Press.

Barry, D., & Elmes, M. (1997). Strategy retold: Towards a narrative view of strategic discourse. *Academy of Management Review, 22,* 429–452.

Bass, B. M. (1985). *Leadership and performance beyond expectations.* New York, NY: Free Press.

Bennis, W. (1984). The 4 competencies of leadership. *Training and Development Journal, 38,* 15–19.

Bennis, W., & Nanus, B. (1997). *Leaders: Strategies for taking charge* (2nd ed.). New York, NY: HarperCollins.

Berson, Y., Shamir, B., Avolio, B. J., & Popper, M. (2001). The relationship between vision strength, leadership style and context. *Leadership Quarterly, 12*(1), 53–73.

Boal, K. B., & Hooijberg, R. (2001). Strategic leadership: Moving on. *Leadership Quarterly, 11,* 515–549.

Cannella, A. A., & Monroe, M. J. (1997). Contrasting perspectives on strategic leadership: Toward a more realistic view of top managers. *Journal of Management, 23,* 213–237.

Chattopadhyay, P., Glick, W. H., & Huber, G. P. (2001). Organizational actions in response to threats and opportunities. *Academy of Management Journal, 44,* 937–956.

Conger, J. A. (1990). The dark side of leadership. *Organizational Dynamics, 19*(2), 44–55.

Conger, J. A. (1991). Inspiring others: The language of leadership. *Academy of Management Executive, 5,* 31–45.

Conger, J. A., & Kanungo, R. N. (1998). *Charismatic leadership in organizations.* Thousand Oaks, CA: Sage.

Dunford, R., & Jones, D. (2000). Narrative in strategic change. *Human Relations, 53,* 1207–1226.

Dutton, J., & Jackson, S. (1987). Categorizing strategic issues: Links to organizational action. *Academy of Management Review, 12,* 76–90.

Dvir, T., Kass, N., & Shamir, B. (2004). The emotional bond. Vision and organizational commitment among high-tech employees. *Journal of Organizational Change Management, 17*(2), 126–143.

Eccles, R., & Nohria, N. (1993). *Beyond the hype.* Cambridge, MA: Harvard Business School Press.

Emrich, C. G., Brower, H. H., Feldman, J. H., & Garland, H. (2001). Images in words: Presidential rhetoric, charisma and greatness. *Administrative Science Quarterly, 46,* 527–557.

Fairhurst, G. T., & Saar, R. A. (1996). *The art of framing: Managing the language of leadership.* San Francisco, CA: Jossey-Bass.

Fiol, C. M., & O'Connor, E. J. (2003). Waking up: Mindfulness in the face of bandwagons. *Academy of Management Review, 28,* 54–70.

Gabriel, Y. (2000). *Storytelling in organizations: Facts, fictions, and fantasies.* Oxford: Oxford University Press.

Gahmberg, H. (1989). Metaphor management: On the semiotics of strategic leadership. In: B. A. Turner (Ed.), *Organizational symbolism.* New York, NY: W. de Gruyer.

Gardner, H. (1995). *Leading minds: An anatomy of leadership.* New York, NY: Basic Books.

Gioia, D. A., & Chittepedi, K. (1991). Sensemaking and sensegiving in strategic change initiation. *Strategic Management Journal, 12,* 433–448.

Greiner, L. E. (1983). Senior executives as strategic actors. *New Management, 1*(2), 11–15.

Grove, A. S. (1999). *Only the paranoid survive.* New York, NY: Doubleday.

Hambrick, D. C. (2001). Upper echelons: Donald Hambrick on executives and strategy (Interview by A. A. Cannella, Jr.). *Academy of Management Executive, 15,* 36–45.

Hambrick, D. C., & Mason, P. A. (1984). Upper echelons: The organization as a reflection of its top managers. *Academy of Management Review, 9,* 193–206.

Hardy, C., Palmer, I., & Phillips, N. (2000). Discourse as a strategic resource. *Human Relations, 53,* 7–28.

Howell, J. M., & Shamir, B. (2005). The role of followers in charismatic leadership: Relationships and their consequences. *Academy of Management Review, 30,* 96–112.

Kotter, J. P. (1996). *Leading change.* Cambridge, MA: Harvard Business School Press.

Maier, C. (2002). *Leading diversity.* St. Gallen, Switzerland: University of St. Gallen, I.FPM Schriftenriehe Band 3.

March, J. G. (1996). A scholar's quest. *Stanford Graduate School of Business Magazine,* June, 1–4.

Meindl, J. R., Ehrlich, S. B., & Dukerich, J. M. (1985). The romance of leadership. *Administrative Science Quarterly, 30,* 78–102.

Pfeffer, J. (1981). Management as symbolic action: The creation and maintenance of organizational paradigms. In: L. L. Cummings & B. M. Staw (Eds), *Research in organizational behavior* (Vol. 3, pp. 1–52). Greenwich CA: JAI Press.

Podolny, J. M., Khurana, R., Hill-Popper, M. (2005). Revisiting the meaning of leadership. In: B. Staw & R. Kramer (Eds), *Research in organizational behavior* (Vol. 26, pp. 1–36). New York, NY: Elsevier.

Pondy, L. R. (1978). Leadership is a language game. In: M. McCall & M. Lombardo (Eds), *Leadership: Where else can we go?* (pp. 87–96). Durham, NC: Duke University Press.

Schein, E. H. (1992). *Organizational culture and leadership.* San Francisco, CA: Jossey-Bass.

Selznick, P. (1984). *Leadership in administration: A sociological perspective.* Berkeley, CA: University of California Press.

Shamir, B. (1991). Self, meaning and motivation in organizations. *Organization Studies, 3,* 405–424.

Shamir, B., House, R. B., & Arthur, M. B. (1993). The motivational effects of charismatic leadership: A self-concept based theory. *Organization Science, 4,* 577–594.

Shenhav, Y. (2000). *Manufacturing rationality: The engineering foundations of the managerial revolution.* Oxford: Oxford University Press.

Smircich, L., & Morgan, G. (1982). Leadership: The management of meaning. *Journal of Applied Behavioral Science, 18,* 257–273.

Smircich, L., & Stubbart, C. (1985). Strategic management in an enacted world. *Academy of Management Review, 10,* 724–736.

Snow, D. A., Rochford, E. B., Worden, S. K., & Benrod, R. D. (1986). Frame alignment processes, micromobilization and movement participation. *American Sociological Review, 51,* 464–481.

Sosik, J. J., Jung, D. I., Berson, Y., Dionne, S. D., & Jaussi, K. S. (2004). *The dream weavers: Strategic leadership in technology-driven organizations.* Greenwich, CT: Information Age Publishing.

Spreitzer, G. M. (1995). Individual empowerment in the workplace: Dimensions, measurement, validation. *Academy of Management Journal, 38*(5), 1442–1465.

Trice, H., & Beyer, J. M. (1993). *The cultures of work organizations.* Upper Saddle River, NJ: Prentice-Hall.

Thomas, K. W., & Velthouse, B. A. (1990). Cognitive elements of empowerment: An interpretive model of intrinsic task motivation. *Academy of Management Review, 15,* 666–681.

Thomas, S., Clark, J., & Gioia, D. (1993). Strategic sensemaking and organizational performance: Linkages among scanning, interpretation, action, and outcomes. *Academy of Management Journal, 36,* 239–270.

Vera, D., & Crossan, M. (2004). Strategic leadership and organizational learning. *Academy of Management Review, 29,* 222–240.

Waldman, D. A., Javidan, M., & Varella, P. (2004). Charismatic leadership at the strategic level: A new application of upper echelons theory. *Leadership Quarterly, 15,* 355–380.

Weber, M. (1946). From Max Weber. In: H. H. Gerth & C. W. Mills (Trans. and Eds), New York, NY: Oxford University Press.

Weick, K. (1979). Cognitive processes in organizations. In: B. M. Staw (Ed.), *Research in Organizational Behavior* (Vol. 1, pp. 41–75). Greenwich, CT: JAI Press.

Weick, K. (1995). *Sensemaking in organizations.* Thousand Oaks, CA: Sage.

CHAPTER 8

MANAGING MEANINGS IN TIMES OF CRISIS AND RECOVERY: CEO PREVENTION-ORIENTED LEADERSHIP

Heike Bruch, Boas Shamir and Galit Eilam-Shamir

ABSTRACT

While there is growing recognition of the role of leaders as managers of meanings, leadership theories have so far focused primarily on the articulation of a positive vision, the framing of organizational issues as opportunities, and emphasizing potential gains and benefits for the organization and its members. However, these positive frames may not be equally valid under all circumstances and with respect to all issues. This chapter concentrates on exploring leadership as management of meanings in times of crisis and recovery, when leaders attempt to stop deterioration, turn the organization around, and lead it to recovery. We label this leadership approach prevention-oriented leadership. On the basis of an analysis of a series of weekly e-mail letters sent by the CEO of a large company to all organizational members over a period of 22 months we suggest that prevention-oriented leaders may use three related ways to manage meanings, namely (1) generating a clear picture of the negative challenge, (2) strengthening the organizational members' self-efficacy

Being There Even When You Are Not: Leading Through Strategy, Structures, and Systems
Monographs in Leadership and Management, Volume 4, 127–153
Copyright © 2007 by Elsevier Ltd.
All rights of reproduction in any form reserved
ISSN: 1479-3571/doi:10.1016/S1479-3571(07)04007-2

*and confidence in the organization's resources available for coping with
the crisis, and (3) creating a sense of progress.*

There is a growing recognition that, to a great extent, strategic leadership in organizations concerns the management of meanings (Pfeffer, 1981; Smircich & Morgan, 1982). Namely, organizational leaders exercise their influence on followers by influencing the way followers perceive both the environment and the leaders themselves. Also, they influence the meanings that followers attach to various events and circumstances and to their own roles within the organization. Leaders engage in the management of meaning in order to justify their actions and the changes they introduce, to recruit followership and motivate members of the organization to support their actions, and to create shared perceptions and interpretations so that members' actions are guided by a common definition of the situation (Alvesson & Willmott, 2002). Reflecting such views, a recent doctoral dissertation defined leadership as "the guidance and facilitation of the social construction of a reality that enables the group to achieve its goals" (Maier, 2002, p. 186).

MANAGEMENT OF MEANINGS IN PROMOTION- AND PREVENTION-ORIENTED LEADERSHIP APPROACHES

Despite this recognition of the management of meanings, we do not know much about the meanings leaders actually manage, the ways by which they manage those meanings, and how they practice this aspect of their leadership role in different situations.

The "New Leadership" theories (Bryman, 1992) or transformational approaches to leadership (Sashkin, 2004) interpret leadership as the management of meanings, but in a limited way. These theories share one component, which focuses directly on the management of meanings, namely the articulation of a vision by the leader. They share the assumption that by articulating and communicating a vivid, attractive, and compelling vision, leaders can influence followers' perceptions of the organizational mission and their motivation to contribute to it. In addition to vision, the new leadership theories also include other behavioral components that may be related to the management of meanings, such as the enhancement of the collective identity (Shamir, House, & Arthur, 1993) or the intellectual stimulation of followers (Bass, 1985). However, all of these behaviors share a positive bias toward the opportunities frame. Extant leadership theories have been limited with respect to the question of how leaders may frame issues as threats and manage meaning related to these issues. There is not a single leadership concept known to us that acknowledges that managing meaning through the framing of issues as threats may have beneficial consequences and may sometimes constitute effective leadership behavior.

While considerable evidence suggests that the opportunity frame, to which the new leadership theories apply, is closely associated with effectiveness and performance (Dumdum, Lowe, & Avolio, 2002; Fuller, Patterson, Hester, & Stringer, 1996; Lowe, Kroeck, & Sivasubramaniam, 1996), the opportunity frame may not be equally valid under all circumstances and with respect to all issues. There are circumstances where the primary task of the organization is survival or recovery, with individuals' perceptions being focused on threats and potential losses for the company and themselves. A leadership approach that concentrates exclusively on an opportunity-laden vision and other behaviors which use a vision for sense-making and the management of meanings may not be realistic in such situations and may not be as effective as an approach that includes the acknowledgement and framing of threats. Moreover, there are situations in which the main danger for the organization is organizational inertia and complacency (Bruch & Ghoshal, 2003; Jansen, 2004). Under such situations, the primary task of the leader may be the identification of potential threats and the framing of issues as threats (Kotter, 1995; Tushman & O'Reilly III, 1996). In line with this, Heifetz and Laurie (1997, p. 124) recommend: "Rather than protecting people from outside threats, leaders should let the pinch of reality stimulate them to adapt." Furthermore, it may be assumed that certain types of employees are unreceptive to visions because their motivational structures are different and they react differently at the emotional level.

In view of these considerations, our aim in the present investigation was to contribute to a better understanding of alternative ways of managing meaning next to and beyond the comparatively well researched leadership approaches – transformational (Bass, 1985) or charismatic (Conger, 1989; Shamir et al., 1993) leadership – which are more oriented toward opportunities for the future and potential gains. Beyond these "promotion-oriented" leadership styles, we are interested in exploring what we call "prevention-oriented leadership."

A first approximation of different forms of managing meaning may be found in the work of Dutton and colleagues (Denison, Dutton, Kahn, & Hart, 1996; Jackson & Dutton, 1988), who investigate differences in the interpretation and labeling of situations. For instance, in a highly influential paper, Dutton and Jackson (1987) suggested that strategic issues can be labeled by organizational decision-makers as either threats or opportunities, with different consequences for the organization. Dutton and Jackson and following studies (e.g., Thomas, Clark, & Gioia, 1993), however, have focused mainly on the impact of this labeling on the actions undertaken by managers to address strategic issues. The broader implications of the Dutton and Jackson (1987) distinction for leadership have not been developed theoretically and have not been studied systematically. While it is possible that the mere labeling of certain issues by leaders will have some effects on followers, the actual management of meanings involves a wider range of leadership activities.

In line with this idea, Bruch and Ghoshal (2003) recently suggested that strategic leaders can motivate organization members and energize their organizations by adopting one of two approaches: (1) "slaying the dragon," which focuses organizational members' attention on the need to overcome threats, problems, or crises, and (2) "winning the princess," which focuses members' attention on opportunities, potential gains, or a vision. Following Bruch and Ghoshal (2003), we suggest that leaders can manage meaning with the help of both threats and opportunities. We propose that it is not only the compelling opportunities and visions that may be a potent motivational force, but that, under certain circumstances, leaders may motivate people more effectively when they help people interpret the situation around a threat or negative challenge.

Support for this suggestion can be derived from Higgins' (1997, 1998) regulatory focus theory which can explain the motivational effect of both threats and opportunities. Higgins and his colleagues (Higgins & Silberman, 1998; Shah & Higgins, 2001) argue that individuals can pursue two types of goals: Promotion goals that take the form of pursuing desirable outcomes and prevention goals that take the form of avoiding undesirable outcomes like failures or disasters. Promotion-focused people are motivated by growth and development needs. Therefore, they tend to show especially high motivation and persistence on tasks that are framed in terms of promotion, and they scrutinize their social world for information that assists their pursuit of success. Prevention-focused people, on the other hand, are motivated by security needs. Therefore, they focus on information relevant to the avoidance of failures, and they tend to show high motivation and persistence on tasks that are framed in terms of prevention. Studies by Higgins and his colleagues (Higgins & Tycocinsky, 1992; Shah, Higgins, & Friedman, 1998) demonstrate that when people have a prevention focus, they do not attend to and do not respond to information concerning possible success and gains, but rather focus on information relevant to the avoidance of failure. These findings suggest that in times of crisis, promotion-oriented leadership, with its emphasis on vision, growth, and gains, may be less relevant than prevention-oriented leadership.

The possible implications of these findings for leadership in organizations stem from the notion that "organizational authorities as 'makers of meaning' may influence members' regulatory focus through the use of language and symbols" (Brockner & Higgins, 2001, p. 58). In terms of regulatory focus theory, transformational and charismatic leadership behaviors, with their emphasis on articulating an attractive vision and on developing followers, can be seen as attempting to induce or reinforce a promotion focus among organization members. Such leadership has received most of the attention in the last 20 years (Boal & Hooijberg, 2001). In contrast, limited attention has been given to prevention-oriented leadership. While Bruch and Ghoshal (2003) point to the significance and the effectiveness of prevention-oriented leadership, they do not investigate what leaders actually do when managing meaning with a prevention focus.

We conceptualize prevention-oriented leadership as leader behavior that focuses on threats, dangers, and possible negative consequences in an attempt to mobilize followers through a prevention-oriented regulatory focus, that is, through focusing their efforts to avoid losses, failures, and other negative outcomes. Defined in this way, prevention-oriented leadership is not a coercive- or punishment-based leadership. It does not threaten followers individually with personal punishments, but rather empowers them and highlights the importance of their effort in order to prevent potential negative consequences for the collective (group, unit, or organization). Prevention-oriented leadership is also different from transactional leadership, which, as originally defined by Burns (1978) and Bass (1985), motivates individuals by promising gains and rewards in exchange for followership. One key element of prevention-oriented leadership is the management of meanings. This becomes particularly relevant in situations of crises.

SIGNIFICANCE OF MANAGEMENT OF MEANINGS IN TIMES OF A PERFORMANCE CRISIS

In this paper, we are primarily concerned with the way strategic leaders practice prevention-oriented leadership. Particularly, we focus on the way such leaders manage meaning in times of crisis that may follow a decline in performance, which threatens the existence of the organization (accumulating heavy losses, large and growing debt, dramatic decline in share prices). In such times, the strategic leadership task is commonly referred to in terms of leading an organizational recovery, renewal, or a "turnaround." We chose to focus on these kinds of situations, because leadership in general and prevention-oriented leadership in particular may be especially relevant under such circumstances. After studying about two dozen turnarounds, Kanter (2003) recently concluded that leadership matters most in these difficult times. Following this thought, we suggest that times of crisis that threaten an organization's existence present strategic leaders with the ultimate test of their management of meaning abilities and skills.

First, crises pose sudden threats to high priority goals with little or no response time (Jick & Murray, 1982). They are, by definition, unexpected, even when they come after a period of declining performance. Hence, they typically cause confusion and uncertainty among organizational members who do not fully understand what happened, why it happened, and what they should do now; organizational members will likely seek answers to these questions from their top leaders. In such situations, it is the strategic leaders' task to help organizational members make sense of their uncertain, confusing, and vulnerable situation. Second, crises are also, by definition, situations in which the organization and its members are expected to handle demands for which their existing resources may not suffice. Therefore, in crisis situations members are likely to have doubts about their own and their organization's ability to successfully handle the situation. Loss of confidence and morale, even despair and paralysis, may develop among members precisely when the organization needs their highest level of effort and self-discipline. Organizational decline typically leads to passivity, rendering it a key task for organizational leaders to restore people's confidence in themselves and in each other and to inspire and empower them to take actions that will renew profitability (Kanter, 2003).

We draw two conclusions from this: First, prevention-oriented leadership as the management of meanings is of special importance in times of crisis and decline. Second, we expect that one of the major challenges of leaders in times of crisis is to balance two seemingly contradictory tasks of managing meaning. Leaders need to calibrate the level of threat experienced by organization members so that it is not so high that it paralyzes them (Staw, Sandelands, & Dutton, 1981), and at the same time is high enough to maintain organization members' prevention-oriented motivational forces.

Since crisis is a stressful situation, the literature on stress and coping is relevant here (Affleck & Tennen, 1996; Folkman & Moskowitz, 2000; Lazarus, 1991; Lazarus & Folkman, 1984; Schwarzer & Knoll, 2003). Dominant theories of coping with stress assign an important role to the interpretation or assessment of the situation by the individual. Lazarus' (1991) transaction theory places emphasis on the meaning of the potentially stressful event for the individual and argues that one's view of the situation determines the coping strategy one may employ to deal with the stress. Blascovich and Mendes (2000) suggest that individuals' interpretations of and their reactions to threatening situations derive from an appraisal process that has two parts: (1) demand appraisal, which involves the appraisal of situational demands (including perceptions or assessments of danger, uncertainty, and required effort inherent to the situation) and (2) resource appraisal, which is an appraisal of the individual's resources (e.g., knowledge and skill).

On the basis of our analysis of theoretical descriptions of situations of crisis and decline and stress theoretical approaches, we suggest that in order to lead an organizational turnaround following a performance crisis, prevention-oriented management of meanings has to focus primarily on the following dimensions in order to combat members' helplessness and foster prevention-oriented motivational forces.

(1) *Influencing members' assessment of situational demands*, namely their perceptions of how the current situation emerged (past), how difficult or serious the current situation is or how dangerous the threats posed by the environment are (present), and how difficult the necessary actions or demands are in order to be able to prevent harm and improve the situation (future).

(2) *Influencing members' assessment of organizational resources*, namely their perceptions of the adequacy of organizational technologies, financial assets, people's knowledge and skills, management competence, customer relations, etc.

(3) *Influencing members' assessment of the coping process*, namely their perception of progress, effects of their efforts and signals of success or failure. To maintain members' sense of mastery and their motivation to engage in efforts on behalf of the organization, they need to feel that their efforts are successful, at least to some extent. It is therefore the strategic leaders' task to highlight successes or achievements, frame them as being signs of progress toward recovery, and link them with members' efforts.

In order to further illustrate these key tasks of prevention-oriented leadership, we present the results of a case study of strategic leadership in a crisis situation in the following.

A CASE STUDY – MANAGEMENT OF MEANING DURING THE TURNAROUND OF A GLOBAL INDUSTRIAL COMPANY

We examine the management of meaning by the CEO of a large multinational company specializing in power and automation technology with headquarters in Zurich, Switzerland. The company enjoyed high rates of growth and profitability in the 1990s but experienced severe decline in the early 2000s, with heavy losses, a huge debt, and a sharp deterioration of its stock value. In the second half of 2002, the company was on the verge of bankruptcy.

The new CEO was appointed in September 2002, after the company had reported a loss of US$700 million and a net debt of US$5 billion amidst un-guaranteed bank loans and impending damage claims from several product-liability lawsuits. He initiated a series of steps to save the company from collapsing, among them a change of strategy, changes in structure, cost cuts (including job reductions), and changes in managerial personnel. By the middle of 2004, the turnaround had been concluded successfully: The company's half-year results came to US$9 billion in sales and earnings of US$90 million. The first quarter of 2004 turned out to be the first profitable quarter for several years.

From his first until his last week in office, the CEO wrote weekly e-mail letters to all company employees around the world. This series of letters constitutes relatively unique naturalistic data regarding the ongoing efforts of a CEO to manage the meanings held by organizational members in a way that will support management strategy and company recovery. In total, the CEO wrote 112 letters, which we have analyzed by asking ourselves the following questions: What are the main messages the CEO tries to convey? Which members' beliefs and perceptions does he try to influence? How does he try to influence these beliefs and perceptions? While we were guided in our reading and analysis by the theoretical considerations presented above, we tried not to be restricted by them and attempted to find additional meanings and principles of meaning management that were not suggested by our theoretical framework.

The Three Dimensions of Prevention-Oriented Leadership as Management of Meaning – an Overview

Our empirical analysis suggests that prevention-oriented leadership as management of meanings consists of three dimensions. Fig. 1 gives an overview of the three dimensions and the leader behaviors which they comprise. The three dimensions represent separate and related leadership activities, which imply influencing the organization members' assessment of the threatening situation, their own coping capabilities, and the success of the crisis management process.

The first dimension of prevention-oriented leadership as managing meanings is influencing the assessment of situational demands. Here the key focus is on creating a vision of the negative challenge implying that leaders generate a clear picture of the situation, its emergence, and the necessary actions to overcome or to avoid the threat. In his letters, the CEO leaves no doubt about the urgency, seriousness, and the unconditional necessity to act. At the same time, however, in his management of meanings he gives a maximum of orientation, reason, and a sense of controllability, which allow the members of the organization the opportunity to make sense of the situation and develop an active stance.

The second dimension of managing meanings in situations of crisis involves influencing the assessment of resources in a way that strengthens the organizational members' confidence to be able to cope with the threatening situation. Prevention-oriented leaders do this not only by expressing their own confidence but also by fostering central elements of empowerment of their followers, namely their self-efficacy or potency as well as their sense of impact (Kirkman & Rosen, 1999).

The third dimension of prevention-oriented leadership as managing meanings involves influencing the assessment of the coping process such that the members of the organization develop a sense of progress. Leaders can do this by emphasizing successes, strengthening peoples' pride in the achievements, and as the process of recovery evolves, adopting an increased future orientation up to a switch toward a promotion-oriented leadership behavior.

When combined, the three dimensions of a management of meanings in times of crisis create a positive tension or organizational energy (Bruch & Ghoshal, 2004) which is unleashed when the organization members clearly see the threat or problem and are confident that (although it may be a long way) they will be able to overcome it because they have the right resources and are on the right track.

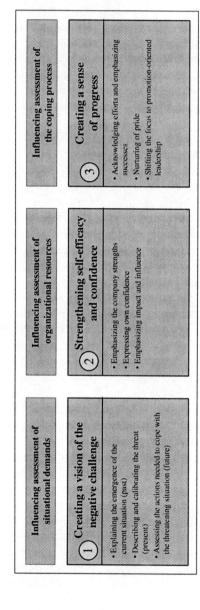

Fig. 1.   The Dimensions of Prevention-Oriented Leadership as Management of Meanings.

Influencing Members' Assessment of Situational Demands – Creating a Vision of the Negative Challenge

According to Shamir, Arthur, and House (1994), organizational members strive for a sense of congruence and continuity between the past, the present, and the future. For promotion-oriented management of meaning it has been argued that it is in the vision of the leader and the articulation for change that the past, the present, and the future come together (Gioia & Thomas, 1996). For prevention-oriented leaders our analysis revealed three activities by which prevention-oriented leaders bridge in their management of meanings the present to the past and the future while actively influencing organizational members' assessment of the situational demands (see Fig. 1). Instead of creating a vision of possible gains and opportunities, a prevention-oriented leader may create a vision of negative challenges, which depicts possible threats, harm, and losses. In order to meet organizational members' need for congruence and help people understand necessary actions or future goals, a prevention-oriented leader can influence members' assessments of situational demands in three related ways, namely by (1) explaining the emergence of the current situation (past), (2) describing and calibrating the threat (present), and (3) assessing the actions needed to cope with the threatening situation (future). Following, we will describe these activities of managing meaning of prevention-oriented leaders in more depth and illustrate how the CEO in our case example practiced them in his letters:[1]

Explaining the Emergence of the Current Situation (Past)
In stressful situations, people seek explanations because understanding increases their sense of mastery and control (Taylor, 1983). A lack of understanding, by contrast, leaves organizational members with feelings of ambiguity, a lack of control, and uncertainty, which can result in negative stress or distress (Selye, 1976), helplessness, or even paralysis. A first task of a prevention-oriented manager of meaning, which helps organizational members assess the demands, is to explain the emergence of threatening situations and developments as well as their own actions taken in the context of the crisis.

In his letters, the CEO invests a lot of time and space analyzing and making sense of factors causing the company's downturn, annual results, or share price development.

"Today we are not competitive as a group because after 15 years of growth through acquisitions our costs are too high, and our portfolio of businesses too broad." (letter 12)

"(...) we grew too broadly. And when we divested major activities – the rail transportation and the power generation businesses – we failed to aggressively readjust our organizational complexity and our structures to the size of our business. That is why our costs are too high today." (letter 15)

"(...) do our problems of today stem from a lack of focus in recent years? Partly. Or do they stem from the fact that our portfolio of activities grew too broadly in our first decade? Partly. [...]

It is also true that our weak margins were caused in part by the failure to drastically adjust our organization after we sold the trains and power generation businesses. And we also should have acted earlier to focus on our industrial activities." (letter 19)

"It was relatively easy in the long early period of expansion by acquisition to integrate new companies into our company. Add the company logo, place our company name in front of their former name, and let them get on with business.

But over time, the downsides outweigh the upsides. Without integration and a shared approach and shared processes, companies lose energy – and create higher costs – through lack of cohesion. And there is too little discipline on key themes.

You know the story. We've lived it. In the end, our cost base was much too high.

So change is needed, even though it may be uncomfortable." (letter 101)

Describing and Calibrating the Threat (Present)

One of the major tasks of prevention-oriented leaders' management of meaning is the description of the actual threat and of possible losses or dangers. Bruch and Ghoshal's (2003) research similarly identified a key task for the management of meaning in crisis situations, namely defining the problem or threat as precisely as possible and making it as clear and vivid as possible. Stress theoretical approaches are in line with this recommendation. They imply that it is important that people get a realistic, authentic, and credible picture of the situation that allows them to assess how serious the organization's situation is, rendering their appraisals of demands is not only subjectively reliable, but also helping them assess the relevance and the possible consequences for themselves (Lazarus & Folkman, 1984).

Accordingly, in his letters, the CEO describes the situation in an unpolished, very straightforward way in order to help the organization's members face reality and understand that their company's mere existence is at stake:

"We are in stormy waters. Deep and fast cost cuts are the only way to improve our operating margins in the short term." (letter 6)

"I don't enjoy implementing austerity programs, but we simply have no choice. It is a matter of survival." (letter 8)

"Hoping that things will get better doesn't work. And trying to be nice – a laudable human quality – is not helpful in the competitive world of business, and certainly totally out of place when survival is at stake." (letter 9)

"Today, we have informed financial analysts and the media – and you – about our targets for this year and the years until 2005, for the group and the core divisions. A lot of hard work will be needed to achieve these targets.

Why do I say this? The general economic conditions, and by this I mean general market-led demand, will not help us much in the next year to 18 months. The capital goods sector, our sector, is facing challenges.

Industrial output is down today to the levels of 1994. We saw brief glimpses of an upturn earlier in the year. No more. If in addition U.S. consumer spending now slows, as some studies suggest, we could even see a real recession. I'd be delighted if I'm wrong. But let's count on difficult economic conditions, and act accordingly." (letter 11)

"Let me stress the need for speed and a sense of urgency in implementing our strategy. This is vital to our future. Unless we act now, and fast – we may jeopardize a great company." (letter 11)

"The near future – the next 18 months – will determine our destiny. The economy will not help us, so we need to spend our time and energy wisely to ensure our survival." (letter 17)

"Despite higher EBIT, we had a net loss of 787 million dollars, because of 853 million dollars of losses in discontinued operations, including charges related to asbestos.

This shows how important it is that we move quickly to implement the Step Change program." (letter 25)

> *"Our markets, too, are affected by the general economic climate, which has been weak for some time. But our customers continue to have needs that must be met, and we are there to meet those needs. At the same time, the uncertainties in the world mean that the pressure on us to lower our cost base remains unchanged – if anything it becomes even more urgent."* (letter 30)

In situations of crisis, one of the first activities of managers of meaning may involve working against complacency or organizational inertia (Bruch & Ghoshal, 2003; Jansen, 2004). In such situations, an important focus of management of meaning may be to identify threats, create a sense of urgency, and drive people out of their comfort zone (Kotter, 1995). Stress theoretical approaches, however, would suggest that leaders in order to prevent distress should not present crises as overly powerful, uncontrollable, or overwhelming.

While the CEO openly emphasizes the severity of the situation and the threat of bankruptcy in his letters and explicitly calls for action, speed, and urgency, he also actively structures and delimits the threat. In doing so, he helps organizational members assess the dimension of the threat as well as the degree of possible damage and he focuses their attention on areas that are relevant for them and thus, helps employees understand priorities and implications for them personally.

> *"I believe we will reduce our workforce by more than 10,000 people. It could be 9,000. It could be 12,000 – but certainly not 20,000 or more, as some have speculated. Is this dramatic? Yes, it may seem so. But it is necessary for the survival of our company."* (letter 2)
>
> *"It will take at least until mid-2004 before we are out of the woods. But we will turn this great company around."* (letter 14)
>
> *"Our finances must be strengthened, so that we can stick to our roadmap and achieve our goal – steady growth based on profitable core businesses.*
>
> *Power Technologies and Automation Technologies are on track, and we need to pay down our debt – as planned – to keep our turnaround on track, too. Specialists are handling the divestments. But when it comes to stabilizing the cash flow, we can all contribute."* (letter 33)
>
> *"Our legal experts will handle the asbestos issue. Our mergers and acquisitions experts will handle the divestments. You and I must look after the ongoing business. That's our job."* (letter 37)

> *"We are also quietly progressing in our plans concerning the group portfolio. We can't share these plans, as you will understand, beyond confirming that we will continue to focus on power and automation technologies. And that we have no plans for any big acquisitions for some years." (letter 97)*
>
> *"Our legal team will deal with the asbestos issue while we continue to ensure that our business improves. Customers, markets, operational excellence, making our targets, ensuring ongoing technology innovation – that is our job." (letter 109)*

Assessing the Actions Needed to Cope with the Threat (Future)
Leaders as managers of meaning also influence organizational members' perception of the actions that are necessary to cope with the threatening situation. This is in line with stress theoretical conceptions, which link the perception of stress closely to the perception of the difficulty of demands placed upon the individual (Lazarus, 1993).

Accordingly, in his letters, the CEO emphasizes not only the seriousness of the situation but he also points out how hard, work intensive, and long the way will be:

> *"We have a tough road ahead, and many obstacles lie in our path." (letter 14)*
>
> *"It'll take hard work, step by step." (letter 19)*
>
> *"As you know, there's still plenty of work to do to get our company back on track. You know what we have to do. At Group level, we must complete the announced divestments to streamline our portfolio, and act forcefully on our plans to lower our cost base. And in the markets, our future lies in remaining close to our customers." (letter 24)*
>
> *"(...) we have a lot of work to do in the next year or two." (letter 33)*
>
> *"Last year was tough, and we still have hurdles to overcome. You know the challenges – the asbestos issue, our liquidity and financial flexibility, our debts, our divestments of activities that no longer form part of our core business, and our high cost base. I also told our shareholders – the owners of our company – that we aim to return our company to profitability in 2003, and that I count on you to make this turnaround happen. It means hard work, but you have seen the results for the first quarter, when we reported some progress." (letter 35)*

> *"We must go beyond the numbers, and work on some real changes in the company culture. The way to start is to ensure greater openness. This is essential in order for us to realize our company's potential in the markets and start off a virtuous circle of constant improvements. My colleagues on the executive committee and myself are trying to create a working environment where all issues are brought up for discussion – on our organization, our products, our projects, on any aspects of your business life. We need to find ways to make this openness spread faster through the organization. There is probably no single change that would have a greater effect than more openness." (letter 45)*

In sum, it should be noted that the CEO deliberately tries to influence organizational members' perceptions of the demands posed by the crisis situation. His prevention-oriented management of meaning aims at giving organizational members a clear picture of the situation and the necessary activities. He emphasizes the severity of the situation in his letters and leaves no room for doubt that urgent actions are required. At the same time, he tries to ensure that the threat is not perceived as excessive, uncontrollable, or insurmountable but as a negative challenge, emphasizing that it can be controlled and overcome, even though hard work is required. Hence, his management of meaning is not supposed to create fear or negative stress, but tries to appeal to employees' prevention focus in an objective, almost sober manner.

Influencing Members' Assessment of the Organizational Resources – Strengthening Self-Efficacy and Confidence

Our analysis of the CEO letters suggests that a prevention-oriented leader may engage in influencing organizational members' assessment of the organizational resources available to cope with the critical demands. We identified three related ways by which prevention-oriented leaders may strengthen self-efficacy and confidence, namely (1) emphasizing the company strengths, (2) expressing their own self-confidence, and (3) emphasizing impact and influence (see Fig. 1).

Our finding can be related to both stress as well as leadership theories. According to stress theory, perceptions of threats do not only depend on the perception of the demands but also on the assessment of resources (Lazarus, 1991). Schwarzer (1999) suggests that a proactive coping with stressful events is more likely when individuals are high in self-efficacy (Bandura,

1997), i.e., they have a strong belief in their own ability to cope with the situation. As coping with crisis situations in organizations affects not only the individual's perception of their own abilities but also the perceptions of the collective resources and social support, the leaders' task of managing meaning will also have to refer to individuals' perception of company resources available for coping with the crisis. Drawing on stress theory, we suggest that leaders as managers of meaning can contribute to avoiding negative reactions to stressful events or situations of crisis by helping organizational members interpret crisis situations as challenges rather than threats. Actively coping with these demands (Blascovich & Mendes, 2000) implies their confidence will be strengthened that the company's resources are sufficient to meet the demands.

Following we will describe the three ways of influencing members' assessment of company resources that the CEO uses in his letter the manage meaning in times of crisis.

Emphasizing the Company Strengths
He strengthens people's self-efficacy and their confidence in the company's resources (organizational technologies, financial assets, people's knowledge and skills, management competence, customer relations, etc.) by emphasizing the company strengths:

> *"Over the years you have built excellent market positions, customer relationships and sales organizations. We need to capitalize fully on these strengths." (letter 1)*
>
> *"Let's continue to build on our strengths, together. Your personal contribution makes a real difference." (letter 4)*
>
> *"We're leaders in our core businesses after more than a century because we do what we do best better than our competitors." (letter 15)*
>
> *"Our technology leadership and customer relationships are second to none, as a result of your work, and of the work of the generations that went before you." (letter 17)*
>
> *"Our core strengths rest on three pillars – technology leadership, a pioneering spirit, and a sustainable approach to business, possible because we are at home where we do business. In other words: strong technologies, strong market presence, strong people." (letter 28)*
>
> *"Few of our competitors possess what is potentially our greatest advantage – the ability to balance our manufacturing base, and to focus on the unique strengths of each region." (letter 66)*

> *"Companies need a strong foundation and certain traits that hold them together. In our company, our leading-edge technology, our can-do spirit and our ability to be at home everywhere form this foundation." (letter 106)*

Expressing Own Confidence

In his letters, the CEO raises organizational members' optimism by expressing his own confidence:

> *"I would like to reassure you that I am confident we will meet our business targets this year." (letter 3)*
>
> *"There is great pride in our company, and a great sense of resolve. This strengthens my conviction that we will master and overcome the tough challenges facing us." (letter 5)*
>
> *"We will emerge from this challenging period even stronger." (letter 8)*
>
> *"Why am I so confident? Simple. I believe we will make a success of our company again." (letter 10)*
>
> *"Peter (CFO) and I sensed renewed confidence in our company." (letter 26)*

Emphasizing Impact and Influence

Bruch and Ghoshal (2004) suggest another task in meaning management, namely to create a perception of personal impact in the members of the organization. Perception of impact is also a key element of both individual as well as collective empowerment (Kirkman & Rosen, 1999). Perception of impact or influence has been found to be associated with people's receptiveness for change (Eby, Adams, Russel, & Gaby, 2000). Emphasizing impact may therefore be an important task for prevention-oriented leaders who aim at empowering people to take action for change (Kanter, 2003).

Our analysis revealed that, in his letters, the CEO strongly emphasizes the influence and the impact that organizational members have on the change process in their company. He repeatedly demonstrates the influence and the impact that peoples' engagement and efforts have:

> *"Working to regain the trust of investors is both a mid-term goal and a daily must. It is something we can all influence."* *(letter 5)*
>
> *"Be aware that responsibility and power go hand in hand – the power to influence, motivate, execute and deliver. The power to change. That power is in our hands – yours and mine. Let us use it. Let us act now."* *(letter 8)*
>
> *"So you see, there is good news here. We can improve our business results through our own efforts, despite a weak market. We have it in our own hands to increase productivity, do more for our biggest customers, leverage our size and scope and explore key market niches."* *(letter 23)*
>
> *"And if you ever feel you have an insurmountable challenge, let us take heart from the great progress made on settling the asbestos issue.*
>
> *It shows that nothing is impossible if we look forward and concentrate on what makes common sense – even if it has never been done before."* *(letter 24)*
>
> *"It is clear to me that it was your determination that pulled us through the hard stretches in the past couple of years."* *(letter 88)*

Influencing Members' Assessment of the Coping Process – Creating a Sense of Progress

Kotter (1995) argues that a frequent stumbling block of change processes is that leaders fail to create short-term wins. Based on this observation, he recommends that leaders create short-term wins, which validate their effort and maintain the level of urgency.

Our findings are in line with this recommendation showing that a prevention-oriented leader may engage in activities of managing meaning that go beyond influencing organizational members' perception of demands and resources, and influence their assessment of the coping process or creating a sense of progress. In his letters, the CEO uses three ways to create a sense of progress, namely (1) acknowledging efforts and emphasizing successes, (2) nurturing of pride, and (3) shifting the focus to a more promotion-oriented leadership (see Fig. 1).

Acknowledging Efforts and Emphasizing Successes
In his letters, the CEO engages in influencing organizational members' assessment of the coping process by highlighting achievements, reconfirming

that the company is on the right track for change. To maintain members'
sense of mastery and their motivation to engage in efforts on behalf of the
organization, he gives them the feeling that their efforts are acknowledged
and at least to some extent successful.

"You are a fantastic fighting force." (letter 9)

*"We're on the right path to a fair solution. It will take some time, but
we'll get there." (letter 11)*

*"The key message in our annual results is that in a difficult market, our
two core divisions performed well in the fourth quarter, and in the full
year." (letter 25)*

"(...) you see that your hard work is paying off." (letter 26)

*"The good news is that in the first quarter, we are on track with our
performance. That is the result of your work." (letter 30)*

*"Come to think of it, this positive momentum and the clear view of the
road ahead itself provide reasons enough for feeling good, even though
hard work remains.*

*So, let's agree to put some champagne on ice. And let's continue our
efforts to make our company great again, while we wait for the right
moment to pop the corks." (letter 41)*

*"So we're steadily moving forward. In fact, we are making more
progress than anyone could have imagined six months ago." (letter 42)*

*"We're not out of the woods yet, but as our results showed, we are well
underway." (letter 46)*

*"These days, I'm asked how we managed the turnaround so quickly."
(letter 62)*

*"Thanks to your efforts, 2003 has really been a key turn-around year."
(letter 69)*

*"This quarter, we were able to report steady progress and results which
underline the fact that our company is on the right track." (letter 92)*

*"Today, our company is a good business partner, an attractive em-
ployer, a good neighbor, and a good share to invest in.*

*That is in large parts thanks to your efforts, and to the energetic
leadership that so many of you demonstrate throughout our company."
(letter 97)*

*"Yesterday we reported our third quarter results. It was the eighth con-
secutive quarter of better results, good growth on the top line, a strong order
book with good margins, and we had a sizeable net profit." (letter 104)*

Nurturing of Pride
A further leadership task of managers of meanings can be observed in the CEO's letters – it is the nurturing of pride. In his letters, he explicitly expresses pride and he nurtures it by emphasizing their contribution to the progress, and thanking them for their efforts.

"These great assets are at the core of our customer relationships, and we should be proud of them." (letter 4)

"I have already told you – and that impression is reconfirmed daily – how strongly I have been struck by the determination, pride and fighting spirit of people in our company." (letter 7)

"You have every reason to be proud of our second quarter efforts, reflected in the results we published on Tuesday." (letter 46)

"I think the road we have traveled in the past year has shown that we were able to achieve this positive momentum – and you should all be proud of that." (letter 62)

"While we should be proud of what we have achieved, we should not be satisfied." (letter 70)

"I take special pride in the fact that we achieved the turnaround together – all of us. Without the contributions of each and every one of you, the turnaround would not have been this swift." (letter 92)

"One of the many reasons that I'm proud of what we have achieved together – and I mean all of us – is that we have injected and channeled focus and energy into our company." (letter 111)

"Your enthusiasm, dedication and your focus on what is important made my period as CEO a great experience. I am proud of what we have achieved together. So should you be." (letter 112)

Shifting the Focus to Promotion-Oriented Leadership
Bruch and Ghoshal (2003) argue that a strong, exclusive orientation towards either promotion- or prevention-oriented leadership is beneficial only in extreme cases such as acute crises, times of enormous growth, or phases of great innovation: Generally, we suggest that a flexible combination of both types of leadership is most effective.

In the letters of the CEO, a change in focus can be observed. Shortly after his appointment as CEO, i.e., in the midst of the turnaround, his management of meaning focuses on an immediate need for action, short-term goals, and concrete tangible problems such as stopping the firm's decline, cost savings, layoffs, and restructuring the company. With the progress of the company's recovery, he gradually switches from a purely prevention-oriented leadership style to a more promotion-oriented leadership style, with increasing emphasis of opportunities, long-term goals, and future orientation:

> *"But now, as the first signs of a broader recovery are showing up in the world economy, I would also like you to think about the next chapter. And that is profitable growth." (letter 51)*
>
> *"The crisis is over in our company. Employees can now breathe a sigh of relief. From here on, it's all about building for the future."(letter 57)*
>
> *"So, as we fight to meet our targets in the short-term, consider this: Raising the performance of our company to a new level will require that we look further ahead from time to time. We must keep our eyes on longer-term goals, too." (letter 67)*
>
> *"Our company needs forward movement and expansion, based on technology innovation." (letter 67)*
>
> *"While we should be proud of what we have achieved, we should not be satisfied." (letter 70)*
>
> *"Let's acknowledge – and act on – the fact that we are seen as a healthy industrial leader again." (letter 76)*
>
> *"Now that we have turned the company around and are stabilizing it, we must shift our motivation and identification from external threat to opportunity." (letter 88)*
>
> *"Our focus now must be on sustained profitable growth." (letter 92)*
>
> *"The message is clear: we have to continue our work to become the clear leader. In all corners of our business. We have just started on the journey to really good levels of performance." (letter 93)*
>
> *"It is only through innovation that we can continue to prosper in our mature markets. In today's global world, no one can compete on cost alone.*
>
> *The tasks awaiting all of us – in finance offices, production units, business centers, laboratories around the world – show that we have challenges and exciting opportunities ahead of us." (letter 105)*

CONCLUSION

Based on a literature review and a first exploratory study, we developed a three-dimensional model of prevention-oriented leadership as management of meanings in times of crises and recovery.

Our study contributes to a better understanding of leadership activities that go beyond a mere labeling of situations as threats (Dutton & Jackson, 1987). While it confirms basic characteristics of Bruch and Ghoshal's (2003) leadership strategy "slaying the dragon," our study illustrates in much more detail how leaders may actually influence the perceptions and interpretations of organizational members during a turnaround.

Boal and Bryson (1988) distinguish between visionary and crisis-responsive charismatic leaders. Visionary leaders start with meanings such as values, ideologies, and beliefs and translate them into required actions and processes. Crisis-responsive leaders, in contrast, start with action and only later provide interpretative schemes to support the actions. If this distinction is taken to mean that crisis-responsive leaders (charismatic or not) do not engage in the management of meaning while handling the crisis, we believe it is not accurate. On the basis of both our theoretical and empirical analysis, we suggest that crisis-responsive leaders are heavily engaged in the management of meanings and the provision of interpretative schemes to organizational members. The meanings they manage are different, however, from those managed by leaders in other situations.

Visionary strategic leaders are promotion-oriented leaders. They focus on "why" questions and provide answers and meanings by connecting organizational actions and members' roles to collective identities, a value-laden vision, and other possible gains such as organizational learning and individual development (Shamir et al., 1993). Crisis-responsive leaders are prevention-oriented leaders. In a crisis situation like the one faced by the CEO we studied when he took over the company, the threat is imminent, and the tasks of survival and recovery are very clear. There is a clear "dragon" in the neighborhood and identifying it, making it known, and then mobilizing people to slay the dragon is imperative for survival (Bruch & Ghoshal, 2003). Therefore, there is a lesser need for the leader to provide meaning to organizational efforts and members' tasks by answering "why" questions. Instead, the meanings he or she has to manage concern organizational members' perceptions of the reasons for the organizational situation, the current environmental demands, the resources available for dealing with the demands, and the progress that is made during the turnaround.

The questions that members of the organization are likely to ask themselves are not "How important is the task?" or "Why is it important?" but rather "How bad is the situation?" "What shall we do?" "Can we do it?" and "Are we on the right track?" It is to these questions that much of the sense-giving effort is directed in the management of meaning during crisis situations or recovery.

Indeed, during the entire period, the CEO we study has refrained from providing a vision to the recipients of his letters. We believe that this was done consciously, perhaps echoing Lou Gerstner's famous assertion when he took over as CEO of IBM in a similar situation, "The last thing IBM needs right now is vision." The content and style of the letters does not reflect charismatic or transformational leadership. For instance, the CEO does not appeal to organization members' emotions. His manner of communication is rational, dry, and factual. He does not use much inspirational language or many colorful metaphors. He never tells a story. More fundamentally, he does not promise a "princess" (Bruch & Ghoshal, 2003) or any other gains beyond "return to profitable growth." Every action is presented as directed toward that goal and almost every message addresses this goal. At least at the beginning of his term, he does not highlight opportunities. It is only after the threat of survival is over and the company appears to be on the road to recovery that he starts to engage in promotion-oriented leadership. As opposed to a promotion-oriented leadership with a one-sided positive bias of managing meaning, prevention-oriented leadership is characterized through a particular combination of negative and positive elements of managing meaning. Thus, the three dimensions of prevention-oriented leadership as management of meanings represent a balance between seemingly contradictory activities of managing meanings – confronting negative truths, possible threats or losses, deficiencies, and maybe even cruel actions on the one hand, while emphasizing strength, nurturing pride and giving hope on the other hand.

There are many circumstances when the primary task of the organization is survival or recovery. We do not mean to imply that the presentation of a vision for the organization, the use of inspirational communication or other components of transformational or charismatic leadership are not relevant in such situations. However, our theoretical analysis and case study suggest that, at least in the initial phases of a turnaround effort, a transformational leadership approach that focuses exclusively on vision, opportunities, growth, development and other behaviors that emphasize "princesses" or potential gains may not be realistic and may not be necessary. An approach that uses threat as a potential motivator, while calibrating its level so that it is not paralyzing, and attempts to increase members' sense of mastery, efficacy, and control through highlighting strengths, amplifying resources, and creating a sense of progress toward recovery may be both required and effective, at least at the beginning of a turnaround situation.

As the organization's situation improves, more components of promotion-oriented leadership need to be inserted and the optimal approach might be a combination of features of transformational leadership and of prevention-oriented leadership. We believe the two leadership styles are not contradictory, as they share some elements in common. For instance, both focus on the empowerment of people through the management of meanings. We believe this issue deserves further study. We shall continue to focus on the management of meaning efforts of the CEO we study and hope other researchers will perform similar studies. Hopefully some of these studies will also be able to assess the impact of the strategic leader's sense-giving efforts on members of the organization.

NOTE

1. In the following quotes all names were substituted (the company name was substituted by the word "company" or "our," the name of the former CEO was substituted by the word "former CEO").

REFERENCES

Affleck, G., & Tennen, H. (1996). Construing benefits from adversity: Adaptational significance and dispositional underpinnings. *Journal of Personality, 64*, 899–922.

Alvesson, M., & Willmott, H. (2002). Identity regulation as organizational control: Producing the appropriate individual. *Journal of Management Studies, 39*, 619–644.

Bandura, A. (1997). *Self-efficacy: The exercise of control.* New York: Freeman.

Bass, B. M. (1985). *Leadership and performance beyond expectations.* New York: Free Press.

Blascovich, J., & Mendes, W. B. (2000). Challenge and threat appraisals. In: J. P. Forgas (Ed.), *Feeling and thinking: The role of affect in social cognition* (pp. 59–82). Cambridge, MA: Cambridge University Press.

Boal, K. B., & Bryson, J. M. (1988). Charismatic leadership: A phenomenological and structural approach. In: J. G. Hunt, B. R. Baliga, H. P. Dachler & C. A. Schriesheim (Eds), *Emerging leadership vistas* (pp. 11–28). New York: Lexington.

Boal, K. B., & Hooijberg, R. (2001). Strategic leadership research: Moving on. *Leadership Quarterly, 11*, 515–549.

Brockner, J., & Higgins, T. E. (2001). Regulatory focus theory: Implications for the study of emotions at work. *Organizational Behavior and Human Decision Processes, 86*, 35–66.

Bruch, H., & Ghoshal, S. (2003). Unleashing organizational energy. *Sloan Management Review, 44*, 45–51.

Bruch, H., & Ghoshal, S. (2004). *A bias for action. How effective managers harness their will-power, achieve results, and stop wasting their time.* Boston, MA: Harvard Business School Press.

Bryman, A. (1992). *Charisma and leadership in organizations.* London: Sage.

Burns, J. M. (1978). *Leadership.* New York: Harper and Row.

Conger, J. A. (1989). *The charismatic leader: Behind the mystique of exceptional leadership.* San Francisco, CA: Jossey-Bass.

Denison, D. R., Dutton, J. E., Kahn, J. A., & Hart, S. L. (1996). Organizational context and the interpretation of strategic issues: A note on CEOs' interpretations of foreign investment. *The Journal of Management Studies, 33,* 453–475.

Dumdum, U. R., Lowe, K. B., & Avolio, B. J. (2002). A meta-analysis of transformational and transactional leadership correlates of effectiveness and satisfaction. An update and extension. In: B. J. Avolio & F. J. Yammarino (Eds), *Transformational and charismatic leadership: The road ahead* (pp. 35–66). Oxford: Elsevier.

Dutton, J. E., & Jackson, S. E. (1987). Categorizing strategic issues: Links to organizational action. *Academy of Management Review, 12,* 76–90.

Eby, L. T., Adams, D. M., Russel, J. E. A., & Gaby, S. H. (2000). Perceptions of organizational readiness for change: Factors related to employees' reaction to the implementation of team-based selling. *Human Relations, 53,* 419–442.

Folkman, S., & Moskowitz, J. T. (2000). Positive affect and the other side of coping. *American Psychologist, 55,* 647–654.

Fuller, J. B., Patterson, C. E. P., Hester, K., & Stringer, D. Y. (1996). A quantitative review of research on charismatic leadership. *Psychological Reports, 78,* 271–287.

Gioia, D. A., & Thomas, J. G. (1996). Identity, image, and issue interpretation: Sense-making during strategic change in academia. *Administrative Science Quarterly, 41,* 370–403.

Heifetz, R. A., & Laurie, D. L. (1997). The work of leadership. *Harvard Business Review, 75*(1), 124–134.

Higgins, E. T. (1997). Beyond pleasure and pain. *American Psychologist, 52,* 1280–1300.

Higgins, E. T. (1998). Promotion and prevention: Regulatory focus as a motivation principle. In: M. P. Zanna (Ed.), *Advances in experimental social psychology* (pp. 1–46). New York: Academic Press.

Higgins, E. T., & Silberman, I. (1998). Development of regulatory focus: Prevention and promotion as ways of living. In: J. Heckhausen & C. S. Dweck (Eds), *Motivation and self-regulation across the life-span* (pp. 78–113). New York: Cambridge University Press.

Higgins, E. T., & Tycocinsky, O. (1992). Self-discrepancies and biographical memory: Personality and cognition at the level of psychological situation. *Personality and Social Psychology Bulletin, 18,* 527–535.

Jackson, S. E., & Dutton, J. E. (1988). Discerning threats and opportunities. *Administrative Science Quarterly, 33,* 370–388.

Jansen, K. J. (2004). From persistence to pursuit: A longitudinal examination of momentum during the early stages of strategic change. *Organization Science, 15,* 276–294.

Jick, T. D., & Murray, V. V. (1982). The management of hard times: Budget cutbacks in public sector organizations. *Organization Studies, 3,* 141–169.

Kanter, R. M. (2003). *The confidence factor: The dynamics of success and decline in business and nations.* Lecture given at the 14th Annual Lecture of the Economic and Social Research Council, London.

Kirkman, B. L., & Rosen, B. (1999). Beyond self-management: Antecedents and consequences of team empowerment. *Academy of Management Journal, 42*, 58–74.

Kotter, J. P. (1995). Why transformation efforts fail. *Harvard Business Review, 73*, 59–67.

Lazarus, R. S. (1991). *Emotion and adaptation.* New York: Oxford University Press.

Lazarus, R. S. (1993). From psychological stress to emotions: A history of changing outlooks. *Annual Review of Psychology, 44*, 1–21.

Lazarus, R. S., & Folkman, S. (1984). *Stress, appraisal, and coping.* New York: Springer.

Lowe, K. B., Kroeck, G. K., & Sivasubramaniam, N. (1996). Effectiveness correlates of transformational and transactional leadership: A meta-analytic review of the MLQ literature. *Leadership Quarterly, 7*, 385–425.

Maier, C. (2002). *Leading diversity.* St. Gallen, Switzerland: University of St. Gallen, I.FPM Schriftenreihe Band 3.

Pfeffer, J. (1981). *Power in organizations.* Marshfield, MA: Pitman Publishing.

Sashkin, M. (2004). Transformational leadership approaches: A review and synthesis. In: J. Antonakis, A. T. Cianciolo & R. J. Sternberg (Eds), *The nature of leadership* (pp. 171–196). Thousand Oaks, CA: Sage.

Schwarzer, R. (1999). Self-regulatory processes in the adoption and maintenance of health behaviors: The role of optimism, goals, and threats. *Journal of Health Psychology, 4*(2), 115–127.

Schwarzer, R., & Knoll, N. (2003). Positive coping: Mastering demands and searching for meaning. In: S. J. Lopez & C. R. Snyder (Eds), *Positive psychological assessment: A handbook of models and measures* (pp. 393–409). Washington, DC: American Psychological Association.

Selye, H. (1976). *The stress of life: Revised edition.* New York: Mc Graw-Hill.

Shah, J., Higgins, E. T., & Friedman, R. (1998). Performance incentives and means: How regulatory focus influences goal attainment. *Journal of Personality and Social Psychology, 74*, 285–293.

Shah, J. Y., & Higgins, E. T. (2001). Regulatory concerns and appraisal efficiency: The general impact of promotion and prevention. *Journal of Personality and Social Psychology, 80*, 693–705.

Shamir, B., Arthur, M. B., & House, R. J. (1994). The rhetoric of charismatic leadership: A theoretical extension, a case study, and implications for research. *Leadership Quarterly, 5*, 25–42.

Shamir, B., House, R. J., & Arthur, M. B. (1993). The motivational effects of charismatic leadership: A self-concept based theory. *Organization Science, 4*, 577–594.

Smircich, L., & Morgan, G. (1982). Leadership: The management of meaning. *Journal of Applied Behavioral Science, 18*, 257–273.

Staw, B. M., Sandelands, L. E., & Dutton, J. E. (1981). Threat-rigidity effects in organizational behavior. A multi-level analysis. *Administrative Science Quarterly, 26*, 501–524.

Taylor, S. E. (1983). Adjustment to threatening events: A theory of cognitive adaptation. *American Psychologist, 38*, 1161–1173.

Thomas, J. B., Clark, S. M., & Gioia, D. A. (1993). Strategic sensemaking and organizational performance: Linkages among scanning, interpretation, action, and outcomes. *Academy of Management Journal, 36*, 239–270.

Tushman, M. L., & O'Reilly, C. A., III (1996). Ambidextrous organizations: Managing evolutionary and revolutionary change. *California Management Review, 38*(4), 8–30.

CHAPTER 9

POSITIVE STRATEGIC LEADERSHIP: LESSONS FROM A UNIVERSITY PRESIDENT

Gretchen M. Spreitzer, Mary Sue Coleman and Daniel A. Gruber

ABSTRACT

In this chapter, two academics from the Stephen M. Ross School of Business at the University of Michigan collaborate with the President of their university to present their experiences and ideas about positive strategic leadership. Positive strategic leadership is derived from the juxtaposition of ideas from the growing stream of research on positive organizational scholarship with what is already known from the literature on strategic leadership. The authors embed new views into current theoretical perspectives on strategic leadership to provide an integrative overview and use the president's experiences during the nationally followed Affirmative Action cases as a vehicle for illustrating five themes: (1) A lifetime of experiences shapes who you are, (2) issues commonly choose you before you choose them, (3) begin with a purpose in mind, (4) appreciate divergent views, and (5) be a beacon for the future. Additionally, the authors provide practitioners with some "takeaways" on positive strategic leadership.

Being There Even When You Are Not: Leading Through Strategy, Structures, and Systems
Monographs in Leadership and Management, Volume 4, 155–170
Copyright © 2007 by Elsevier Ltd.
All rights of reproduction in any form reserved
ISSN: 1479-3571/doi:10.1016/S1479-3571(07)04008-4

Our goal in this chapter is to apply a Positive Organizational Scholarship (POS) perspective to the scholarly literature on strategic leadership. Strategic leadership is traditionally defined as a series of decisions and activities by a top manager (CEOs, presidents, and senior executives) in which the past, the present, and the future of the organization coalesce (Boal, 2004). Strategic leadership researchers have provided remarkable insights in several areas. First, much research has focused on what leaders do (Hambrick, 1989; Finkelstein & Hambrick, 1990). That is, how do strategic leaders go about "making decisions; creating and communicating a vision of the future; developing key competencies and capabilities; developing organization structures, processes, and controls; managing multiple constituencies; selecting and developing the next generation of leaders; and sustaining an effective organizational culture" (Boal & Hooijberg, 2001, p. 516). Second, strategic leadership researchers have focused on the role of leader cognitions in strategic change (Rajagopalan & Spreitzer, 1997). That is, how do leaders perceive and make sense of their environment in order to determine the appropriate course of strategic action (Walsh, 1995).

What is largely absent in the literature on strategic leadership, however, is a focus on the importance of how who the leader is shapes what the leader thinks and does. We know little about how the life experiences, character, and values of the leader shape his/her approach to strategic leadership. Quinn (2004) suggests that the foundation of leadership is not behavior, competencies, techniques or position; rather, the foundation of leadership comes from who we are, or the "person within" the leader.

To begin to understand the "person within" the strategic leader, we seek to learn from the experiences of a manifest leader – Mary Sue Coleman, President of the University of Michigan and a co-author of this chapter. The University of Michigan was established in 1817; it has an enrollment of 53,000 across three campuses with 3,700 faculty and more than 420,000 alumni around the world.

We are particularly interested in learning from President Coleman, because she arrived at Michigan just as the nationally contentious affirmative action lawsuits were playing out in the courts. In 1997, three students filed two separate suits in the U.S. District Court (Detroit), alleging unlawful consideration of race in the University of Michigan's undergraduate and law school admissions policies (*Gratz and Hamacher v. The Regents of the University of Michigan/Grutter v. The Regents of the University of Michigan*). These lawsuits received national attention as test cases for the permissible use of race in university admissions and generated considerable controversy.[1] In late 2000 and early 2001, two separate U.S. District Courts ruled that the use of race in admissions in the undergraduate case was constitutional, but that the use of race in the law school case was unconstitutional.

When President Coleman came to the office in 2002, the Sixth Circuit Court of Appeals had just overturned the earlier district court decision in the law school case by ruling that the law school's use of race was in fact constitutional. The plaintiffs appealed both cases to the Supreme Court for a final ruling in 2002. In June 2003, the Supreme Court ruled that the law school's use of race was narrowly tailored to achieve the compelling educational benefits of diversity, but that the undergraduate policy was not so tailored and therefore did not pass constitutional muster. The court's recognition that universities can consider race in admissions to achieve a diverse student body was considered to be a big victory, not just for the University of Michigan, but also for affirmative action more generally. As such, the affirmative action lawsuits provide a "looking glass" into how who President Coleman is as a leader significantly impacted the actions she undertook in this case of national importance. In sharing her experiences, she can enrich our understanding of the "person within" the strategic leader.

From President Coleman's commentary on her leadership of the affirmative action lawsuits, we evince five principles of what we term "positive strategic leadership." Positive strategic leadership is derived from the juxtaposition of ideas from the growing perspective on POS with what we already know from the literature on strategic leadership. POS is an emerging perspective within organizational studies – drawing from the fields of organizational studies, psychology, and sociology. This perspective focuses on the generative dynamics in leadership and organizations that promote human strength, resiliency, restoration, and the extraordinary (Cameron, Dutton, & Quinn, 2003), and positive deviance (Spreitzer & Sonenshein, 2004). We draw from several POS perspectives to gain insights into President Coleman's experiences with the goal of expanding the notion of positive strategic leadership.

We close the chapter by embedding these new views into current theoretical perspectives on strategic leadership to attempt an integrative overview. Additionally, we provide practitioners with some "takeaways" on positive strategic leadership.

POSITIVE STRATEGIC LEADERSHIP: LESSONS FROM PRESIDENT COLEMAN

In this section of the chapter, President Coleman shares some lessons of experience as a strategic leader. The five themes of positive strategic leadership we evince include:

- A lifetime of experiences shapes who you are;
- Issues commonly choose you before you choose them;
- Begin with a purpose in mind;
- Appreciate divergent views; and
- Be a beacon for the future.

Following the words of President Coleman on each theme, Gretchen Spreitzer and Daniel Gruber provide a brief discussion on the links between President Coleman's commentary and conceptual aspects of positive strategic leadership.

A Lifetime of Experiences Shape Who You Are
(The Voice of Mary Sue Coleman)

As a child who was raised in the South in the late 1940s and early 1950s, segregated schools and segregated daily living were facts of life. In elementary school in Tennessee and Georgia, I was not aware of the great injustice of the social system, but I certainly knew that the African-American children with whom I played in our rural neighborhood were not permitted to attend my university-operated school. Looking back, I remember how the streets in the areas of the town where most African-American families lived lacked pavements, sidewalks, and street-lamps. Like towns throughout the South, there were signs for "colored" and "white" in commercial establishments and on drinking fountains.

To those of us who were children, this façade seemed calm, but the "normality" of this way of life began to crumble with the critical, successful challenge to school segregation in the 1950s, culminating with the monumental Supreme Court decision in the Brown v. Board of Education case in 1954. Ironically, the consequences of that decision provided the impetus that propelled my family out of Georgia, raising my awareness of the terrible injustices segregation had wrought.

Officials in the State of Georgia did not acquiesce readily to the ruling handed down by the Supreme Court. In fact, political leaders in the state entered into discussions and debates that could have resulted in the abandonment of all public education, including the de-funding of schools in order to avoid desegregation altogether. There was a genuine fear that public schools would not survive, so my parents uprooted our family and sought employment in a state where "equal education for everyone" was a core value. We moved to Iowa in 1955 after listening to a full year of the divisive, vicious rhetoric that followed the Brown decision.

What a contrast Iowa provided to Georgia! While the African-American population in Iowa was small, it had deep roots and was fully integrated in schools and businesses. Social justice in Iowa was not perfect, but it was immeasurably more equitable than we had seen in the South. In my school, the faculty did address issues of racial discrimination and social injustice. Through their efforts, and because of the new social landscape of Iowa, I was finally able to begin to understand the terrible legacy of slavery and discrimination in our country.

My experience in college and graduate school only enhanced the lessons I learned about social justice in Iowa. At Grinnell College and the University of North Carolina, I met African-American students with a broader range of first-hand experience of the inequities and humiliation of segregated schools and towns. When I was a child in Georgia, no one I knew was able to articulate the depth of feeling on this issue. The Brown decision provided much more than the starting point for the end of school segregation. It allowed us to enter the continuing public discussion that has informed so much of the social policy of our government in the past 50 years, and the decisions I have made as a faculty member and administrator. It was these critical experiences that shaped the passion and energy in which I embraced the affirmative action lawsuits as the new President of the University of Michigan. I knew from my life experiences growing up in the South that these lawsuits provided a critical response to the years of racial discrimination in our country and our universities.

Insights for Positive Strategic Leadership (The Voice of the POS Scholars)
The positive strategic leader does not work in a vacuum, but everything that one thinks and does is embedded in a lifetime of experiences. Positive psychologists have defined authenticity as both owning one's personal experiences and acting in accord with the true self (Harter, 2002). Personal authenticity in adolescents has been demonstrated to be positively associated with adaptive psychological characteristics including self-esteem, affect, and hope for the future (Harter, 2002; Harter, Marold, Whitesell, & Cobbs, 1996). President Coleman illustrates how formative experiences, challenges or triggers in life shape one's authenticity as a leader (Avolio & Luthans, 2003). These life experiences create strong impressions because they take people out of their comfort zone by stretching them in new ways (Quinn, 2004). These jolts can also stimulate the leader to revise one's sense of self and personal identity (Roberts, Dutton, Spreitzer, Heaphy, & Quinn, 2005).

The jolt President Coleman experienced in her move to Iowa as a child exposed her to positive possibilities in race relations. And it is from sense-making about these life experiences that leaders learn about their authentic self. For President Coleman, witnessing discrimination in the South while growing up imparted a critical sensitivity and propensity for action in her future role as a senior administrator.

Issues Commonly Choose You Before You Choose Them
(The Voice of Mary Sue Coleman)

In every leadership position, new administrators need to enter with a zeal for innovation and a responsibility for the institutional agenda that exists in any organization. When I was approached about the presidency at the University of Michigan, I knew about the admissions lawsuits that the University had committed to defend, and knew that it would be a major focus of the presidency. The Michigan Regents and the search committee clearly indicated that they were dedicated to finding a president who would be able and willing to lead the final stages of the admissions lawsuits (already five years old at that point).

They saw that I was completely committed to the principle and the practice of diversity in higher education, and I viewed the opportunity to provide leadership for the lawsuits as a great expression of my personal and professional beliefs. This was just one of several continuing issues that awaited me, but it was the one with the most significant potential impact, not just for this University, but also for higher education throughout the nation.

This University is justifiably proud of its historically strong commitment to diversity, and it was actually one of the attributes that convinced me to come to Michigan. At that time, I had no idea of how consuming these lawsuits would become in my first year. I not only needed to become involved with the legal complexities of the cases, but also had to become the public face of the University on this issue. With the strong support of the administrators, faculty, and students I found at Michigan, I was able to take on this critical issue and to identify it as my own.

Three months after I arrived, the United States Supreme Court decided to hear our admissions cases. Preparing for the oral arguments in April, and the final successful rulings in June, provided me with a full docket of significant and national-level matters in my first year at Michigan. Ultimately, by making the institutional agenda my own agenda, I was able to work with our constituencies to advance our issues in ways that productively defined my inaugural months, enriched my experience, and greatly benefited the University.

Insights for Positive Strategic Leadership (The Voice of the POS Scholars)
The literature on strategic leadership emphasizes the importance of leaders crafting their own vision or agenda for change. The assumption is that leaders must make their mark right away to command the respect of others. The conversation rarely considers the importance of the leader completing any unfinished business when they begin a new role. But President Coleman explains how critical it was for her to forego setting her own agenda for the University of Michigan. She put all of her energy into the Affirmative Action cases and other lingering issues, knowing that it was the right thing to do for the University but also knowing that it would table any agenda items of her own for some time. This left her open to potential cynics who could complain that she didn't have a vision of her own – that she wasn't a strong leader with her own point of view. But President Coleman was ready to live with that possibility, because she knew it was the right thing for the institution.

Quinn (2004) calls this humble approach the fundamental state of leadership. In the fundamental state, a leader transcends his or her own ego, moves outside the comfort zone, clarifies the results he or she wants to create, and aligns values and behaviors. President Coleman was able to transcend her own vision for the future and focus on bringing the final stages of the lawsuits to a successful conclusion by taking ownership and responsibility for them. Rather than laying out her own strategic plan from the start of her Presidency, President Coleman had to "build the bridge as she walked on it" – having faith that she would be able to shape her own agenda for the University as time passed. And as time has shown, by spring of 2004, almost one year after the landmark decision was issued by the Supreme Court, President Coleman announced her own strategic vision for the University. Thus, as President Coleman's stories have illustrated, positive strategic leaders often transcend their own ego and agenda, putting the common good and welfare of the institution first.

Begin with a Purpose in Mind (The Voice of Mary Sue Coleman)

My entire professional life has unfolded in public universities, the character of which I find fascinating and inspiring. Because these institutions were created to be supported by the public and to support the public, they have an obligation to address important societal issues as well as to educate the citizens of the state.

The University of Michigan, as one of the oldest, largest, and most eminent of the great public universities, has always displayed a special commitment to its mission of social responsibility. A stirring example of this is Michigan's stance on diversity, extending to the defense of the use of affirmative action in admissions at universities. Leading the University, as these cases found their way to the Supreme Court, was one of the most important honors of my life, one that was accomplished because of the extraordinary talent and dedication of the entire leadership team and Regents of the University.

I was keenly aware of the high stakes these lawsuits represented. My childhood, my entire educational life, and my experience in administrative positions at the University of North Carolina, the University of New Mexico, and the University of Iowa taught me the value of diversity and the challenge of creating diverse learning environments when K-12 schools and opportunities are not equal for all racial and ethnic groups. In fact, de facto segregation in some cities in our country has created a college-age population in which students have rarely encountered classmates from a race other than their own.

By the time I arrived in Ann Arbor, the leadership of the University had been speaking openly about the importance of affirmative action for creating diversity in classrooms. Additionally, several prominent faculty members at the University undertook social science research on the impact of classroom and campus diversity on learning and on our students' ability to function well in careers and community after graduation. The conclusions of these studies were persuasive, and we felt our arguments about taking a stand on this important principle were sound. Our legal team worked diligently to translate difficult analyses about our admissions processes into terms that could be more easily comprehended by the public. In short, the University embarked on a comprehensive, information-based public awareness program about affirmative action.

This meant that I also had to educate myself thoroughly about the contents of the massive amount of material that had emerged in the five years the two cases had been reviewed, were argued, and appealed. Being trained as a biological chemist, I had only a basic understanding of the legal process. I spent almost every waking hour being briefed and reading background materials on the case. This was essential because I needed to be able to speak with confidence on the issues with reporters, boards, external organizations, and alumni groups. Almost always, I discovered recognition and pride about the public defense of this issue by the University. Even when members of an audience did not agree with the premise of affirmative action, they understood that the University was taking a principled stand on an issue its Regents and leadership believed was critical. Indeed, I firmly believe that a consequence of this broad educational effort by the University eventually led to a more reasoned debate in the media about the ongoing legacy of discrimination and the importance of achieving diversity in our educational institutions. This massive educational effort also provided the impetus for a record number of amicus briefs (a brief filed with the court by someone who is not a party to the case) filed on our behalf by educational and civil rights organizations, corporations, and former military officers.

Insights for Positive Strategic Leadership (The Voice of the POS Scholars) President Coleman had a clear purpose in mind as the leader of a public university. She believed there was a social responsibility as a public university to take a stand on diversity – her actions began with a purpose in mind. It might have been an easier road not to undertake the controversy and expense of the affirmative action lawsuits, but this leader lives out her presidency with clear purpose because she takes the mission of a public university to serve the public so seriously.

Authentic leaders are grounded with a purpose and a mission – living their values and using discipline and commitment to achieve great results (George, 2003). They know the true north of their moral compass. Quinn (2004) describes this as being purpose-centered. The leader clarifies the result they want to create, are committed and engaged, with unwavering commitment to pursue that purpose. Cameron (2003) talks about purposefulness as leading with virtue for human impact, moral goodness, and social betterment. And being purpose-centered is the engine of personal empowerment for leaders to take action and have real impact (Spreitzer, 1995). Thus, a hallmark of the positive strategic leader is leading with purpose.

Appreciate Divergent Views (The Voice of Mary Sue Coleman)

The affirmative action debate also provided ample opportunity for me, as a new president, to engage with campus stakeholders who held widely divergent views. While we enjoyed broad campus support for our position, we also realized that like any university, strongly held views would be part of our community discussion. Prominent faculty members and some student organizations at the University had reservations about using affirmative action as a tool for admissions. At the other end of the spectrum, other faculty members engaged in social science research to investigate the impact of a diverse student body on the educational environment of the University.

Students also held widely divergent opinions about affirmative action. Large numbers of students supported the University and its stand on this issue. Some believed that the leadership was not aggressive enough in defending these lawsuits. A number joined the effort as interveners in the lawsuits, attempting to create a more activist defense of the lawsuits. On the other side, some students were opposed to the policies of affirmative action. Public debates among students were vigorous throughout the six years the lawsuits traversed the court system.

Alumni, likewise, expressed intense interest in the cases, mirroring the range of opinions found on the campus. What held us together was our dedication to the ideals of the excellent academic traditions of the University of Michigan, a dedication on which I promised never to yield. I knew then, and I continue to see in our post-decision era, that we can be both diverse and excellent in our academic endeavors.

From my arrival on campus in August 2002, there was intense interest in my stance on the Affirmative Action cases. I was questioned vigorously by students, by faculty, and certainly by alumni groups. In each instance, I talked openly about my beliefs and often referred to my own background and experiences in segregated communities and in preparing for a field of study not common among women. With personal stories, I attempted to explain my strong support for diversity on the campus. I always listened to divergent views and invited people to share their perspectives with me. But in the end, sometimes we had to agree to disagree.

Insights for Positive Strategic Leadership (The Voice of the POS Scholars)
Quinn (2004) describes positive strategic leaders as being externally open. Like President Coleman, they move outside their comfort zone, appreciate others' points of view, and are open to learning from others who hold different conflicting perspectives. By seeking to understand the perspective of others, particularly those who hold divergent points of view, the positive strategic leader can not only demonstrate empathy, but can also learn important things from others that may strengthen the leader's own perspective. And in some cases, their openness can also create openness to those with divergent views to temper or even change their perspectives. Recent research has indicated that respectful engagement with others is critical for personal growth (Spreitzer, Sutcliffe, Dutton, Sonenshein, & Grant, 2005). Positive

strategic leaders can display respectful engagement with others by conveying presence (i.e., "just being there"), being genuine (i.e., reacting from a real and honest place), and confirming affirmation (i.e., actively looking for the positive core in another) (Dutton, 2003). So while the positive strategic leader may not agree with others, they seek to hear, understand, appreciate, and learn from divergent perspectives.

Be a Beacon for the Future (The Voice of Mary Sue Coleman)

The University of Michigan undertook a unique role in advancing diversity and civil rights. The six-year journey of the admissions lawsuits, and the landmark decision of the Supreme Court, placed us in the center of the public debate about affirmative action. Because we staked out such a public presence with our defense of the lawsuits, our subsequent actions are receiving intense scrutiny, and we need to turn that scrutiny to our advantage as we move forward, continuing to lead the way on the issue of diversity.

An outstanding university that is diverse has a strength that comes from the hybrid vigor of a multitude of ideas and perspectives. I expect us to have a university that continues to provide an intellectually engaging and challenging environment that other universities will want to emulate. We are committed to the core principles that will inform our next steps: a real commitment to a welcoming climate, accountability to diversity on both an institutional and an individual level, and the recognition that the vigor of diversity will create a better and more intellectually rich university.

There are several areas we are exploring as we bring these principles to life. We must develop institutional best practices to create a diverse academic community and a truly welcoming environment. We need to focus on aggressive recruitment and retention efforts for diverse and exceptional faculty, students, and staff, and we need to understand better how issues of climate are affecting those who decide to join us, or to leave. We also need to infuse our curriculum with multicultural and interdisciplinary content, so the richness of our intellectual environment is deepened. To accomplish all of this, we need to establish a broad strategy for an institutional commitment to a diversity that is effective and long-lasting.

I have said on many occasions that the true impact of any landmark decision is determined by the actions taken in the eras between decisions. I will continue to advance the principles of the University by reminding our many constituents that we can never rest, and we must continue to reinvent the meaning of diversity at this University and in our broader society.

Insights for Positive Strategic Leadership (The Voice of the POS Scholars)
Positive strategic leaders are bullish on the future. They lead with a hope for
a better tomorrow, even when tomorrow is potentially threatening or dis-
concerting. Rather than dwelling on the negative, positive strategic leaders see
opportunities rather than threats (Jackson & Dutton, 1988). They invent
possibilities for the future (Zander & Zander, 2000). They discover and dream
about their positive destinies through techniques, such as appreciative inquiry
– a positive methodology for strategic organizational change (Cooperrider,
Whitney, & Stavros, 2003). For example, after the successful decision on the
lawsuit, it might have been easy to take a breather on diversity issues after
the frenetic pace of her first year. But President Coleman worked hard to keep
the University community focused on creating a community that would be
welcoming to people from all backgrounds – how Michigan could become the
university of choice for minority students. In this way, positive strategic
leaders are resilient (Sutcliffe & Vogus, 2003) and keep their sights looking
forward with hope rather than cynicism (Spreitzer & Mishra, 2000).

CONCLUSION

When we started to work on this chapter on the Affirmative Action cases
with President Coleman, we thought that our focus would be on addressing
rather esoteric questions, such as: "How do leaders create and sustain
identity when they are managing multiple divergent stakeholders?" or "How
do leaders manage to craft their own agenda while tending to the inevitable
fires that flare up unexpectedly?" These kinds of topics are embedded in the
more traditional strategic leadership literature. However, as we spent time
with President Coleman and learned more about her, we expanded not only
our perspective on her as a person and as a leader, but also our perspective
on the larger issue of strategic leadership.

We began to see how we could juxtapose a growing body of research on
positive organizational scholarship with current frameworks on strategic
leadership. This pointed us toward the idea of the person within – that who
the leader is as a person matters. For example, in defining strategic leadership, Boal (2004, p. 1,503) states: "Strategic leadership forges a bridge
between the past, the present, and the future, by reaffirming core values and
identity to ensure continuity and integrity as the organization struggles with
known and unknown realities and possibilities."

If we look at the same passage of Boal's definition from the perspective of
"who the strategic leader is as a person," we could adapt the definition to

define who positive strategic leaders are. Positive strategic leaders bridge the past, the present and the future by reaffirming their core values and identity to ensure their own continuity and integrity as they struggle with known and unknown realities and possibilities. In this way, positive strategic leaders are themselves strategic about bringing their whole person – past experiences, values, purpose, and personal vision – to their role as a leader who contributes to the collective good.

In order to illustrate how positive strategic leadership informs the strategic leadership discussion, we have adapted Rajagopalan and Spreitzer's (1997) integrative model of strategic change. Their original model (see Fig. 1) demonstrates how an organization and its environment are perceived by the leader and influence the actions that he or she takes. Those actions then determine the impact that leader has and ultimately the organization's outcome. While their model goes far in helping us understand strategic leadership, we believe it is incomplete. What is missing is who the leader is as a person – how they are shaped by their life experiences, their character, and their values. As such, we add the shaded circle to their model to reflect the role that the person within the leader plays in strategic leadership. The person within their experiences, character, and values underlie the thoughts, actions, and ultimately the impact of the leader. By adding these characteristics to the model, we are not suggesting that they are an additional node and/or step the leader takes in his or her leadership process, but rather they illustrate the

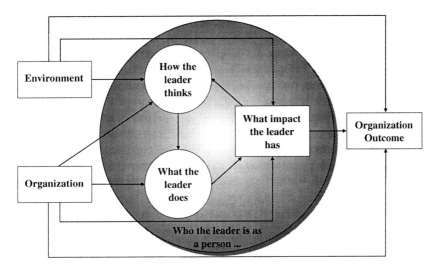

Fig. 1. A Model of Positive Strategic Leadership.

gestalt of who they are as a person, or what Quinn (2004) called the fundamental state of leadership. As we have described throughout the chapter, we believe that President Coleman's life and leadership experiences enabled her to adroitly guide the University at such a turbulent and critical time.

It is our hope that by using Mary Sue Coleman as a learning vehicle we have not only offered new insights to the literature on strategic leadership, but also to the POS body of knowledge. In the foundational book on POS (Cameron et al., 2003), there is only one chapter related directly to the topic of leadership (Avolio & Luthans, 2003), and none that focus specifically on senior-level leadership in organizations. Future work can move beyond this kind of qualitative work to more quantitative work that measures positive strategic leadership. This work could explore how these kinds of leaders may bring significant value to their organizations in terms of more effective strategic change and organizational performance. Additionally, future case studies and academic/executive collaborations focused on understanding the strategic leader and their impact would help to develop these theoretical ideas in greater depth.

We believe that practitioners can also learn from these ideas on positive strategic leadership. Whether a senior executive, a middle manager or a front-line employee, life experiences, personal character, and values shape how people think and what they do. Only when the person within a leader is congruent with their behaviors can leaders feel authentic. And we know from a growing body of research in POS that authenticity is critical for people to feel empowered, engaged, and be able to relate to others (Avolio & Luthans, 2003; Quinn, 2004). The five themes also provide practitioners some direction about how to create more alignment and authenticity between who they are and what they do as leaders. These lessons are relevant not only for themselves, but for also regarding how leaders can develop and grow their employees into positive strategic leaders.

In closing, our hope is that this work will inspire a new direction for strategic leadership research as well as leadership at all levels of the organization. Paraphrasing perhaps the most famous positive strategic leader, Mahatma Gandhi, positive strategic leaders must take the initiative to "be the change they wish to see" by becoming more humane and authentic leaders (Quinn, 2000).

NOTE

1. The former University of Michigan President Lee Bollinger, a constitutional law expert, helped to craft the admissions policies to pass constitutional muster.

ACKNOWLEDGMENT

We thank Peter Anderson, Robert Hooijberg, and Elmer Spreitzer for their guidance on an earlier version of the chapter.

REFERENCES

Avolio, B., & Luthans, F. (2003). Authentic leadership development. In: K. Cameron, J. Dutton & R. Quinn (Eds), *Positive organizational scholarship: Foundations of a new discipline* (pp. 241–258). San Francisco, CA: Berrett-Koehler.

Boal, K. B. (2004). Strategic leadership. In: G. R. Goethals, G. J. Sorenson & J. M. Burns (Eds), *Encyclopedia of leadership* (pp. 1497–1504). Thousand Oaks, CA: Sage.

Boal, K. B., & Hooijberg, R. (2001). Strategic leadership: Moving on. *Leadership Quarterly, 11*(4), 515–549.

Cameron, K. (2003). Organizational virtues and performance. In: K. Cameron, J. Dutton & R. Quinn (Eds), *Positive organization scholarship: Foundations of a new discipline* (pp. 48–65). San Francisco, CA: Berrett-Koehler.

Cameron, K., Dutton, J., & Quinn, R. (Eds) (2003). *Positive organization scholarship: Foundations of a new discipline*. San Francisco, CA: Berrett-Koehler.

Cooperrider, D. L., Whitney, D., & Stavros, J. M. (Eds) (2003). *Appreciative inquiry handbook: The first in a series of AI workbooks for leaders of change*. Bedford Heights, OH: Lakeshore Communications.

Dutton, J. E. (2003). *Energize your workplace: How to create and sustain high-quality connections at work*. San Francisco: Jossey-Bass.

Finkelstein, S., & Hambrick, D. C. (1990). Top management team tenure and organizational outcomes: The moderating role of managerial discretion. *Administrative Science Quarterly, 35*, 484–503.

George, W. (2003). *Authentic leadership: Rediscovering the secrets to creating lasting value*. San Francisco, CA: Jossey-Bass.

Hambrick, D. C. (1989). Putting top managers back into the strategy picture. *Strategic Management Journal, 10*, 5–15.

Harter, S. (2002). Authenticity. In: C. R. Snyder & S. J. Lopez (Eds), *Handbook of positive psychology* (pp. 382–394). Oxford, UK: Oxford University Press.

Harter, S., Marold, D. B., Whitesell, N. R., & Cobbs, G. (1996). A model of the effects of parent and peer support on adolescent false self-behavior. *Child Development, 67*, 360–374.

Jackson, S., & Dutton, J. (1988). Discerning threats and opportunities. *Administrative Science Quarterly, 33*, 270–287.

Quinn, R. E. (2000). *Change the world: How ordinary people can achieve extraordinary results*. San Francisco, CA: Jossey-Bass.

Quinn, R. E. (2004). *Building the bridge as you walk on it: A guide for leading change*. San Francisco, CA: Jossey-Bass.

Rajagopalan, N., & Spreitzer, G. (1997). Toward a theory of strategic change: A multi-lens perspective and integrative framework. *The Academy of Management Review, 22*(1), 48–79.

Roberts, L. M., Dutton, J., Spreitzer, G., Heaphy, E., & Quinn, R. (2005). Composing the reflected best self: Building pathways for becoming extraordinary in work organizations. *Academy of Management Review, 30*(4), 712–736.

Spreitzer, G. M. (1995). Psychological empowerment in the workplace: Dimensions, measurement, and validation. *Academy of Management Journal, 38*(5), 1442–1465.

Spreitzer, G. M., & Mishra, A. (2000). An empirical examination of a stress-based framework of survivor responses to downsizing. In: R. J. Burke & C. Cooper (Eds), *The organization in crisis: Downsizing, restructuring, and privatization* (pp. 97–118). Oxford, UK: Blackwell Publishers.

Spreitzer, G. M., & Sonenshein, S. (2004). Toward the construct definition of positive deviance. *American Behavioral Scientist, 77*(6), 828–847.

Spreitzer, G. M., Sutcliffe, K. M., Dutton, J. E., Sonenshein, S., & Grant, A. M. (2005). A socially embedded model of thriving at work. *Organization Science, 16*, 537–549.

Sutcliffe, K. M., & Vogus, T. (2003). Organizing for resilience. In: K. Cameron, J. Dutton & R. Quinn (Eds), *Positive organizational scholarship: Foundations of a new discipline* (pp. 94–110). San Francisco: Berrett-Koehler.

Walsh, J. P. (1995). Managerial and organizational cognition: Notes from a trip down memory lane. *Organization Science, 6*, 280–321.

Zander, R. S., & Zander, B. (2000). *The art of possibility*. Boston, MA: Harvard Business School Press.

PART IV: LEADERSHIP DISCRETION

Organizational structures, systems and processes can and do limit the discretionary decision-making space of all involved in organizational life. However, high up in organizations leaders have significant discretion in making decisions. Robert Kaiser and Robert Hogan explore the dark side of what might happen if strategic leaders use their discretionary freedom for personal rather than organizational benefit. Timo Santalainen and Ram Baliga present a real example of discretionary leadership gone bad in an NGO that looks quite healthy on the outside. They refer to the phenomenon of a financially successful company with a sick leader as the "healthy-sick organization." We juxtapose this chapter with the one by Corey Billington and Michèle Barnett Berg to show how Duncan Covington at computer products, services, and solutions company IQ used his discretionary freedom for the good of the company. Covington inherited a sick organization and introduced key systems, structures, and processes to bring it back to health.

CHAPTER 10

THE DARK SIDE OF DISCRETION: LEADER PERSONALITY AND ORGANIZATIONAL DECLINE

Robert B. Kaiser and Robert Hogan

ABSTRACT

We review the literature to determine how discretion, defined as the free-dom to make decisions, moderates the relationship between leader per-sonality and organizational performance. Discretion increases with level in organizations so that top executives have the most discretion and the greatest opportunity to impact organizational performance. We describe how personality drives executive actions and decision making, which then impacts organizational performance; the more discretion a leader has, the more leeway there is for his or her personality to operate. Finally, using research and contemporary business examples, we illustrate the dynamics linking personality, discretionary freedom, and destructive leadership in and of organizations.

Power tends to corrupt, and absolute power corrupts absolutely.
Great men are almost always bad men.

Lord Acton, 1834–1902

Discussions of leadership typically glorify senior managers, a practice that seems increasingly suspect (Kellerman, 2005). This chapter examines the

Being There Even When You Are Not: Leading Through Strategy, Structures, and Systems
Monographs in Leadership and Management, Volume 4, 173–193
Copyright © 2007 by Elsevier Ltd.
All rights of reproduction in any form reserved
ISSN: 1479-3571/doi:10.1016/S1479-3571(07)04009-6

concept of discretion, defined as the degree of choice or "latitude of action" available to managers (Hambrick & Finkelstein, 1987). We propose that, although discretion is necessary for leaders to make positive contributions to their organizations, it also provides the potential for leaders to disrupt and destroy them. This dilemma has possible implications for the fate of organizations and even societies. Thus, given the tendency for academics to romanticize senior leaders, we focus on the dark side of discretion and how it links leader personality to organizational failure.

Consider Harry Stonecipher, an executive at General Electric (GE) in the 1980s, an organization that tolerated, if not actually reinforced, his intimidating management style. Although he earned a reputation for integrity by taking strong positions on ethical issues, media accounts of his career at GE, and later at Sundstrand and McDonnell Douglas, indicate that his abrasiveness earned him many enemies. (The details of this case are based on several media reports, particularly Isidore, 2005.) Stonecipher joined Boeing in 1997 when it acquired McDonnell Douglas. He retired in 2002, but as Boeing's single-largest shareholder, he remained on the board of directors. In December 2003, amid an ethics scandal that led to the resignation of the CEO, Phil Condit, and sent two other executives to prison, he returned as CEO. Wall Street approved of his return and Boeing's stock rose by 52% during his tenure.

In the spring of 2005, Stonecipher's many detractors finally caught up with him. An anonymous letter informed the board that he was having an extramarital affair with another Boeing executive. According to the Associated Press, "The board concluded that the facts reflected poorly on Harry's judgment and would impair his ability to lead the company." Stonecipher was fired, and Boeing became the subject of yet another public scandal.

This case illustrates three points about leader personality. First, personality matters – who leaders are determines how they lead, for better or worse. Second, personality flaws shape judgment and sometimes lead to ill-advised decisions; they also prompt behaviors that create enemies, alienate coworkers, and undermine teams. Third, leader personality is most consequential at the top, where there is great freedom of choice and much is at stake.

This chapter is organized as follows. First, we review the literature on managerial discretion, which indicates that discretion moderates the relationship between leader personality and organizational performance. Second, we present a model for conceptualizing the links between leader personality and organizational performance. Third, we present a particular viewpoint on personality that may be useful in research concerning how leaders harm organizations. Finally, we use empirical research and examples from the business press to illustrate how dark side personality characteristics impact and possibly destroy organizations. Our argument is that, under conditions of high discretion, organizations come to resemble their leaders – warts and all.

DISCRETION

Discretion is a multifaceted variable that reflects the degree to which managers can turn their intentions into reality – what Hambrick and Finkelstein (1987) call "latitude of action." When discretion is low, managerial judgment and behavior are constrained. When discretion is high, managers are relatively free to do as they wish. Thus, discretion is a situational variable that moderates how much leaders can affect organizational processes and outcomes. Three lines of research show how discretion influences leadership.

Social Psychology of Discretion

In an influential critique of traditional personality psychology, Mischel (1968) argued that behavior is determined by situational factors rather than personality variables. He later conceded that personality may influence behavior, but only in "weak situations." According to Mischel (1977), strong situations provide clear, unambiguous cues about appropriate behavior, and that leads to less variability in how people respond. Weak situations provide only ambiguous cues for action; these conditions allow greater opportunity for personality to influence behavior.

Situation strength has been used to analyze organizational behavior (Weiss & Adler, 1984). Research shows, for example, that job autonomy moderates the relationship between personality and performance (Barrick & Mount, 1993). However, the concept of situation strength has not been widely used in the study of leadership. The concept of situation strength is obviously related to discretion. Thus, situation strength should be inversely related to organizational level because, with increasing organizational status, autonomy increases and roles and performance criteria become less clearly defined (Zaccaro, 2001).

Mischel's ideas about situational strength are consistent with *agency theory* and *strategic leadership theory*, two management models that were developed independently of Mischel.

Agency Theory

Jensen and Meckling (1976) introduced a model for reconciling the conflicts of interest in public corporations between principals (shareholders and owners) and agents (executives). Agency theory proposes mechanisms to deter senior managers from pursuing personal gain at the expense of shareholder value. Agency theory predicts that executives prefer to drive revenues because their pay is tied to revenue, and profitability primarily benefits the owners/investors; research supports this prediction (Cannella & Monroe, 1997; Gray & Cannella, 1997).

Agency theory leads to several conclusions; we will highlight two. First, certain structural mechanisms can reduce executive selfishness and promote greater manager–owner alignment. Specifically, self-interested executive behavior is inversely related to the power of boards of directors, governance structure and activity, shareholder activism, and the extent to which executive pay is tied to firm performance (Cannella & Monroe, 1997; Eisenhardt, 1989; Tosi, Katz, & Gomez-Mejia, 1997). Note that these mechanisms are designed to reduce executive discretion. Second, these controls are rarely enforced in practice. For instance, executive compensation is unrelated to firm performance across public corporations (Gomez-Mejia, 1994) and, prior to the Sarbanes-Oxley act, boards were reluctant to discipline executives. This lack of accountability partially explains the rash of executive fraud and malfeasance described in the business press in the first years of the 21st century.

Strategic Leadership Theory

In contrast with social psychology and agency theory, strategic leadership theory (SLT) assumes that executive behavior is a product of individual psychology (Hambrick & Mason, 1984). Personality, values, and beliefs shape how leaders perceive, interpret, and use information to decide what business to compete in, what goods or services to offer, how to allocate resources, and what policies to implement. SLT further maintains that these choices are consequential for organizations. But this claim appears controversial: Some studies report no relationship between leadership style and organizational performance, while others report a substantial relationship (see review in Day & Lord, 1988).

Hambrick and Finkelstein's (1987) analysis of leader discretion resolves this apparent contradiction. They argue that discretion determines the impact leaders have on organizations. Specifically, three general classes of factors restrict executive discretion: environmental, organizational, and individual. Environmental factors vary by industry and are considered to be the most potent (Hambrick & Abrahamson, 1995). They include product commoditization versus differentiation, monopolistic versus oligopolistic industry structure, market growth, degree of government regulation, and capital intensity. Organizational factors – age, size, culture, and control mechanisms – also impose constraints on executive choice. Finally, characteristics of leaders affect how much discretion they seek and how they use their level of discretion. Hambrick and colleagues point to locus of control and tolerance of ambiguity as important personality variables associated with a preference for greater discretion.

The empirical research on discretion in the SLT paradigm is nicely coherent (see reviews in Cannella & Monroe, 1997; Finkelstein & Hambrick, 1996). This research shows that who is in charge affects organizational strategy, structure, policy, and culture. Discretion also consistently moderates the relationship between leader characteristics and organizational outcomes. When discretion is low, there is little relationship between leader characteristics and organizational performance; when discretion is high, there is a strong relationship. For example, this has been shown for tenure and strategy distinctiveness (Finkelstein & Hambrick, 1990) as well as locus of control and strategy formation (Miller, Kets de Vries, & Toulouse, 1982).

The fact that discretion links individual leaders to organizational outcomes poses a dilemma: Without discretion, leaders are unable to influence firm performance, but with discretion leaders can put self-interest ahead of their other responsibilities and obligations.

Summary

The literature on managerial discretion yields three generalizations relevant to the present discussion. First, discretion increases with hierarchical level – in any given company, executives enjoy more freedom of choice than supervisors – and senior executives have the most discretion. Second, some companies allow executives more discretion than others. In particular, discretion is highest in organizations that are younger, smaller, have weaker cultures, and limited governance or control mechanisms and in companies in the computer, engineering, telecommunications, pharmaceutical, and entertainment industries (Hambrick & Abrahamson, 1995). Finally, the prospect of retribution is the best way to prevent greedy managers from abusing their authority.

The foregoing suggests that executive personality can affect organizational performance. However, two problems in the literature obscure this point: incomplete or ad hoc definitions of personality and poor personality measurement. For example, SLT researchers routinely use demographic variables as proxy measures of personality (Cannella & Monroe, 1997). A clear definition of personality should help advance our conceptual understanding, and good measures should advance our empirical understanding, of how senior leaders affect organizational performance. Before turning to that issue, however, we need to discuss the means by which leaders affect organizational performance.

LEADERS AND ORGANIZATIONAL EFFECTIVENESS

Several studies report that who is in charge of for-profit businesses makes a difference in firm performance (e.g., Barrick, Day, Lord, & Alexander, 1991; Barney, 1991; Day & Lord, 1988; Thomas, 1988). What is needed is a clearer account of *how* leaders affect organizational performance. Hogan and Kaiser (2005) proposed a model for integrating the literatures on personality, leadership, and organizational effectiveness. They suggest that personality predicts leadership style, leadership style impacts employee attitudes and team functioning, and these variables then predict organizational effectiveness. Fig. 1 illustrates these relationships and also incorporates the moderating role of discretion and the distinction between leadership *in* organizations and leadership *of* organizations (cf., Dubin, 1979).

Leadership involves persuading individuals to give up their purely selfish interests for a while and contribute to the overall performance of the organization (Hogan, 2006; Hogan, Curphy, & Hogan, 1994; Hogan & Kaiser, 2005). In other words, leadership concerns building and motivating a team to outperform the competition. In an organizational context, it is important to distinguish between two types of leadership influences (cf. Zaccaro & Horn, 2003). The first is the influence that leaders exert in direct social interaction; this is leadership as face-to-face social influence, leadership *in* an organization. The second is the indirect influence that leaders exert through their decisions about direction, organizational structure, and objectives. This is leadership *of* an organization, guiding collective action impersonally by setting goals, defining roles and staffing positions, acquiring and allocating resources, and establishing policies. Although direct influence is an important activity for all leaders in an organization, indirect influence is a key activity for strategic senior leadership (Zaccaro & Horn, 2003).

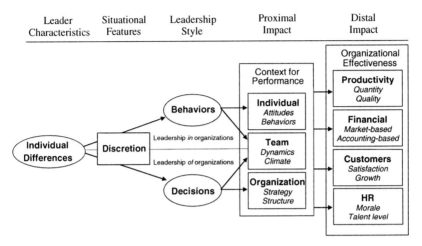

Fig. 1. How Leaders Impact Organizational Effectiveness.

Leader Characteristics

Discretion moderates the effect of leader attributes. Although this applies to individual differences in cognitive ability, knowledge, skills, and experience, we believe personality is the most potent source of individual differences in leadership. We say this for three reasons. First, meta-analyses show that, when organized in terms of an adequate taxonomy (e.g., the Big Five), the validity for personality is greater than the validity of cognitive ability for predicting leadership (cf. $R = 0.48$ for personality, Judge, Bono, Ilies, & Gerhardt, 2002, $\rho = 0.27$ for cognitive ability, Judge, Ilies, & Colbert, 2004). Second, personality is a broader domain than cognitive ability; there is, in principle, more variance to personality. And third, other scholars also argue that personality is the primary source of differences among leaders (e.g., Hambrick & Mason, 1984; Kets de Vries & Miller, 1985).

Leadership Style

The more discretion leaders have, the more their leadership style will reflect their personalities. Leadership style can be characterized in terms of inter-personal behavior and preferred patterns of decision making. The psychological study of leadership focuses on behavior – being considerate, showing initiative, transforming followers, and other direct methods of interpersonal influence (Bass, 1990), whereas the managerial literature emphasizes decision making with regard to strategy, structure, staffing, and policy – all of which influence a workforce in indirect and impersonal ways (Finkelstein & Hambrick, 1996).

The behavioral and the decision-making aspects of leadership style are complementary; they are unique direct and indirect influences. This distinction is represented in Fig. 1. Above the line, leadership *in* organizations concerns the behaviors that directly motivate employees and galvanize teams – versus the behaviors that demoralize employees and weaken teams. Below the line, leadership *of* organizations involves making decisions about strategy, structure, staffing, and policy that indirectly influence employees by creating a "strong situation" in their work environment.

Impact of Leadership

Leadership style affects organizational performance directly and indirectly through its impact on the organizational unit. Put simply, leaders get things done through other people. Influencing people, teams, and organizational features is the proximal effect of leadership; like falling dominoes, the proximal effects create business results as a distal impact.

Proximal impact: Organizational process

Recent theoretical and empirical work suggests conceptualizing the effects of leadership at three levels of analysis (e.g., Yammarino & Dansereau, 2002): the individual employee, the team or group, and the organization itself.

Leader behaviors directly influence the attitudes (e.g., commitment, satisfaction) and behaviors (e.g., performance) of individual employees (Dansereau, Graen, & Haga, 1975). Leader behaviors also directly affect team dynamics and climate – for instance, by facilitating communication and coordination, resolving intragroup conflict, and rewarding or sanctioning certain behaviors (Peterson, Smith, Martorana, & Owens, 2003). Leader decisions also indirectly influence teams by establishing goals, by assigning people to roles, and by distributing resources (Antonakis & House, 2002). And leader decisions impact organizations by defining strategic direction, organizational structure, resource allocation, and formal policy (Zaccaro, 2001).

Thus, the mechanisms through which leadership style affects organizational performance operate at the individual, team, and organizational level of analysis. A leader's impact across these three levels can be seen as creating a context for performance, because the leader's role is to facilitate team performance. On the one hand, this promotes an internal focus – with an emphasis on activities within the group. On the other hand, because contexts are more or less conducive to performance, these actions affect a team's performance in competition with rivals, and that translates directly into organizational effectiveness.

Distal Impact: Organizational Effectiveness
Although psychologists have tended to ignore the topic of organizational effectiveness, it is the ultimate measure of leadership effectiveness (Hogan & Kaiser, 2005). The managerial literature has taken the topic more seriously. A survey of this literature reveals four general classes of variables that constitute a "balanced scorecard" (Kaplan & Norton, 1996) and that apply to a wide range of business organizations: productivity, finances, customer service, and human resources.

Productivity measures reflect relative efficiency in transforming inputs (capital, people, materials) into outputs (goods and services). This is the concept of organizational effectiveness in classic social psychology (Katz & Kahn, 1978) and includes such indices as quantity and quality, sales per employee, and rate of innovation. There are two distinct kinds of financial measures, market-based and accounting-based. Market-based metrics (e.g., total shareholder return, price-to-earnings ratio) reflect profitability and value to shareholders whereas accounting-based measures (e.g., return on equity, assets, or sales; economic value added) are more internally focused and are easier to manipulate (Anderson & Tirrell, 2004). Customer service indices concern customer satisfaction, retention, and growth. Finally, human resource-based measures reflect how well an organization manages talent. Metrics in this group include rate of turnover and morale. Bench strength – the number and quality of future leaders – belongs here as well. An important point about customer service and human resource-based measures is that, although they are not reflected directly in the bottom line, they are crucial to the sustainability of productivity and financial performance. That is, when production goals and financial results are achieved while alienating customers and demoralizing employees, the organization will inevitably suffer a reversal of fortune.

Taken together, these measures of business results map the domain of organizational effectiveness, the distal impact of leadership. We now turn to a discussion of how leaders use their discretion to affect organizational performance.

PERSONALITY

Leadership researchers routinely talk about personality but rarely define the term. Moreover, they routinely confuse description with explanation (e.g., they argue that domineering behavior – description – is caused by a trait for dominance – explanation). Furthermore, leadership research is typically based on mini-theories of personality (e.g., locus of control) rather than more comprehensive models (e.g., psychoanalysis). We turn next to a brief overview of *socioanalytic theory* (Hogan, 2006) – a model of personality designed to account for occupational performance that is well suited to examining performance in leadership roles.

Socioanalytic Theory

The theory attempts to integrate the best insights of sociology and psychoanalysis. According to this view, personality concerns two things: (1) generalizations about human nature and (2) generalizations about individual differences – which are important and how they arise. With regard to human nature, a review of sociology, anthropology, and evolutionary psychology yields two major generalizations. First, humans evolved as group-living animals and are inherently social. Second, every group has a status hierarchy; there are people at the bottom, many in the middle, and a few at the top and everyone knows who is where. This suggests that the big problems in life concern building relationships and achieving status – getting along and getting ahead. It is worth noting that effective leaders are skilled at both of these while ineffective leaders come up short in one or both (Kaplan & Kaiser, 2003, 2006).

In terms of individual differences, personality should be defined from two perspectives: (1) how people think about themselves – which is their identity and (2) how others think about them – which is their reputation. Identity – a person's self-concept – is composed of goals, values, and strategies for getting along and getting ahead. Reputation concerns how observers evaluate that person's efforts to get along and get ahead. Identity is the "you that you know;" reputation is the "you that we know." These are very different constructs. George H. Mead (1934) emphasized reputation because it is the basis on which others interact with us. Freud was probably right when he argued that we make up our identities to justify self-serving goals and beliefs. Nonetheless, identity is important because it *explains* why you do what you do – even if your behavior is self-defeating.

Reputation *describes* what you have done and *predicts* what you are likely to do. It determines some of the most consequential outcomes in life: promotions, mates, and allies. It is important to distinguish two aspects of reputation, "the bright side" and "the dark side." The bright side reflects people's social performance when they are at their best – during a job interview or a first date. The Big Five is a taxonomy of the bright side; it reflects common themes observers use to describe others in the early stages of a relationship (McAdams, 1995): outgoing and assertive (extraversion); congenial and cooperative (agreeableness); reliable and rule-abiding (conscientiousness); stable and rewarding to be with (emotional stability); curious and worldly (openness). But there is more to one's reputation than the bright side.

The Dark Side

The dark side of personality refers to the impression we make on others when we let down our guard – i.e., when we do not care how we are perceived. The bright side describes the person we meet in an employment interview, and the dark side describes the person we evaluate at the end of the year. Dark side tendencies concern agenda-driven efforts to get along and get ahead (Hogan & Hogan, 2001), and they are usually effective in the short run. However, they rest on flawed assumptions about others' impressions (e.g., "other people find me irresistible") and they are usually problematic in the long term (Baumeister & Scher, 1988). They are otherwise attractive tendencies that are overdone; for example, confidence turns into arrogance, creativity becomes eccentricity, tact becomes obsequiousness, and so on.

The dark side is the key to understanding managerial failure. Bentz (1985) pioneered the topic with an interview study of derailed managers at Sears. He noted that they were chosen on the basis of a rigorous assessment center and they were all bright, ambitious, and self-confident; nonetheless, they had "over-riding personality defects." Subsequent researchers have replicated Bentz's findings (Leslie & Van Velsor, 1996; McCall & Lombardo, 1983). Based on this "derailment literature," Hogan and Hogan (1997) proposed that the standard personality disorders, as described in the DSM-IV (American Psychiatric Association, 1994), provided a taxonomy of the most important causes of managerial failure. They further noted that these behavior patterns were extensions of the Big Five and resembled Bentz's (1985) "personality defects."

Dark side tendencies are not forms of mental illness – they are flawed interpersonal strategies that prevent managers from building a team, forming alliances, and gaining support for their vision and plans. Hogan and Hogan (2001) developed an inventory of the 11 key dimensions of the dark side; subsequent research shows that the inventory is a valid predictor of derailment. This taxonomy is presented in Table 1.

There are three points to note about these dark side characteristics. First, although high scores on the dimensions in Table 1 have negative consequences in the long run, they often have positive consequences in the short run. For example, Bold managers make unusually positive first impressions and Excitable managers convey great passion and intensity. On the other hand, low scores on these dimensions are not necessarily desirable. Low Imaginative suggests lack of vision, low Bold suggests indecisiveness, low Dutiful suggests problems with authority figures and so on. Optimal performance is associated with more moderate scores. In several executive samples, Kaplan and Kaiser (2003, 2006) have shown that very high or low levels of most performance dimensions are undesirable and that the ideal lies somewhere in between.

Second, these 11 dimensions form three higher-order factors that closely resemble the three self-defeating styles that Horney (1950) identified for managing anxiety in relationships (Hogan & Hogan, 1997). According to Horney, these dysfunctional coping strategies are motivated by excessive concerns for security, recognition, and approval. Each pattern rests on a particular interpersonal strategy: Gaining security by intimidating others; winning recognition through flirtation and seduction; and obtaining approval by becoming indispensable.

Our final point about the dark side characteristics is that they do not predict when a leader will self-destruct. A key lesson from the person-situation debate of the 1970s concerns the fact that it is difficult to predict behavior in a specific episode. Rather, stable individual differences emerge from cumulative performance and aggregate trends in behavior (Epstein, 1979). Thus, dark side personality factors capture the general themes regarding how a leader is likely to fail. For example, Excitable leaders fail because they are volatile and unpredictable. Bold leaders are doomed by their arrogance and inability to learn from experience. Diligent executives micromanage and then drive off talented people. Most importantly for our purposes, however, the discretion literature suggests that dark side tendencies will be most apparent in "weak situations" – senior positions where there are fewer constraints. Executives who are aware of their dark side tendencies can develop ways to minimize their disruptive influence (Kaiser & Kaplan, 2006). At the top of big organizations, however, this type of development appears to be the exception and not the rule.

Table 1. Taxonomy of the Dark Side of Leader Personality.

Dimension	Definition	Short-Term Strengths	Long-Term Weaknesses
Higher-order factor: Motivational strategy			
Factor 1 – Intimidation: Gaining security by threatening people and scaring them away			
Excitable	Inappropriate anger and outbursts; unstable and intense relationships alternating between idealization and devaluation	Energy and enthusiasm	Others begin to avoid him/her
Cautious	Hypersensitivity to criticism or rejection	Makes few mistakes	Indecisiveness and risk-aversion
Skeptical	Mistrustful and suspicious; others' motives are interpreted as malevolent	Insightful about organizational politics	Mistrustful; vindictive and litigious
Reserved	Cold, detached, tough, and uncommunicative	Tough and resolute under pressure	Uncommunicative and insensitive to morale issues
Leisurely	Stubborn, procrastinating, and passively resistant to requests for improved performance	Charming and apparently cooperative	Passive aggressive meanness
Factor 2 – Flirtation and seduction: Winning recognition with self-promotion and charm			
Bold	Arrogant sense of entitlement; grandiose sense of competence and self-importance	Courage, confidence, and charisma	Inability to admit mistakes or learn from experience
Mischievous	Manipulative, dissembling, impulsive, and limit testing	Willing to take risks; charming	Lying; ignoring rules; exploiting others
Colorful	Attention seeking; self-dramatizing, and theatrical	Entertaining, flirtatious, and engaging	Attention-seeking, overly dramatic, and distracting
Imaginative	Interesting and sometimes eccentric flights of ideas	Visionary out-of-the-box thinking	Bad judgment leading to loss of credibility
Factor 3 – Ingratiation: Ensuring approval by being loyal and becoming indispensable			
Diligent	Perfectionist and hard to please	Hard working, high standards; self-sacrificing	Over controlling, rigid, micromanaging
Dutiful	Difficulty making independent decisions and unwillingness to disagree with superiors	Team player; considerate; keeps boss informed	Indecisive; overly concerned about pleasing superiors

DARK SIDE PERSONALITY, DISCRETION, AND ORGANIZATIONAL INEFFECTIVENESS

We close this chapter with some examples of the links between the dark side of personality, bad business behavior, and organizational ineffectiveness. The examples are organized around the three higher-order dark side factors.

Factor 1: Intimidation

Leaders with these dark side characteristics are often described as aloof, inflexible, insecure, and mean-spirited. Their problems are caused by their insensitivity to morale issues, emotional volatility, and inability to build bonds with their constituents. Failing to build a team is a key factor in derailment (Leslie & Van Velsor, 1996). These managers also make strategic decisions that ignore the human consequences and they seem nearly impervious to feedback regarding their performance.

Consider the case of Philip J. Purcell, a textbook example of a Reserved personality. Purcell began his career with the McKinsey consulting group. He did some early work with Dean Witter, a retail brokerage firm. He was popular with senior management at Dean Witter and became CEO in the late 1970s. In 1997 he orchestrated a merger with Morgan Stanley, a merchant banking firm, a merger that was widely criticized on the grounds of poor culture fit. According to the *New York Times* (June 16, 2005), as a CEO, Purcell was "ruthless, autocratic, and remote. He had no tolerance for dissent or even argument. He pushed away strong executives and surrounded himself with yes men and women. He demanded loyalty to himself over the organization. He played power games ...," had little contact with the rank and file, and stayed in his office to plot strategy. "He belittled the investment bankers [at Morgan Stanley]. Executives learned that it was pointless to argue with Mr. Purcell about anything – all it did was make him mad and he didn't even pretend to be listening."

Disgusted Morgan Stanley executives began leaving in droves, and Purcell used their departures as a chance to give their jobs to people who were loyal to him. Former Morgan Stanley executives, infuriated by the way they had been treated, created enough shareholder agitation that the Morgan Stanley board fired Purcell in the week of June 13, 2005, but only after the stock had dropped precipitously and the company had lost some of the most talented investment bankers in the United States.

Michael Eisner of Disney is a combination of Excitable and Skeptical personalities. He is widely regarded as politically insightful, passionate, and aggressive. He hired new executives in a fit of enthusiasm, immediately began to distrust them, then drove them away. For example, he impulsively hired his one-time friend, Michael Ovitz, with much fanfare. He then became disappointed and fired Ovitz 14 months later. Ovitz's $140 million severance package caused a revolt among shareholders who, in March 2004, demanded Eisner's resignation.

Factor 2: Flirtation and Seduction

These dark side characteristics are perhaps the most common in the executive suite. Most charismatic leaders score high on Bold, Colorful, Mischievous, and Imaginative, which is reflected in their extreme self-confidence, dramatic flair, willingness to test the limits, and expansive visionary thinking. They make a strong initial impression, especially in the hiring process. They are often chosen for leadership roles but subsequently fail due to overwhelming arrogance (Paulhus, 1998). This is the "dark side of charisma" – although charismatic leaders have great appeal and personal magnetism, it is often used for self-aggrandizement rather than the good of the organization (Conger, 1990; Hogan, Raskin, & Fazzini, 1990). It is noteworthy that studies of CEOs find no direct relationship between charisma and firm performance (Tosi, Misangyi, Fanelli, Waldman, & Yammarino, 2004; Agle, Nagarajan, Sonnenfeld, & Srinivasan, 2006; Waldman, Ramirez, House, & Puranam, 2001). Not surprisingly, however, charisma is directly related to a CEO's level of compensation (Tosi et al., 2004).

Kets de Vries and Miller (1985) note that narcissistic leaders present grandiose visions that initially seem bold and compelling. Ultimately these visions cause waste and distress because they defy successful implementation. Two studies of executive "hubris" and "overconfidence" demonstrate this in the case of acquisitions. Using different methodologies, both studies show that arrogant CEOs are more likely to make acquisitions, make riskier purchases, and pay considerably more than market value (Hayward & Hambrick, 1997; Malmendier & Tate, 2005). Furthermore, these investments are likely to add value for acquired firms but lose money for the acquiring firms. Consider, for example, the failed merger of computer manufacturers Hewlett-Packard and Compaq. The deal was orchestrated by Carlton S. "Carly" Fiorina, who was hired because the board wanted a CEO with a big ego (and rock-star status) to change the corporate culture. Her constant self-promotion at the expense of day-to-day operations caused a dramatic drop in HP stock value, which led to her highly publicized removal.

Factor 3: Ingratiation

This cluster of dark side characteristics – the Diligent and Dutiful personalities – is less common among executives, probably because their lack of independent thinking and initiative prevents them from rising to the top. A common theme in the derailment literature concerns relying on a particular boss for too long (McCall & Lombardo, 1983).

Diligent managers make ideal subordinates because, with their high standards and strong work ethic, they deliver results. But their perfectionism, need for control, and tendencies toward micro-management alienate their subordinates, while delighting their superiors. Diligent and Dutiful managers have a difficult time making decisions in a timely manner (Kaplan, 1999), and their strong need for consensus magnifies the problem. For example, Ken Olsen of Digital Equipment insisted on long strategic planning processes designed to produce complete agreement among his entire management team. Many analysts regard his consensus-driven style as the primary reason Digital Equipment was so late entering the personal computer market.

Consider also Douglas Ivester, the former CEO of Coca-Cola. The board believed that Ivester would be the ideal CEO for Coca-Cola because he grew up in the company and had been both CFO and COO. But his extraordinary attention to detail, which was key to his earlier success, proved lethal in the CEO role. Mired in minutiae, Ivester was unable to focus on the bigger picture and strategic issues, and the board requested his resignation in 1999, not quite two years into the job.

CONTAINING THE DARK SIDE

We have focused on managerial derailment to highlight the down side of leader discretion. People are inherently both altruistic and selfish, tendencies that emerge at different times and in different circumstances. To say that people are inherently selfish is to suggest two things. First, left to their own discretion, people will focus on advancing their own interests rather than the interests of the larger social group. Second, most people are selfish some of the time and some people are selfish most of the time. The question then is how to contain selfishness? We see three general strategies that can be used to limit the dark side potential of executive personality. These involve selection, governance, and compensation.

The most obvious way to minimize the influence of dark side personalities is to screen them out in the selection and succession process. However, two factors make this difficult. First, dark side characteristics coexist with well-developed social skills (Hogan & Hogan, 2001). For example, Bold managers are also charming and self-confident and Reserved managers are cool under pressure. Thus, dark side tendencies are extremely difficult to detect in an interview; in fact, they typically come across as positive attributes in the short run. Hogan and Kaiser (2005) showed how many executives are hired for the very same qualities that get them fired. Second, dark side tendencies are best detected with valid assessment instruments. However, real executive selection decisions rarely involve standardized psychological assessment tools (Sessa, Kaiser, Taylor, & Campbell, 1998). Better decisions may result from more extensive background checks, particularly with former subordinates, and individual assessments conducted by psychologists who explicitly seek information on dark side tendencies.

There is empirical evidence indicating that governance mechanisms can better align executive action and decisions with stakeholder interests (Cannella & Monroe, 1997; Eisenhardt, 1989). Boards of directors represent a potentially powerful constraining force. However, for boards to govern effectively, certain conditions are necessary – historically, these conditions have not been the norm (Gandossy & Sonnenfeld, 2004). They include relative board independence, where a critical mass of members are from the outside and not chosen by the CEO; regular and active oversight by the board in company affairs, including performance reviews and succession processes; and board accountability, where the board is responsible for executive and organizational performance and also has the power to sanction executives. In the wake of the wave of corporate scandals since 2001, governance reform has been a hot topic. Time will tell how effective such reform is. However, the May 24, 2006 issue of the *New York Times* featured an article by Julie Creswell, showing how Robert L. Nardelli, the CEO of Home Depot, has staffed his board with CEO friends who have awarded him $245 million in five years. Over that same period of time the company's stock slid 12% while shares of its competitor, Lowe's, have risen 173%.

Finally, better alignment between managers and stakeholders can be achieved by performance-contingent compensation (Tosi et al., 1997). As noted earlier, executives prefer to grow revenues rather than maximize profitability, because their pay is related to revenues while shareholder value is reflected in profitability. Principals could reasonably expect better performance from their managerial agents to the extent that their incentives are congruent. For instance, tying executive compensation to profitability and decoupling it from top-line revenues seems to be a promising strategy for minimizing risky acquisitions and promoting value-added initiatives that enhance profitability. Furthermore, this seems to be a ripe opportunity because executive compensation is typically unrelated to firm performance (Gomez-Mejia, 1994).

Of course, these solutions involve a balancing act: Too much discretion, and leaders tend to pursue self-interest at the expense of the organization and its stakeholders. But too little discretion, and leaders may be constrained in their opportunities to contribute to organizational success. So the question becomes how much discretion is ideal for senior leaders? It probably is somewhere between agency theory and strategic leadership theory, but surely not in the middle. The right amount is most likely closer to the former, with its emphasis on accountability and external control.

REFERENCES

Agle, B. R., Nagarajan, N. J., Sonnenfeld, J. A., & Srinivasan, D. (2006). Does CEO charisma matter? An empirical analysis of the relationships among organizational performance, environmental uncertainty, and top management team perception of CEO charisma. *Academy of Management Journal, 49*, 161–174.

American Psychiatric Association (1994). *Diagnostic and statistical manual of mental disorders* (4th ed.). Washington, DC: American Psychological Association.

Anderson, J. R., & Tirrell, M. E. (2004). Too good to be true: CEOs and financial reporting fraud. *Consulting Psychology Journal: Practice and Research, 46*, 35–43.

Antonakis, J., & House, R. J. (2002). An analysis of the full-range leadership theory: The way forward. In: B. J. Avolio & F. J. Yammarino (Eds), *Transformational and charismatic leadership: The road ahead* (pp. 3–33). Greenwich, CT: Elsevier Science/JAI Press.

Barney, J. B. (1991). Firm resources and sustained competitive advantage. *Journal of Management, 17*, 99–120.

Barrick, M. R., Day, D. V., Lord, R. G., & Alexander, R. A. (1991). Assessing the utility of executive leadership. *Leadership Quarterly, 2*, 9–22.

Barrick, M. R., & Mount, M. K. (1993). Autonomy as a moderator of the relationship between the Big Five personality dimensions and job performance. *Journal of Applied Psychology, 78*, 111–118.

Bass, B. M. (1990). *Bass and Stogdill handbook of leadership*. New York: Free Press.

Baumeister, R. F., & Scher, S. J. (1988). Self-defeating behavior patterns among normal individuals. *Psychological Bulletin, 104*, 3–22.

Bentz, V. J. (1985). A view from the top: A thirty year perspective of research devoted to the discovery, description, and prediction of executive behavior. Paper presented at the 93rd annual convention of the American Psychological Association, Los Angeles, August.

Cannella, A. A., & Monroe, M. J. (1997). Contrasting perspectives on strategic leaders: Toward a more realistic view of top managers. *Journal of Management, 23*(3), 213–237.

Conger, J. A. (1990). The dark side of leadership. *Organizational Dynamics, 19*, 44–55.

Dansereau, F., Jr., Graen, G., & Haga, W. J. (1975). A vertical dyad linkage approach to leadership within formal organizations: A longitudinal investigation of the role making process. *Organizational Behavior and Human Performance, 13*, 46–78.

Day, D. V., & Lord, R. G. (1988). Executive leadership and organizational performance. *Journal of Management, 14*, 453–464.

Dubin, R. (1979). Metaphors of leadership: An overview. In: J. G. Hunt & L. L. Larson (Eds), *Crosscurrents in leadership* (pp. 225–238). Carbondale, IL: Southern Illinois University Press.

Eisenhardt, K. (1989). Agency theory: An assessment and review. *Academy of Management Review, 14*, 57–74.

Epstein, S. (1979). The stability of behavior I: On predicting most of the people most of the time. *Journal of Personality and Social Psychology, 37*, 1097–1126.

Finkelstein, S., & Hambrick, D. C. (1990). Top-management-team tenure and organizational outcomes: The moderating role of managerial discretion. *Administrative Science Quarterly, 35*, 484–503.

Finkelstein, S., & Hambrick, D. C. (1996). *Strategic leadership: Top executives and their effects on organizations.* St. Paul, MN: West Publishing.

Gandossy, R., & Sonnenfeld, J. A. (2004). *Leadership and governance from the inside out.* San Francisco, CA: Wiley.

Gomez-Mejia, L. R. (1994). Executive compensation: A reassessment and future agenda. In: K. Rowland & J. Ferris (Eds), *Research in personnel and human resources management* (Vol. 12, pp. 161–222). Greenwich, CT: JAI Press.

Gray, S. R., & Cannella, A. A., Jr. (1997). The role of risk in executive compensation. *Journal of Management, 23*, 517–540.

Hambrick, D. C., & Abrahamson, E. (1995). Assessing managerial discretion across industries: A multi-method approach. *Academy of Management Journal, 38*, 1427–1441.

Hambrick, D. C., & Finkelstein, S. (1987). Managerial discretion: A bridge between polar views of organizational outcomes. In: L. L. Cummings & B. M. Staw (Eds), *Research in organizational behavior, 9* (pp. 369–406). Greenwich, CT: JAI Press.

Hambrick, D. C., & Mason, P. A. (1984). Upper echelons: The organization as a reflection of its top managers. *Academy of Management Review, 9*(2), 193–206.

Hayward, M. L. A., & Hambrick, D. C. (1997). Explaining the premiums paid for large acquisitions: Evidence of CEO hubris. *Administrative Science Quarterly, 42*, 103–128.

Hogan, R. (2006). *Personality and the fate of organizations.* Mahwah, NJ: Erlbaum.

Hogan, R., Curphy, G. J., & Hogan, J. (1994). What we know about leadership: Effectiveness and personality. *American Psychologist, 49*, 493–504.

Hogan, R., & Hogan, J. (1997). *Hogan development survey manual.* Tulsa, OK: Hogan Assessment Systems.

Hogan, R., & Hogan, J. (2001). Assessing leadership: A view from the dark side. *International Journal of Selection and Assessment, 9*, 40–51.

Hogan, R., & Kaiser, R. B. (2005). What we know about leadership. *Review of General Psychology, 9*, 169–180.

Hogan, R., Raskin, R., & Fazzini, D. (1990). The dark side of charisma. In: K. Clark & M. Clark (Eds), *Measures of leadership* (pp. 343–354). West Orange, NJ: Leadership Library of America.

Horney, K. (1950). *Neurosis and human growth.* New York, NY: Norton.

Isidore, C. (2005). Boeing CEO out in sex scandal. *CNN/Money.* Retrieved March 14, from http://money.cnn.com/2005/03/07/news/fortune500/boeing_ceo/

Jensen, M., & Meckling, W. (1976). Theory of the firm: Managerial behavior, agency costs and ownership structure. *Journal of Financial Economics, 3,* 305–360.

Judge, T. A., Bono, J. E., Ilies, R., & Gerhardt, M. W. (2002). Personality and leadership: A qualitative and quantitative review. *Journal of Applied Psychology, 87,* 765–780.

Judge, T. A., Ilies, R., & Colbert, A. E. (2004). Intelligence and leadership: A quantitative review and test of theoretical propositions. *Journal of Applied Psychology, 89,* 542–552.

Kaiser, R. B., & Kaplan, R. E. (2006). The deeper work of executive development. *Academy of Management Learning and Education, 5,* 463–483.

Kaplan, R., & Norton, D. (1996). *The balanced scorecard.* Boston, MA: Harvard Business School Press.

Kaplan, R. E. (1999). *Internalizing strengths: An overlooked way of overcoming weaknesses in managers.* Greensboro, NC: Center for Creative Leadership.

Kaplan, R. E., & Kaiser, R. B. (2003). Rethinking a classic distinction in leadership: Implications for the assessment and development of executives. *Consulting Psychology Journal: Research and Practice, 55,* 15–25.

Kaplan, R. E., & Kaiser, R. B. (2006). *The versatile leader.* San Francisco, CA: Pfeiffer.

Katz, D., & Kahn, R. L. (1978). *The social psychology of organizations* (2nd ed.). New York, NY: Wiley.

Kellerman, B. (2005). *Bad leadership: What it is. How it happens. Why it matters.* Cambridge, MA: Harvard Business School Press.

Kets de Vries, M. F. R., & Miller, D. (1985). Narcissism and leadership: An object relations perspective. *Human Relations, 38,* 583–601.

Leslie, J. B., & Van Velsor, E. (1996). *A look at derailment today.* Greensboro, NC: Center for Creative Leadership.

Malmendier, U., & Tate, G. (2005). CEO overconfidence and corporate investment. *Journal of Finance, 60,* 2661–2700.

McAdams, D. (1995). What do we know when we know a person?. *Journal of Personality, 63,* 365–395.

McCall, W. M., & Lombardo, M. M. (1983). *Off the track: Why and how successful executives get derailed.* Greensboro, NC: Center for Creative Leadership.

Mead, G. H. (1934). *Mind, self, and society.* Chicago, IL: University of Chicago Press.

Miller, D., Kets de Vries, M. F. R., & Toulouse, J. M. (1982). Top executive locus of control and its relationship to strategy-making, structure, and environment. *Academy of Management Journal, 25,* 237–253.

Mischel, W. (1968). *Personality and assessment.* New York, NY: Wiley.

Mischel, W. (1977). The interaction of person and situation. In: D. Magnusson & N. S. Endler (Eds), *Personality at the crossroads: Current issues in interactional psychology* (pp. 333–352). Hillsdale, NJ: Erlbaum.

Paulhus, D. L. (1998). Interpersonal and intrapsychic adaptiveness of trait self-enhancement. *Journal of Personality and Social Psychology, 74,* 197–1208.

Peterson, R. S., Smith, D. B., Martorana, P. V., & Owens, P. D. (2003). The impact of chief executive officer personality on top management team dynamics. *Journal of Applied Psychology, 88,* 795–808.

Sessa, V. I., Kaiser, R. B., Taylor, J. K., & Campbell, R. J. (1998). *Executive selection.* Greensboro, NC: Center for Creative Leadership.

Thomas, A. (1988). Does leadership make a difference to organizational performance? *Administrative Science Quarterly, 33,* 388–400.

Tosi, H. L., Katz, J., & Gomez-Mejia, L. (1997). Disaggregating the agency contract: The effects of monitoring, incentive alignment, and term in office on agent decision-making. *Academy of Management Journal, 40,* 584–602.

Tosi, H. L., Misangyi, V. F., Fanelli, A., Waldman, D. A., & Yammarino, F. J. (2004). CEO charisma, compensation, and firm performance. *Leadership Quarterly, 15,* 405–420.

Waldman, D. A., Ramirez, G. G., House, R. J., & Puranam, P. (2001). Does leadership matter? CEO leadership attributes and profitability under conditions of perceived environmental uncertainty. *Academy of Management Journal, 44,* 134–143.

Weiss, H. M., & Adler, S. (1984). Personality and organizational behavior. In: B. M. Staw & L. L. Cummings (Eds), *Research in organizational behavior 6* (pp. 1–50). Greenwich, CT: JAI Press.

Yammarino, F. J., & Dansereau, F. (2002). *Research in multi-level issues* (Vol. 1). New York, NY: Elsevier Science.

Zaccaro, S. J. (2001). *The nature of executive leadership.* Washington, DC: American Psychological Association.

Zaccaro, S. J., & Horn, Z. N. J. (2003). Leadership theory and practice: Fostering an effective symbiosis. *Leadership Quarterly, 14,* 769–806.

CHAPTER 11

VIRAL STRATEGIC LEADERSHIP AND ORGANIZATIONAL CONSEQUENCES: IS YOUR *HEALTHY* ORGANIZATION *SICK*?

Timo J. Santalainen and B.R. Baliga

ABSTRACT

This chapter focuses on "healthy-sick" organizations. We define them as those organizations that appear to be healthy to the outside world but are sick at their core. We identify and discuss, in detail, singular attributes of healthy-sick organizations and their path to failure. As senior organizational leaders are responsible for creating and maintaining the set of interactions that creates the healthy-sick phenomenon, our elaboration will necessarily focus on these leader(s). We conclude with a set of recommendations to mitigate the probability of organizations falling into the healthy-sick trap.

Consider the case of Omega,[1] an NGO[2] that governs – some would argue rules – an international sport. Omega was established shortly after World War II. Consistent with the spirit of its mandate to oversee and promote its sport, it was located in Switzerland, a country favored by many

Being There Even When You Are Not: Leading Through Strategy, Structures, and Systems
Monographs in Leadership and Management, Volume 4, 195–215
Copyright © 2007 by Elsevier Ltd.
All rights of reproduction in any form reserved
ISSN: 1479-3571/doi:10.1016/S1479-3571(07)04010-2

international organizations and NGOs for its political neutrality. For the first 30 years of its existence it operated out of a small office staffed by the president and his two secretaries, handling its affairs in a sedate, bureaucratic fashion, with emphasis on oversight and maintenance rather than growth. Aggressive growth became the mantra after the appointment of a new head – only the second one in Omega's history. Since his ascension in 1980, Omega's assets, annual income, and profits have grown 60-fold. Corporate and TV sponsorships for the next decade, valued in excess of US$140 million, have already been negotiated and signed. With this comfortable financial position, and more than 200 national organizations from five continents currently affiliated with it, Omega has become the envy of less successful international sports organizations.

By almost any conventional definition or metric, Omega appears to be an organization in the pink. But a close look at Omega reveals a different reality, a sort of wonderland where nothing is quite what it seems. A gaping chasm exists between corporate illusion and reality: Rather than focusing on organizational issues and concerns, Omega's organization and its members concentrate primarily on serving the personal goals of the president. Anyone who is seen as a threat to Omega's way of functioning or a challenge to the authority of the president or his inner circle is immediately ousted. With each passing day, organizational members' perception of reality becomes more and more distorted owing to the president's insistence on controlling, exclusively, all key (political and corporate) contacts with the outside world and member interactions. The president's control of member interactions is so complete that organizational members are forbidden from leaving Omega's premises for meetings without express consent. If this were not enough, to further control the behavior of organizational members, the president has instituted policies, rules, and regulations that are so complex that it would be all but impossible for any member to strictly adhere to them and function effectively. Organizational members who find themselves in the president's bad books quickly realize that his interpretation of the rules and regulations is fluid enough that no matter what they do their actions can be – and usually are – defined as "wrong." Not surprisingly, these interpretations create confusion, disorientation, and physical stress (Kinicki, McKee, & Wade, 1996); erode organizational members' psychological states of autonomy, competence, and social worth (Ryan & Deci, 2000); and diminish their ability to thrive (Spreitzer, Sutcliffe, Dutton, Sonenshein, & Grant, 2005).

When stress becomes unbearable, organizational members who have options leave Omega. Those who choose to stay quickly realize that their ability to survive depends on their ability to play their assigned role in various organizational games that are initiated by the president to boost his power and influence. Street-smart players quickly realize that the super-ordinate objective of every game is to stoke the president's image and vociferously support his ever-changing positions. As few competent people are willing to play such games over an extended period of time, resignations and departures are frequent, diminishing Omega's ability to attract top talent. Consequently, Omega's pool of competence becomes shallower and shallower as do its adaptive capabilities.

How does one characterize Omega – an organization whose internal competencies and adaptive capabilities are being eroded even as its current performance, by almost any output metric, is stellar? While most outside observers would characterize Omega as a "healthy, high-performance or-ganization," most insiders would characterize Omega as a "sick" organi-zation. Reflecting this duality and recognizing the fact that the long-term viability of the organization is under threat,[3] we prefer the oxymoronic label "healthy-sick" to refer to such organizations.

THE DYNAMICS OF SICK ORGANIZATIONS

Fig. 1 traces the path leading to organizational sickness.

Viral leaders set in motion *viral dynamics* by playing organizational games designed to reinforce their power, improve their standing and image, and create a culture of sycophancy. Such behaviors are difficult for competent and/or ethical organizational members to stomach and those who have op-tions leave the organization, reducing its adaptive capability. As long as it appears to be healthy and performing "well," there is little incentive for any of the stakeholders to intervene in organizational functioning.

Over a period of time organizational performance starts dropping because of declining organizational adaptability. Rather than deal with the root causes of performance decline, leaders see the decline as a potential threat to their survival. They start engaging in a preemptive strategy, nominally to save the organization but in reality to preserve their position. This pre-emptive strategy often involves reinterpretation of organizational rules and regulations to reinforce their power and authority, shadow boxing – pursuit of imaginary critics – and building up sycophants to ensure protection from challenges by competent organizational members. If the preemptive strategy is successful it causes an even greater exodus of competent members. This exodus further isolates the leaders from reality, leading to further decreases

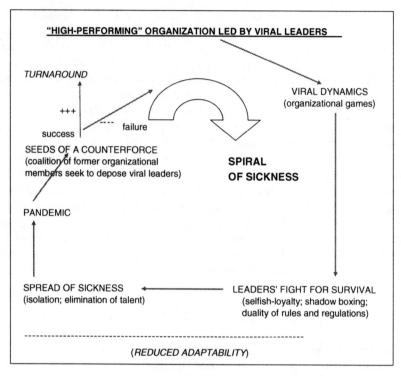

Fig. 1. The Dynamics of "Healthy-Sick" Organizations.

in adaptability. This creates a pandemic which encourages previously frustrated stakeholders (competent members who have quit the organization and others concerned with the growing sickness) to create a countervailing force to challenge the machinations of the viral leaders. If the countervailing force succeeds in deposing viral leaders it leads to organizational turnaround. If it fails, the organization descends into a spiral of sickness, with all the attendant dynamics, until a new counterforce emerges.

In the following sections of the chapter we identify and discuss, in detail, singular attributes of healthy-sick organizations and their path to failure. As we will show, there is no one distinctive element that characterizes a healthy-sick organization; rather it is a set of elements acting in concert. We utilize fine-grained data from Omega for explicatory purposes and complement these with insights from other healthy-sick organizations. We conclude with a set of recommendations for organizations to mitigate the probability of falling into the healthy-sick trap.

SINGULAR ATTRIBUTES OF HEALTHY-SICK ORGANIZATIONS

Viral Leaders: The Master Puppeteers

Healthy-sick organizations are characterized by senior leaders,[4] particularly the CEO, who have a strong negative influence on the long-term viability of the organization. We label such leaders as *viral leaders* because they infect the organization with a sickness which, if left unchecked, ultimately leads to its demise. Our notion of viral leaders is somewhat different from the notion of *toxic leader* developed by Frost (2003) in that the organizational impact of the toxic leader is rather immediate, whereas that of the viral leader becomes evident only with the passage of time. We hypothesize that given the greater visibility and impact of the toxic leader, developing an antidote for dealing with his or her negative impact is likely to be easier than for the viral leader.

Viral leaders are often *charismatic leaders who have become destructively narcissistic*. While a certain amount of *productive narcissism* (Maccoby, 2000) is invaluable in reinforcing leadership effectiveness in terms of creating visions, acquiring resources, and pushing through significant changes, being too narcissistic can be detrimental to the organization. Overly narcissistic or viral leaders essentially see themselves as being either "beyond" their organizations or utterly indispensable to their organization's success (Emmons, 1987). They use organizational resources to reinforce their narcissism and see *organizational members as puppets* to be exploited for their pleasure. As puppet masters, they have an elevated sense of vanity and do everything to be front and center and are unwilling to let anyone else share the limelight. For instance, the president of Omega did his utmost to feed his narcissism by creating a larger-than-life image of himself. He did this through skillful manipulation of images of his public appearances. Media and promotional activities such as meetings with heads of state, cabinet ministers and VIPs were used relentlessly to build up his image, increase his prestige, and create more opportunities for interaction with the rich and famous.

A favorite tactic was to publicize photos of himself being greeted by world leaders and corporate CEOs. Another image-boosting technique was his acquisition of "honorary" degrees and then lording it over people who had legitimately earned their degrees.

He was also prone to creating a scene when he considered some public events or actions were below the level he was entitled to. A vivid example of such behavior was his cancellation of his papal appointment when he found out that the meeting was not going to be televised. On another occasion he rejected a limousine that had been sent to meet him at the airport as it was not a Mercedes – which was the only car that befitted his status. Another example was his constant dissatisfaction with hotel suites reserved in advance; "the president" always wanted "something better." The embarrassment that this caused his hosts was clearly of no concern to him. What mattered most was that he be received and honored in a manner befitting his status as head of an international sports body.

Viral leaders consistently demonstrate *willful arbitrariness*, which they use to keep organizational members on tenterhooks and to reinforce their own invincibility and power. Not surprisingly, such arbitrary actions create significant paranoia in organizational members. Omega's president, for example, was very active on the "firing front" – firing people routinely on the faintest of pretexts. Committee assignments and their functioning were also handed out in an arbitrary manner. If a particular committee was functioning effectively, the president would often choose to disband the committee or minimize its importance. This was particularly true when these committees were headed by individuals who were considered a threat. For instance the lead member of a team that was working on some new developmental initiatives for Omega and had apparently done an excellent job was fired an hour before he was to make his presentation to Omega's board.

Probably the most harmful characteristic of viral leaders is their *demand for blind obedience and a marked intolerance for criticism*. Despite repeatedly assuring organizational members that Omega had an open culture and that he welcomed criticism, the president immediately punished anyone who criticized any initiative or action he had proposed. On one vivid occasion when an Australian member of parliament was critical of some of Omega's actions, the president's wife grabbed his microphone and threatened to throw him out of the meeting if he continued to make such remarks.

Though such demands for blind obedience certainly reinforce the leader's feelings of invincibility, it rapidly disconnects the organization from reality. It creates and reinforces a culture of rampant self-delusion where problems are pushed under the carpet and members who call for critical evaluations and changes in organizational strategies and/or actions are labeled "disruptive" and silenced. Over time, this decreases the organization's adaptive capabilities which, in turn could lead to its demise (Lubit, 2002).

Organizational Games

Healthy organizations have a clear strategic intent (Hamel & Prahalad, 1996). Organizational members focus their energy on this and rarely, if ever, engage in disruptive games or behaviors. In contrast, unhealthy organizations are characterized by an absence of a clear strategic intent and superordinate goals, creating opportunities for organizational members to push their own agendas. In the case of Omega, given that almost all of its media offerings had been "presold" and the organization was already the apex body in its sport, it was difficult – if not impossible – to create meaningful strategic intents, though vague ones such as "Being a leading business type NGO" were constantly being bandied about.

Consistent with Morf and Rhodewalt (2001), the president filled the strategic intent vacuum with the goal of bolstering his own prestige and standing and exploiting organizational resources to do so. Organizational members, in turn, used the president's personal goals to initiate and play *organizational games* designed to push their own agendas. One popular game at Omega was to curry favor with the president by generating proposals that ostensibly were substantive but were really designed to get into his good books by making him look good. One such proposal was to create and strengthen ties with academic institutions, an idea that had nothing to offer Omega as an organization but did give the president an opportunity to increase his standing among his peers and credibility as a successful leader.

A common tactic employed by viral leaders is to engage in games that, on the surface, are designed to boost the perception that the organization is well run and effective but at a deeper level are designed to gain "control" over organizational members and other stakeholders so that they could never be a threat to the leader. This game was played brilliantly by Jeff Skilling at Enron – the epitome of a healthy-sick organization. Over his entire career Skilling ensured that the "performance" of his division was consistently "excellent" and used this not only to boost his image but also to ensure that questions regarding his activities or those of his division were never raised (McLean & Elkind, 2003).

Another common game in healthy-sick organizations is to weaken the governance mechanisms and usurp control systems generally by coopting the key person(s) involved in the control function – the CFO/treasurer and, in some cases, members of the board of directors. Recent corporate scandals at Tyco, WorldCom and Adelphia were all characterized by the cooption of CFOs in cooking the books (Colvin, 2004). Omega's president also sought to contain his CFO/treasurer by providing him with significant perks such as an apartment in Omega's luxury villa, unlimited first-class travel, and a percentage of the commission that the president took when he signed long-term media deals. Under these circumstances the treasurer was only too happy to create fake transactions to cover up the president's shenanigans.

The negative effects of such organizational games are not too evident to outsiders until the underlying sickness becomes so great that it cannot be covered up by apparently healthy performance. When this happens, stake-holders lose faith in the organization and it begins its downward spiral. This creates substantial uncertainty for organizational members who, seeing their very survival at stake, initiate the blame game even going to the extent of challenging the president, a situation that Omega encountered recently. When this happened the president initiated a counter-game to gain control of the organization by using perks and promises to "retain or buy the loyalty" of members who were threatening to rebel.

Viral leaders are not afraid of playing games with any stakeholder, in-ternal or external. Omega's president obtained great media coverage by pledging to pay $3 million to the UN for rebuilding schools and sports facilities destroyed in the 2004 Indian Ocean tsunami. However, the NGO never followed through on the pledge because of "internal power games at the organization," referring to illegal gains accusations made by a national board member against the president (discussed below).

Selfish-Loyalty

Healthy-sick organizations are characterized by a culture of sycophancy. Sycophants strive to be in close physical proximity to the leader, praising his or her every position and action. In return the leader is generous in re-warding and promoting them, i.e. becomes a sycophant in return. Not sur-prisingly, such rewards and promotions continue only as long as the leader does not perceive these sycophants to be a threat. Thus, each party is loyal to the other, only as long as each party gains something from the other – a phenomenon we term *selfish-loyalty*. Organizational actions are designed to convey and reinforce this loyalty. For example, newly elected members of Omega's executive board were asked to step in front of the president and swear an oath of "fidelity, loyalty, and integrity" in front of the delegates of the Congress. Organizational members were constantly reminded that microphones and/or cameras could be installed in employees' offices for random loyalty checks. Employees were also discouraged from interacting with each other, presumably because they could plot against the president.

As the following example from Omega illustrates, leaders can act aggressively to deal with perceived disloyalty: A high-performing employee, who had recently resigned from Omega following disagreements with the president, had invited selected board members to a small farewell party. The president, upon learning of this party, communicated to the invitees that the ex-employee had been a poor performer and disloyal to Omega. Following this message none of the board members had the guts to accept the invitation. They were all worried about appearing disloyal and falling out of favor with the president!

The primary reward for sycophants was psychological rather than monetary: Omega's president made a point of publicly thanking sycophants for their "excellent" contributions and pointedly ignored the real contributions made by competent organizational members. Sycophants were always given attractive assignments irrespective of whether they were competent or not. When the sycophants failed to deliver, the competent people were made to take the fall. Ironically, the inability to get these assignments done did not matter much in terms of organizational performance, given the substantial organizational slack. They did, however, serve to demonstrate that it was valuable to be on the right side of the president.

Shadow Boxing

An interesting characteristic of healthy-sick organizations is the manner in which the leaders seek to keep key organizational members off balance by creating "enemies" both inside and outside the organization. Business media and government agencies are often labeled the "enemy," particularly if the leader and/or other senior managers interpret media and governmental reports as being overly critical. Likewise "threatening" organizational members are targeted as the "enemy" for being "disloyal." Such enemies provide the pretext for the leader and his or her group to take action against the "enemies" and deal with a "crisis of confidence," a crisis that can easily be escalated to monumental proportions if the leader finds his or her power base threatened. Even though dealing with these "enemies" and "crises" dissipates large amounts of organizational energy, by engaging in and controlling the game, the leader can demonstrate "commitment to the organization and its welfare."

In Omega's case, journalists, current and former organization members, other international organizations, and even governments were typical targets of shadow boxing when they were perceived as being hostile to the interests of Omega and/or the president. In order to show that he meant business, the president filed libel lawsuits against some Italian journalists who criticized his actions. Likewise, when a national board member accused the president of acting inappropriately, Omega filed lawsuits against this member with the primary intention of silencing him.

Duality of Rules and Regulations

A characteristic feature of sick organizations is *duality of rules and regulations* – duality in the sense that viral leaders see themselves as being above organizational policies, rules, and regulations even as they seek to selectively impose them on other members of the organization. Clearly what is good for the goose is not good for the gander. Moreover, as stated earlier, policies and rules are often interpreted in such a manner as to punish organizational members who challenge the leader and reward personnel who are in his or her good books.

Healthy-sick organizations also demonstrate an ability to create and interpret policies in such a way that leaders can never be challenged. Often serious challenges to the organization's leadership and functioning are deflected under cover of vague policies or by challenging the challenger's interpretation of these policies. Such selective usage is consistent with the Czech proverb, "If you want to hurt a dog you can always find a stick."

An excellent example of such selective use of rules is evident at Omega. The NGO had drawn up an extensive set of rules, including a code of conduct governing its activities and the activities of its affiliates. In winter 2002, the Swiss press reported that a national member of Omega's executive board had been "initially suspended and then expelled from all positions in sports worldwide due to violations of statutes and regulations of Omega." Ironically, this action was taken after the member in question had filed a criminal complaint accusing Omega's president, his wife (incidentally on Omega's payroll without any formal position) and the general manager of falsifying documents connected with the Sports World Congress 2002, and of buying for Omega, at a significant premium, a villa owned by the president's wife. To compound the irony, a couple of days after the Swiss police had seized documents pertaining to the charges laid by this board member, Omega's general manager was reported to have made a presentation to the sports community on Omega's code of conduct, strict rules governing the behavior of Omega's members, financial and operational transparency, and its excellent ethical behavior. Clearly, the viral leader and his spouse were beyond these!

Given the threat to his legitimacy posed by the board member's accusations, Omega's president successfully orchestrated, at the next international congress, a vote of "no confidence" and expelled the board member who had blown the whistle. The majority of the congress delegates, who owed their position and privilege to Omega's president, accepted "an analysis and explanation of the facts at the core of misleading claims made by the expelled board member." The delegates also accepted that claims about the falsified accounts were wrong and approved "a new way of presenting accounts and commissions in the interest of greater transparency." Ironically all these resolutions were orchestrated by the president before judgment was passed by the various independent judicial bodies investigating the board member's accusation of misappropriation of funds. To top off this stellar performance, the president proposed and gained approval for several amendments to Omega's code of conduct. "Our Code must be respected at all levels of our sport, and if we discover breaches of the Code, we must investigate them fairly and thoroughly, and not be afraid to take any necessary measures even though it may affect our image," declared the president without any embarrassment whatsoever.

This duality of rules and regulations is also used to drive political/hidden agendas that have absolutely no relationship to the functioning of the organization, i.e. the specific decisions made and actions undertaken are justified as being consistent with the policies, rules, and regulations of the organization. For example, at Omega, the president justified taking a significant percentage of corporate sponsorship revenues as his personal commission, claiming that "the rules provide for this" even though there were no such rules in place. In fact, the "Rule on Commissions" was passed and made effective retroactively when it was brought to the president's attention that his receipt of commissions could be considered illegal!

Isolation

Healthy-sick organizations minimize members' boundary-spanning activities, as they fear that such openness could expose their sickness. They do this by minimizing member interactions and, as noted earlier, restricting contacts that organizational members can have outside the organization. The net result is *isolation*. Omega, for example, went so far as to restrict organizational members' (be they employees or trustees) ability to interact with friends inside or outside the organization even in their own time. If the president heard that anyone had violated this norm, he or she was *persona non grata* for an extended period of time.

Long-term partnerships, other than those reinforced by personal gains of top leaders, are also hard for healthy-sick organizations to establish and manage. If partners perceive the organization to have healthy-sick characteristics they are quick to withdraw from the relationship. In the case of Omega its auditors, PricewaterhouseCoopers, resigned soon after lawsuits concerning falsified accounts were filed.

Viral leaders also leave organizations with which they are affiliated if they fear exposure. This is well illustrated in the "voluntary" retirement of Omega's president from the International Olympic Committee (IOC) following his interrogation by IOC's Ethics Committee on accusations that he had misused IOC money. "Voluntary" retirement took place only a couple of days before it would have been required by the Ethics Committee. Even here Omega's president skillfully reversed the course of history for his own benefit. He said that he was leaving because he was disappointed with IOC's work morale. This was applauded by his blinded followers at Omega.

Elimination of Talent

The apparent health (from the outside) of a healthy-sick organization attracts competent people to the organization at the outset. When they discover how sick the organization is, they face a dilemma – leave the organization, or stay and start engaging in a sycophantic relationship with the viral leaders. Those who choose to engage in sycophantic behavior, i.e. those whose competencies are complemented by a measure of insecurity and desire for power and prestige, are well rewarded in terms of ego-boosting positions and titles. For example, Omega developed its own system of titles. The president insisted on being addressed as "Doctor" immediately after assuming his position, despite the fact that his doctorate was honorary and not earned. Members who were favored by the viral leader were also designated as "Doctors" even if they did not possess a doctoral degree. People who had fallen out of favor, even those who had earned a doctorate, were addressed as "Mister" – or only their last name was used to downgrade their non-Omega related achievements and emphasize their lowly status in the eyes of the viral leader. "Real" doctors never became "Omega doctors."

Seating arrangements at public functions were also designed to indicate the "closeness" of organizational members to the viral leader. Falling out of favor was invariably signaled by a change in seating arrangements, and if one was nowhere on the seating chart it was a clear signal of banishment. As a result of these actions, it was always possible to gauge one's standing with respect to the viral leader.

Viral leaders also use "transactional calculus" to buy "loyalty" with money and perks. Thus members who liked to travel were provided business class tickets and five star hotel stays in exchange for their fealty to the leader. Other members' loyalty was bought by giving them "spending money" when they attended Omega meetings or by providing "scholarships" for their children to study abroad. The "scholarships" were much favored by Omega members from third world countries. In exchange for these scholarships these members were willing to throw their support behind the viral leader without examining the rightness of their position. Competent organizational members who perceived such actions as being inequitable left at the first available opportunity. The net result was the reinforcement of mediocrity.

Viral leaders also manipulate *succession plans* to ensure that their protégés are selected over more qualified persons. Such actions not only project the viral leader's power and reinforce the culture of sycophancy but also ensure that he or she can continue to manipulate key decisions from behind the scene. There is another benefit to this mode of succession: It ensures that prior machinations and illegal or unethical actions undertaken by the viral leader are not exposed. Numerous examples of this can be seen in the functioning of global NGOs (the IOC, for example) where people without any real expertise, often from third world nations, are elected to key positions to ensure that the viral leader can continue to project and perpetuate his or her agenda. Ironically, while benefiting personally from such appointments, viral leaders skillfully use them to signal to the world that the organization and its leadership are "non-discriminatory" and truly open to all.

Overall, viral leaders do not tolerate competent, strong performers; they do not allow others to "shine." Such leaders *eliminate talent* if they suspect that it is a threat – real or imaginary – to their leadership.

Creating a Pandemic

Viral leaders invariably spread their virus through the organization. In short order the organization has a cadre of infected members – viral members – who in turn spread the sickness. They create a *pandemic* by spreading the virus through their active support of viral leaders and becoming complicit in questionable activities. A truly alarming situation – from the standpoint of

1

TIMO J. SANTALAINEN AND B.R. BALIGA

the organization's long-term viability – arises when several viral members combine to generate negative synergy – synergy that leads the organization into a downward spiral of destruction. When such a spiral is set in motion, it reinforces the hand of senior viral leaders who intervene to "correct" the situation. Rather than correcting the situation, the viral nature of their intervention only serves to exacerbate the downward spiral. Ironically, people on the outside who are not privy to the internal organizational dynamics may incorrectly perceive that the leader is on top of the situation.

A recent example of such a pandemic took place at Computer Associates – the world's largest software support company. Charles Wang and Sanjay Kumar, the chairman and president respectively, set in motion a series of "false sales," in order to improve the firm's reported performance. Rather than objecting to such moves, people at lower levels widely and actively supported them. When rumors of the irregularities started to surface in the business press and questions were raised about the long-term viability of the organization, Wang and Kumar engaged in a very public process to demonstrate their leadership and signal to the stakeholders that they were on top of the very situation that they had created in the first place (*Newsday*, April 22, 2004, p. A44).

A Growing Cadre of Frustrated Former Affiliates

A major fallout (generally unacknowledged by viral leaders) from casting off competent/high-performing employees and other affiliates is that these people could communicate a "true" picture of the organization to external constituents, i.e. *a growing cadre of frustrated former allies may become a major counterforce.* As such a counterforce could clearly endanger the organization's legitimacy and survival, viral leaders go to great lengths to discredit former employees and affiliates, even resorting to lawsuits to undermine their credibility. The problem with such lawsuits is that they can backfire, especially if the defendants are able to work together to demonstrate, accurately and clearly, the sickness pervading the organization. However, it is difficult to coordinate the actions of the various parties involved, as evidenced by the trouble the expelled board member had in obtaining widespread support for his efforts to expose Omega's president's ill-gotten gains.

In some instances, viral leaders even fear "normal" departures (retirement, for example), particularly if the person knows of some of the leader's shenanigans. In such instances, viral leaders do their utmost to bind the "departing" people to the organization. Such was the case at Omega upon the retirement of the treasurer, a person intimately familiar with the financial manipulations of the president. Fearful that the treasurer would spill the beans, the president "hired" him back as a "special advisor" within a year of his retirement.

ALTERNATIVE SCENARIOS TO SICKNESS

Our discussion up to this point raises two fundamental questions: (1) Why do organizations move down the path from healthy to healthy-sick and ultimately sick? (2) Can organizations moving down this path be identified in a timely manner so that corrective action can be taken? We postulate that either of the two scenarios discussed below – the "easy life scenario" or the "extreme-stretch scenario" – could lead to the type of sickness discussed above.

In the "easy life scenario," the focal organization resides in a relatively munificent environment in terms of obtaining resources and disposing of its output. As long as the environment remains like this there is no real pressure for change or renewal as strong organizational performance is almost guaranteed, despite any action or inaction by the leader. Several public, non-governmental, and other international organizations as well as dominant firms enjoy resource-rich environments. As a result, leaders enjoy significant organizational slack to pursue their own interests using the organization's resources. Activities and actions designed for "the good life" supplant work-related challenges, with the organizational slack shielding them from scrutiny. With declining board and stakeholder oversight, leaders tend to become even more overt in acting for personal gain and developing a complex web of policies, rules, and regulations to protect their interests. They also grant themselves long tenures, or substantial payoffs (golden parachutes) in the event they are forced out. A munificent environment coupled with weak governance is a fertile field for seeds of viral leadership. Omega followed this path toward becoming healthy-sick. As the apex body of its sport (a sport with global interest and following), Omega benefited from the surge of interest in sports and corporate and media willingness to pay substantial sums of money to televise the games. Omega's president capitalized on this interest to sell global media rights for the next couple of decades, rights that generated substantial sums for Omega and provided it with considerable organizational slack.

At the opposite end of the spectrum is the "extreme-stretch scenario." Organizations in this scenario face a very hostile environment and there is strong pressure on management to deliver results in a relatively short period of time, for example to please Wall Street in the US (Berenson, 2003). This pressure generates and reinforces a "perform at all costs" mentality in organizational leaders, which spreads rapidly to the rest of the organization. This virus is so powerful that it generates a culture of self-interest in its wake, which is justified as "just compensation for coping with the enormous pressures." Enron exemplified this phenomenon by employing practices such as market-to-market accounting to create a perception of performance that was totally unrelated to reality. Organizational members who went along with such practices were praised for their "efforts and performance" and richly rewarded. The self-interest culture became so ingrained that 25 senior executives had no hesitation in awarding themselves a bonus of $55 million the week before Enron declared bankruptcy (McLean & Elkind, 2003).

These two scenarios suggest that extremely munificent or extremely hostile environments are most likely to lead to sickness, with intermediate levels of environmental munificence creating more healthy and stable organizations. Though both scenarios ultimately lead to sickness, we hypothesize that the "extreme-stretch scenario" leads to sickness more rapidly than the "easy-life scenario," where pressure for performance and scrutiny is reduced because of the considerable organizational slack.

While a sick organization is relatively easy to discern in retrospect, it is relatively difficult to identify in time to be able to deal with it. A good example of this is the Catholic Church in the US, which had all the attributes of a healthy-sick organization – sick at its core even as it performed yeomen service in social work, education, and health and enjoyed considerable standing in the community. Had symptoms of its "real" sickness been surfaced and identified earlier, it is conceivable that corrective action could have been taken before the very survival of the organization was placed in jeopardy. Clearly, indicators of inherent organizational sickness would be invaluable from a governance and management perspective.

We can summarize our discussion in Fig. 2 utilizing the 2×2 organizational leadership organizational performance matrix discussed below.

If a healthy-sick organization is not diagnosed, it is only a matter of time before it follows path A, i.e. becomes a dying organization. Clearly turning a dying organization around calls for radical surgery and tends to be extremely painful and expensive and will happen only with a change in the viral leader. This is clearly the path along which both Enron and WorldCom are moving – a path that has led to significant downsizing and loss in shareholder value and the replacement of their viral leaders by new leaders

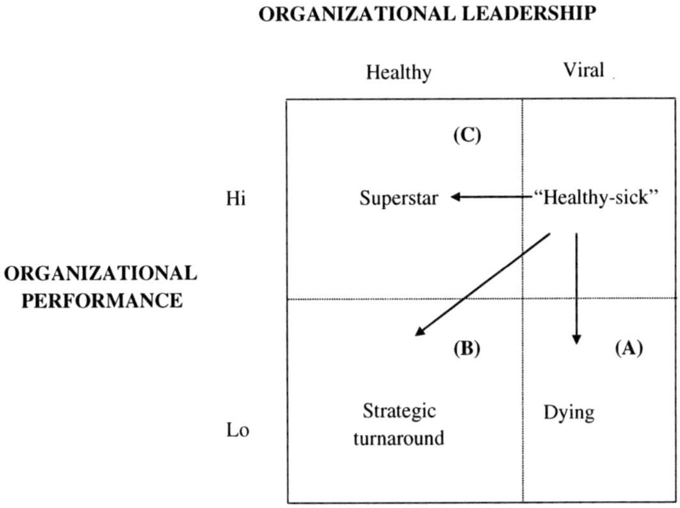

ORGANIZATIONAL LEADERSHIP

Healthy　　　　　　　Viral

Fig. 2. Four Alternative Performance Trajectories.

who have to deal with a messy situation expeditiously. Path B where a healthy-sick organization moves into a strategic turnaround phase is certainly preferable to path A, but this requires viral leaders to be removed before the organization is on its death bed. As discussed earlier, a national board member attempted to redirect Omega along the turnaround path, but these efforts were thwarted by the viral leader and the member expelled. Consequently, Omega could not be deviated from its path toward demise.

When Omega's president was battling legal problems arising from the deposed national board member's allegations, he consistently spoke about his impending retirement and his desire to pick a successor. Following his success in deflecting these charges, all talk of retirement and succession ceased. It is our contention that, given his narcissism, he will continue to hold on to his position even if has to buy loyalty and change the rules to do so.

As Omega continues to possess considerable organizational slack and the viral leader has been able to contain rebellious tendencies by buying loyalty, it is unlikely to die any time soon. Rather, the failure of the national board member and his supporters to oust him is likely to have emboldened Omega's president to be even more viral in his actions and behaviors.

In Fig. 2, we have also shown a path – path C – indicating a move from healthy-sick toward becoming a "superstar." While this is certainly a theoretical possibility, we deduce that the probability of this happening in reality is extremely low as this would take (1) a radical self-transformation on the part of the viral leader or (2) a coordinated uprising from organizational stakeholders to depose the viral leader – an act that is extremely difficult to pull off when the organization's nominal performance is excellent.

An interesting issue is whether it is possible for parts of healthy-sick organizations to be truly healthy? In our judgment this is feasible if and only if the part is reasonably well isolated from the viral dynamics. Geographically distant or peripheral parts of little strategic interest to the viral leader could certainly fall into this category. However, even these "healthy" parts are likely to become infected if the viral leader is in a leadership position for a sufficiently long time.

CAN HEALTHY-SICK ORGANIZATIONS BE PREVENTED?

Given the difficulties involved in nursing a healthy-sick organization to health, it would be better overall for an organization never to fall into the healthy-sick trap. How does one prevent such a phenomenon from occurring? In our judgment, an organization becomes healthy-sick when the *governance role is usurped by the viral leader and his cronies.* Preventing such usurpation is thus the key. This can be done by

(1) *Restricting the tenure of top officials to a predetermined period with no extensions permitted.* Though this appears to be a relatively simple rule, it is routinely violated in NGOs where the top officials are elected rather than appointed. For instance, in the case of Omega though rules restricted the president's tenure to two consecutive four-year terms, the restriction was easily manipulated by the president with support from organizational members whose loyalty had been bought. Omega's president got these members to amend the by-laws arguing that "if any president happened to have an exceptionally good performance during his first and second terms he can be elected for a third term." Following his reappointment to the third term, the president managed to postpone the next scheduled election by two years, arguing that "a new strategy was in the process of being implemented and that a change in leadership would be disruptive to strategy implementation." Following this delay, he got himself reelected again, stating that "the new strategy

implementation was in a delicate stage and since he had created the strategy he should be responsible for implementing it." The irony was that there was no new strategy to implement! He continued in this vein, getting reelected over and over again. After 14 years of viral leadership nobody appeared to remember that a rule restricting his reelection existed.

(2) *Ensuring that the board is truly independent of organizational leaders.* This requires that the board be comprised solely of people with high levels of integrity and true independence. This provides checks and balances and ensures that the machinations of viral leaders are checked before they create a pandemic. Had such a system been in place, the excesses at Omega would never have happened. Unfortunately, from a governance point of view, the board was stacked with people who were indebted to Omega's president in one way or another. Hence they were unable to exercise independent judgment and keep his viral leadership in check.

(3) *Strengthening board governance further by appointing activist "lead-directors"* – knowledgeable people of impeccable integrity – who have the time, energy and willingness to question management actions without fear of retribution or loss of status (Baliga, Moyer, & Rao, 1996).

(4) *Requiring transparency in finances and compensation and setting clear compensation rules.* If there is the slightest doubt about whether accounts are being massaged or compensation rules being violated, a special audit should be carried out. In the case of private corporations it is particularly important that the board of directors pay particular attention to the creation of special entities, moving items off the balance sheet and setting up of multiple accounts when there does not appear to be a sound ethical business reason for doing so.

(5) *Pushing for international laws to govern NGOs.* Many NGOs (Formula 1, FIVB, and IOC, for example) have become sick because their actions do not fall strictly under the purview of any national law. It is imperative that corporations, institutions, and individuals who support these NGOs push for the creation of a set of international laws to ensure that such organizations do not fall victim to viral leaders because of lax legal oversight.

(6) *Encouraging and providing protection to whistle-blowers.* Generally the first ones to be aware of viral dynamics are organizational members. Their willingness to blow the whistle is increased if they are convinced that other stakeholders, both inside and outside the organization, will support them. This support is particularly critical given that the viral

leader can bring substantial organizational resources to bear to defend himself. It was this failure to gain support from sufficient stakeholders that meant that the national board member's efforts to expose Omega's president's viral leadership bore no fruit.

In spite of this, the expelled national board member has been seeking to create an alternative to Omega in its sport, a Nova Omega so to speak. He has succeeded in obtaining some support, but at the time of writing it is not certain whether he has sufficient moral and financial support to make it a reality. Furthermore, with the declining importance of the big global multimedia players owing to competing technologies for distribution of information, it is not clear whether the new organization will ever be able to sign a monetary contract of the type that Omega was able to do.

Despite the suggestions advanced above, we are not confident that the phenomenon of healthy-sick organizations can be avoided if the viral leader is extremely strong and is able to repeatedly deflect counterforces. This is precisely what has happened at Omega. Despite repeated promises to step down in 2006, after 26 years of tenure, Omega's president has decided to run again for the presidency. In our minds his reelection is a foregone conclusion, ensuring that Omega will continue to be stuck in the healthy-sick mode.

NOTES

1. Omega is a real organization. Omega's true identity is not being disclosed to protect the identities and interests of its members – members who provided crucial personal insights that serve as the basis of this chapter.
2. An NGO is a non-governmental organization. The Red Cross and Doctors without Borders are examples of NGOs, as are a number of sports organizations such as the International Olympic Committee.
3. Scholars working in the area of complex adaptive systems identify this characteristic as "declining fitness" (cf. Clippinger, J. H. (Ed.) (1999). *The biology of business*. San Francisco, CA: Jossey-Bass).
4. The term "leader" is used here to denote an individual's position in the organization without any reference to the individual's leadership qualities.

REFERENCES

Baliga, B. R., Moyer, R. C., & Rao, R. (1996). CEO duality and firm performance: What's the fuss?. *Strategic Management Journal, 17*, 41–53.
Berenson, A. (2003). *The number*. New York, NY: Random House.

Clippinger, J. H. (Ed.) (1999). *The biology of business: Decoding the natural laws of enterprise.* San Francisco, CA: Jossey-Bass.

Colvin, G. (2004). Why countries and companies need good cops. *Fortune, 149,* 172.

Emmons, R. A. (1987). Narcissism: Theory and measurement. *Journal of Personality and Social Psychology, 52,* 11–17.

Frost, P. J. (2003). *Toxic emotions at work.* Boston, MA: Harvard Business School Press.

Hamel, G., & Prahalad, C. K. (1996). *Competing for the future.* Boston, MA: Harvard Business School Press.

Kinicki, A. J., McKee, F. M., & Wade, K. J. (1996). Annual review, 1991–1995: Occupational health. *Journal of Vocational Behavior, 49,* 190–220.

Lubit, R. (2002). The long-term impact of destructive narcissistic managers. *Academy of Management Executive, 16,* 127–138.

Maccoby, M. (2000). Narcissistic leaders: The incredible pros, the inevitable cons. *Harvard Business Review, 78,* 68–77.

McLean, B., & Elkind, P. (2003). *Smartest guys in the room: The amazing rise and scandalous fall of Enron.* New York, NY: Portfolio Publishers.

Ryan, R. M., & Deci, E. L. (2000). Self determination theory and the facilitation of intrinsic motivation, social development and well being. *American Psychologist, 55,* 68–78.

Spreitzer, G., Sutcliffe, K., Dutton, J. E., Sonenshein, S., & Grant, A. M. (2005). A socially embedded model of thriving at work. *Organization Science, 16,* 537–549.

CHAPTER 12

THE POSITIVE DISCRETION OF LEADERSHIP: PROVIDING STRUCTURES FOR ORGANIZATIONAL TRANSFORMATION AND SUCCESS

Corey Billington and Michèle Barnett Berg

ABSTRACT

After a decade of continuous success within IQ, a $79.9 billion technology company, Duncan Covington faced one of his greatest career challenges. He was tasked with turning around a procurement organization that was underperforming, had a vacancy rate of 45%, and a tarnished internal reputation. Just five years earlier this same organization had been considered an outstanding contributor to the company and had received numerous awards and accolades. He used leadership discretion to redesign the organization and created six new structures to motivate and lead his staff to success: (1) value creation; (2) improving workgroup productivity; (3) succession planning; (4) long-term value for employees; (5) fee-for-service; and (6) contributing to innovation. By using these structures Covington was able to transform and restore the organization to a high performing and a contributing division within the company.

Being There Even When You Are Not: Leading Through Strategy, Structures, and Systems
Monographs in Leadership and Management, Volume 4, 217–227
Copyright © 2007 by Elsevier Ltd.
All rights of reproduction in any form reserved
ISSN: 1479-3571/doi:10.1016/S1479-3571(07)04011-4

The positive side of leader discretion allows for creating structures that offer people more benefit, choice, and value. When done correctly, people are empowered to contribute a greater effort and benefit from a greater freedom. The story of Duncan Covington and his experience at IQ[1] illustrates how Covington created and implemented six specific structures around the principles of value creation, improved workgroup productivity, succession planning, long-term value for employees, fee-for-service, and contributed to innovation to revitalize and turn around a failing organization. By creating the right processes and structures to support people in his organization, he effectively led and brought about change. His efforts illustrate how fostering structures that allow for choice and accountability can positively impact an underperforming organization with high turnover, low morale, and poor performance. Additionally, these six structures help leaders reorient and re-engineer their staff to their best professional level.

COVINGTON'S EXPERIENCE AT IQ

After almost a decade of continuous success within IQ, a global multibillion dollar provider of products, technologies, and customized solutions to small, medium, and enterprise clients, Duncan Covington was handed one of his greatest career challenges. He was selected to take over the central procurement services (CPS) group, which was underperforming and experiencing a number of problems. Covington had a reputation as a "fix-it guy," having turned around many low-functioning organizations during his tenure at IQ.

Five years earlier, CPS had been considered an outstanding contributor to the company. It had received numerous awards and accolades, including the coveted medal of excellence from *Purchasing* magazine. Its leadership had been greatly admired and internal departments had viewed the procurement team as high performing, providing good value, and helping the departments to meet their business objectives. However, at its pinnacle of success, the head of CPS left IQ to pursue a new opportunity and took several key staff with him. Due to the lack of leadership of the newly appointed successor, the organization lost its focus and direction and many employees left.

Furthermore, Covington was told that he would not receive additional resources or a budget increase. He was facing a vacancy rate of 45% and the group's morale was at an all-time low. Additionally, CPS's internal contribution was being widely disputed by the operating units, which were lobbying for the group to be disbanded and the parts spread over the five major operating groups of the company. Covington knew from experience that if procurement was totally decentralized, overall purchase costs would rise; the complexity and costs to suppliers, who sold to many parts of IQ, would substantially increase; product development would become slower and more difficult; and overall customer satisfaction would suffer. He was a fundamental believer in the power of collaboration and wanted to get this group back on track and highly functional before disbanding could become a reality.

Prior to taking over CPS, Covington had been managing IQ's corporate consulting organization, which included the usability labs, organizational design teams, supply chain strategy, and corporate marketing groups. He was responsible for 150 employees in three geographic locations – the United States, Germany, and Singapore. The additional responsibility of central procurement would add 600 more employees – geographically spread in 16 global locations – to his organization. At the same time as Covington was taking on this new role, IQ was spinning off one of its business units, which would result in a new organization that would be about 20% of IQ in size. This was relevant to CPS, as it created an additional distraction because many employees were interested in finding opportunities in the new organization.

USING LEADERSHIP DISCRETION TO DESIGN A NEW ORGANIZATION

For an organization to be socially viable and thrive it must serve its members.

This was Covington's mantra. He repeatedly told this to his managers and reminded them that their jobs were service oriented. Managers should serve those doing the work, and the most important role in the organization is that of the first-line supervisor. His doctrine was that people had choices and it was up to him and his management team to structure an organization where people wanted to be and where they felt they had choices and were empowered to be successful. He often asked his staff, "How well do you serve your people?" He believed that when people experience an organizational structure that offers them choice, provides support, and empowers them to be successful, they are motivated to follow its leadership. These structures should allow for financial objectives and results to be visible so that people understand their contribution and its overall impact on the organization. When Covington took over, he put in place the six structures – discussed in more detail below – to address the various issues of the organization and set it back on course.

Structure 1: Value Creation

Covington's first structure involved asking each department within CPS to create a charter, a strategic marketing plan, and a value delivery plan and to estimate its return on investment. Expectations were outlined, including the criterion that each department must have a 10×1 return of value creation relative to investment. Covington wanted his managers to understand the challenge of overhead and feel empowered to be creative and come up with new and better ways to reach their targets. He encouraged managers to take ownership and set direction using the structures he introduced, as success would bring them greater freedom.

By creating a collaborative mindset, he allowed his managers the flexibility to individualize their processes to reach their goals. Some departments needed to reduce expenses; others to define and increase their value contribution. Once the charter, strategic marketing, and value delivery plans were created, they would be reviewed on a quarterly basis in a document that was easy to update and follow. It was crucial that reviews took place, and Covington made this a top priority so that objectives stayed on course. Fig. 1 shows a sample charter.

Structure 2: Improving Workgroup Productivity

The second structure Covington used was with managers, getting them to commit to and work with their existing resources and develop their individual departments within CPS for better productivity and results. He delegated to his management team a method of keeping staff development constant and consistent. Managers were to work with all of their employees on professional development. In cases where employees were struggling, managers coded them red and those whose performance was good but should be great were coded blue. These coded segments received coaching and training from their direct managers and HR, and in addition, Covington and other senior managers within CPS committed a minimum of one hour a month to help develop them into better performers.

Covington's philosophy was that most problem employees were the result of a lack of management attention and if these situations were rectified their

VISION: CPS is the pre-eminent leader in the procurement services industry, providing competitively superior procurement services that create and enable trade revenue and profits for the IQ businesses and the communities we serve.

FY06 MISSION: Leverage CPS's assets and capabilities into *essential* procurement services and solutions for IQ's businesses.

CLIENT BASE:
• IQ Businesses
• Supply Chain Council
• Worldwide Supply Chain Operations
• Central Direct Procurement
• IQ Councils: Tax, Procurement, Planning, Logistics

GOVERNANCE: CPS is governed by the initiatives and needs of the IQ businesses as expressed through IQ's
- WWO Supply Chain Operations group
- Supply Chain Council (SCC),
- Businesses

SCOPE:
• Execute *buy-sell services* on behalf of IQ businesses enabling:
  - advantage pricing for IQ strategic commodities
  - IQ to leverage local tax laws
  - better assurance of supply
  - increased standardization in administration and application, where feasible.
• Establish and deploy an integrated, enterprise network of procurement and supply chain *IT solutions and services* that enable IQ's businesses and supply chain community to:
  - collaborate on PO, forecasting and supplier managed inventory
  - support sourcing and disposition of products and product material
  - consolidate and analyze material purchases and pricing data for improved planning and cycle times, cost reductions, and AOS.
• Provide *local supplier management and engineering services* that enable, for example:

Supplier Mgmt & Audits	Design Consulting & Support	Emerging Mkts/Bus. Devlpt
- regional balancing of inventory & local spot buys during material shortages	- supplier selection and qualification	- market intelligence, analysis and newsletters
- factory audits and supplier performance management	- technology roadmaps and prototype management	- country and market risk assessment
- effective escalation and resolution of local supplier engineering issues	- contract negotiation	- screening of new products and technologies
- engineering change mgmt.		

OPERATING PRINCIPLES:
• Provide only those services contracted by IQ businesses or SCC via Lev1-3 funding & MOUs.
• Offer one-stop access to all CPS service groups through an efficient account management infrastructure.
• Strive to connect CPS service value to IQ's external customers & share holders.

Fig. 1. CPS Sample Charter.

performance would improve by a measurable, visible change in the employees' performance. Covington subscribed to the theory of developing staff by taking ownership of their performance and success. He disagreed with the method of just firing one's lowest performers; instead he believed that with the right leadership, coaching, and training, performance would improve and lead to significant organizational change. His ultimate goal was to create a collaborative environment where everyone's involvement and effort would be for the greater good of the organization. These employees' codes were maintained in a confidential document, which was never e-mailed or distributed among staff, and Covington himself stored this information. The list was reviewed every six months, and ideally most employees would have improved their performances; if not, plans would then be made to remove them from the organization.

Creating Group Norms

Covington had used group norms as an effective tool in the past to get individuals to cooperate with one another and with the management. He had seen performance and output improve, as well as an increase in creativity and renewed commitment to innovation. He began to look externally and analyze what the business units actually wanted from CPS and started to address these needs by making certain organizational changes. It appeared that parts of CPS were duplicating their efforts, therefore not realizing any economies of scale. CPS had two engineering groups – one devoted to component quality and another to manufacturing quality. Covington made specific organizational changes such as combining teams that were doing the same type of work, but for different business units within IQ. He decided which services were better suited to being done by the internal organizations themselves and then transferred them to a specific group or division. After the changes, a list of norms (see Fig. 2) was created and distributed to all employees within CPS to hallmark their commitment to how they would treat each other and their customers.

Improved Hiring Practice

Covington felt that the group's processes should be supported by empirical evidence and that hiring was one of the most vital processes in any organization. He advised his managers that hiring should be viewed as their most valued investment, and he made the hiring process more predictive of success on the job.

Covington was influenced by research that showed that the classic interview process had little ability to predict success on the job. He wanted

1) COMMUNICATE PROACTIVELY

2) MAINTAIN INTEGRITY, BE HONEST AND DIRECT– CALL EACH OTHER ON

 NORMS VIOLATIONS

3) RESPECT ONE ANOTHER– EVERYONE'S OPINION IS EQUALLY IMPORTANT

4) TRUST FIRST, SEEK TO UNDERSTAND SECOND, AND ONLY THEN CHALLENGE

5) EVERYONE TAKES RESPONSIBILITY FOR BRINGING EVERYONE ALONG

6) AVOID THIRD-PARTY COMMUNICATIONS

7) MAKE DECISIONS RAPIDLY AND STICK BEHIND TEAM AND DECISIONS

Fig. 2. Group Norms for Central Procurement Services.

managers to be more strategic and investigative than just using typical and surface interviewing techniques. He challenged his staff to hire the people best able to do the job, not the ones that they thought were the nicest or who shared the same experience or education. Therefore, Covington asked each of his managers to include tests such as cases (mock examples) and role plays to improve the predictability of the hiring process on job success. The goal was to have job candidates prove in the interview that they had the specific and necessary skills to handle the position. This structured process helped managers better calibrate candidates and proved to be an effective hiring tool for better skill matching.

In order to ensure that this structure stayed intact, Covington attended case result presentations, which were held as a final step before making a job candidate an offer of employment. Also, before any new employee started, Covington would schedule time to meet with them or speak by phone. Managers knew that he expected to come away from these meetings impressed and without any doubts about hiring the person.

Structure 3: Succession Planning

As the organization was quite fractured, Covington saw the need to formulate long-term planning in addition to addressing the immediate structural and process changes. Covington had all of his managers prepare succession plans for their roles, even though they had no immediate plans to leave. He asked each manager to designate a "right hand" and "left hand" person on his/her staff. The "right hand" person was someone who could assume the manager's position and who was in the process of being groomed for such a role. Covington made it clear to the managers that they had to explicitly tell the named "right hand" person how valuable he/she was to the organization and share the professional opportunities that lay ahead for him/her. The designated "left hand" person was unlikely to be the manager's successor, played a vital role in the organization due to skill, historical knowledge, and/or interpersonal connection with other employees. Again managers were to communicate to the "left hand" person their importance and value and create a plan that would help keep them motivated and contributing. Besides improving retention and staff morale, this practice created an environment within CPS where employee contribution was discussed and solutions were found for potential succession issues, ensuring the organization would be better prepared and have more freedom to respond.

Structure 4: Long-Term Value for Employees

Covington wanted to change the reputation of his organization from being one full of dissatisfaction and high turnover to being a place that was career enhancing, where employees were developed and, when they did leave, it was for a better job. When he took over, the vacancy rate was 45%, an all-time high, and there was no structure or process in place to find out why people left and where they were going. Besides meeting personally with all employees who planned to leave his department, Covington empowered a trusted individual to conduct exit interviews. He wanted to capture data on what type of positions these employees were taking after leaving CPS. By gathering this information, managers were better informed on how best to motivate and develop their staff.

Covington set a benchmark of 80% as the desired percentage of people who should move on to better positions or promotions after they left CPS. The mindset of the organization began to evolve, as there was now an effort and interest in developing people to go on to better positions either internally or externally. This target was reached, and within 18 months of Covington taking over, the vacancy rate had fallen to almost 0%, with turnover among the lowest in the company.

Structure 5: Fee-For-Service

Covington's philosophy was that there was a direct link between CPS's budget and its customers – the profit and loss (P&L) organizations of IQ. In IQ, P&L accountability resided with the independent product organizations. He decided to revamp the cost structure of CPS. Previously, central procurement was a tax item on the product organizations' P&L statement. This had left many line executives grumbling that they were paying for services they deemed of little value and that they were being charged for things they did not use. The value was not transparent and no accountability was created.

In an attempt to change this, Covington decided to gamble that if CPS used a fee-for-service model instead of being an automatic tax item on the P&L statements, it could actually increase its budget ("revenues") while improving P&L "customer" satisfaction and impact the company's overall value and innovation. He structured new levels of service to be offered to P&L "customers" depending on their needs. "Fee-for-service" made CPS's value transparent, and the structure gave managers a high degree of accountability as they now had to successfully sell their services, and it gave the P&L organizations an option to buy only when they felt there was value. Covington used this structure to motivate his staff and reinforce the idea that there is no such thing as a "free lunch."

Testing "Fee-For-Service" in the Field
Since Covington completely changed the way CPS charged its customers, he wanted to go out into the field and discuss this new approach with them and get their reactions. Also, he needed to make sure that there would be enough business to keep his group viable. One of his earliest meetings was with Cameron Howe, the recently appointed head of IQ's test and measurement group. Howe's organization represented approximately 20% of IQ's total size and paid Covington's group around $7 million per year. Covington knew this would be a strategic meeting. If CPS could partner with this organization and rebuild its credibility, it would be that much easier to illustrate its value within the rest of IQ. Covington was prepared for the worst. He knew Howe had been very vocal on the internal debate of whether or not CPS should be disbanded; he was a fan of decentralized procurement.

As Covington expected, the meeting did not get off to a good start. Howe was frank:

> Bottom line, Covington, is that I am cutting our budget by 25% and making plans to completely cut the budget over the next four years. I am not satisfied with what your group does for us and I believe we can do it better on our own. There has been little value added, just cost and I intend to put an end to that.

Covington sat back in his chair and rather than making a quick exit, began to engage some of Howe's managers in discussion. He then spent the next three hours breaking down all the services that procurement had been providing Howe's team and had Howe's managers provide illustrated examples of where the partnering had helped them meet their objectives. Once Howe heard how his team actually needed CPS to do their jobs and learned more about what Covington was proposing, he retracted his 25% budget cut and eventually signed on for a 10% increase in services. Experiences like these became the model of how Covington wanted his team to structure the value they brought to internal customers. He emphasized that they needed to create a value system that was transparent not just a resource consumption system.

Structure 6: Contributing to Innovation

Besides trying to lead the organization back to health, Covington wanted to create a source of funding that would benefit his managers, provide staff protection, and spur innovation. This structure was called the Development Fund, to which all CPS managers contributed 2% of their budgets to participate. Covington knew if managers participated in this fund they would make smarter decisions when working with customers and not have the undue influence of revenue dependence or resource constraints. The fund would help provide budget stability in the new "fee-for-service" environment. Additionally, the Development Fund could be a source for those departments looking to try something new and innovative – the experimental projects which Covington strongly encouraged his staff to try. "You need to prove value everyday and there is no success if there is no possibility of failure," Covington said to his staff.

WINNING AGAIN

After four years, IQ's CPS was back on top and once again won the coveted *Purchasing* medal of excellence. This was a great feat not only because it marked the organization's turnaround but also because IQ was the only company ever to have won twice. By exercising positive discretion, Covington had established the six structures on the principles of value creation, improving workgroup productivity, succession planning, long-term value for employees, fee-for-service, and contributing to innovation, which would serve CPS not only in the short term but also for the future. Results were transparent and measurable, and the staff was motivated to follow leadership. During his tenure, vacancy rates fell to an all-time low and employees viewed experience with CPS as career enhancing. Credibility had been restored to the organization and value was being given to and acknowledged by P&L managers. Additionally, CPS was aiding in IQ's overall innovation – as a participant rather than a spectator.

NOTE

1. All names of individuals and companies are fictitious.

PART V: TRANSLATING THE LEADERSHIP OF ORGANIZATIONS INTO THE LEADERSHIP IN ORGANIZATIONS

One of the key questions leaders at the top face is how to get their vision for the organization implemented throughout the whole organization. Especially in large, geographically dispersed companies with diverse products and markets, such implementation requires careful consideration and attention as well as considerable local interpretation and adaptation. The challenge of cascading the vision down in a meaningful way while maintaining its intent is the focus of this chapter and the following two specific cases.

CHAPTER 13

CASCADING VISION FOR REAL COMMITMENT

John Antonakis and Robert Hooijberg

ABSTRACT

We explore how leaders get real commitment for their visions. We propose that leaders need to pay significant attention to and get broad involvement in three stages of the vision creation and dissemination process. First, they need involvement in the creation of the vision and buy-in from the senior levels. Second, when cascading the vision further down the organization, they need to allow for real discussion and input. Third, leaders need to seriously track and assess the impact of the vision implementation.

LEADING THROUGH VISION

When we talk about leading through vision, we find it important to clarify the key assumptions underlying our approach to leadership and what motivates followers. We believe that you need more than economic exchanges to motivate people to follow a vision. The notion of leadership through exchanges is strongly embedded in the economic-rational perspective (see Bass, 1985; Burns, 1978; Downton, 1973; Shamir, House, & Arthur, 1993). The economic-rational perspective looks at leadership from the basis of transactions and exchanges and assumes that followers react only to

Being There Even When You Are Not: Leading Through Strategy, Structures, and Systems
Monographs in Leadership and Management, Volume 4, 231–244
Copyright © 2007 by Elsevier Ltd.
All rights of reproduction in any form reserved
ISSN: 1479-3571/doi:10.1016/S1479-3571(07)04012-6

"carrots and sticks." The nature of the exchange (transaction) that occurs depends on the extent to which the players have lived up to their side of a particular deal.

Researchers have labeled this form of leadership "transactional leadership" and have shown that it works. However, research has also shown that it is less strongly related to outcome measures than are other forms of leadership based on vision, charisma or other emotional-based influencing processes (Lowe, Kroeck, & Sivasubramaniam, 1996). Furthermore, transactional leadership does not work well in equivocal situations and it is limited in terms of the commitment that it will induce in followers (Bass, 1985; Shamir, 1995; Shamir et al., 1993; Weber, 1947). Research on motivation highlights one of the reasons that transactional leadership does not show as strong an impact on outcome measures as other forms of leadership.

Motivation researchers have shown that extrinsic rewards can undermine intrinsic motivation (Deci, Koestner, & Ryan, 1990) and do not necessarily cause superior performance (Gneezy & Rustichini, 2000). Extrinsic rewards are not predictive of performance in challenging jobs or with employees who are innovative and creative thinkers (Baer, Oldham, & Cummings, 2003). Granted, the relation of monetary rewards with performance, irrespective of job-type or situation, is positive but it is rather weak (Jenkins, Mitra, Gupta, & Shaw, 1998). It seems to work best with a combination of behavior-management approaches (e.g., social recognition and feedback). Finally, transactional methods also tend to emphasize self-interest and greed (Argyris, 1957; Burns, 1978). To be clear, we are not suggesting that organizational leaders should not implement reward systems. We believe that they could be useful, probably if used in moderation (i.e., forming a small part of compensation packages), and if they are promoting collective-level goals.

In order to provide meaningful ideas about leading through vision, we need to take a broader perspective on leadership and follower motivation than the economic-rational model offers us. Research has shown that individuals seek not only to maximize their economic utility but also to self-express, to reinforce an identity of who they are or who they are aspiring to be, and to do what is ideally or morally correct (Shamir et al., 1993). Oftentimes, and in particular in situations that are equivocal – which characterizes today's typical economic milieu – individuals might be motivated to act irrespective of apparent external (economic) rewards linked to their actions (Shamir et al., 1993).

Thus, when we discuss leading through vision, we will examine how leaders can effect follower commitment and positive organizational outcomes by exercising three distinct and complementary leadership styles (Antonakis & House, 2002, 2004):

(1) *Transformational leadership*, which refers to value-based, visionary, inspirational, emotional, intellectually stimulating, and charismatic leader actions, predicated on the leader's symbolic power.
(2) *Transactional leadership*, a quid pro quo influencing process based on reward and coercive power.
(3) *Instrumental leadership*, centered on strategic use of the organization's systems, structures, and processes.

Instinctively, most leaders tend to rely on reward/coercive power to ensure that followers do what they should be doing, a kind of *coerced contagion* approach. In order to generate real commitment to the vision and real results, the leadership of the organization has to use transformational and transactional and instrumental leadership. This will mean a greater upfront investment in terms of time and energy compared to the coerced contagion approach, but it also creates more energy, ideas, and follow-through.

LEADERSHIP: CASCADING THE VISION

As discussed in Chapter 1, leadership has typically been looked at from the leadership "in" organizations perspective (i.e., direct or face-to-face leadership) (Hunt, 1991). However, equally important, if not more so, is leadership "of" organizations or what can be termed as indirect or strategic leadership (Hunt, 1991). The nature of the influencing process varies as a function of leadership being "close" or "distant." Political leaders or CEOs, for example, are distant leaders, influencing their subordinate leaders – who in turn influence others in the hierarchy and ultimately followers – as well as organizational systems and followers (Antonakis & Atwater, 2002; Peterson, Smith, Martorana, & Owens, 2003). Important here is that leader's distal individual differences (e.g., leader personality, values) affect leader behavior (Zaccaro, Kemp, & Bader, 2004) and are manifested in and affect organizational structure (e.g., see Hambrick & Mason, 1984; Miller, Kets de Vries, & Toulouse, 1982). Thus, the influencing process is not confined to followers but also to organizational and social structures, systems and processes as well as subordinate leaders (see Fig. 1; adapted from Antonakis & Autio, 2006).

We contend that successful cascading leadership depends first and foremost on generating a sense of ownership of the vision throughout the

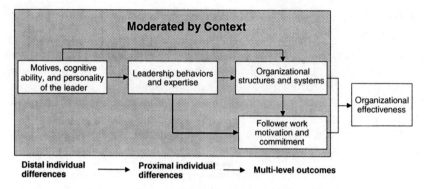

Fig. 1.   Leadership "of" and "in" Organizations.

company. This sense of ownership is created by engaging, directly and in-directly, all members of the organization in the adaptation of the vision to the local context. While this may sound cumbersome and time consuming to many, this upfront investment will generate positive returns in terms of the efficiency and effectiveness of the implementation process. This process can be seen as taking place in three stages: setting the stage, cascading the vision and key strategies, and assessing the impact of the cascading process. In the following pages, we outline these three stages in more detail. This process is depicted conceptually in Fig. 2.

Before we turn to a more detailed discussion of these three stages, we first ask why it is useful to formulate a vision and what makes people pay attention to it.

WHY CREATE A VISION AND HOW TO GENERATE ATTENTION TO IT

What precisely is vision and why is it useful? From a strategic perspective, organizations must anticipate and react to outside opportunities and threats by using and cultivating their organizational strengths while minimizing or eliminating their weaknesses (Hill & Jones, 1998). This function does not and should not occur haphazardly; leaders, through their actions on subordinate leaders and followers and on organizational systems, allow organizational adaptation to occur. The vision should express how the organization could best take advantage of those opportunities.

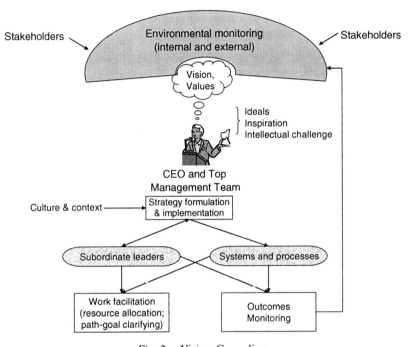

Fig. 2. Vision Cascading.

This means that leaders must understand the systems in which they operate and how they can best integrate independent organizational functions toward the organization's vision (Katz & Kahn, 1978; Senge, 1990; Zaccaro, 2001). The effectiveness of the leader's[1] vision is based on the ability of the leader to influence his or her direct and indirect employees, as well as other stakeholders, to follow. One key element that needs to be in place for people to pay serious attention to the vision is that they must trust the leader, especially in situations characterized as equivocal (or close to crisis).

Having faith in or trusting a leader depends on who the leader is and what the leader does. Antonakis and Atwater (2002) argued that trust in the leader depends on whether the leader:

(1) Has domain-relevant expertise; the street smarts and expertise relating to the organizational system and the organizational milieu (i.e., instrumental leadership);
(2) Exhibits values that are congruent to those of the stakeholders, challenges the status quo for the better, and demonstrates moral conviction (i.e., transformational leadership);

(3) Is honest and reliable in terms of fulfilling his or her contractual obligations (i.e., transactional leadership).

The "trustability" of the leader is an important but not sufficient condition for effective cascading of the vision. The leader also needs to demonstrate that he or she understands the sentiments of the collective group and that their sentiments are expressed in the vision. If the leader manages to do this, then the vision starts to act as the glue that binds the future ideals of the leader and the followers. This makes it more likely that the vision actually guides follower action (see Mio, Riggio, Levin, & Reese, 2005; Willner, 1984).

In order to guide the behavior of followers in constructive ways, leaders need to then mobilize resources and direct collective efforts so as to ensure that the vision becomes a reality. To dedicate the resources and collective efforts in the right way, the vision must be carved up into tangible and operational objectives that can be pursued and measured. This means that the leader must not only have good face-to-face skills but must also be an expert in the organizational system, understanding its resources, constraints, and so forth. The leader must have the appropriate cognitive and behavioral skills (Hooijberg, Hunt, & Dodge, 1997) as well as complex causal models of the operating environment to understand condition-action links (Cianciolo, Antonakis, & Sternberg, 2004). By virtue of their cognitive and behavioral skills and their organizational expertise, leaders make the future happen in ways that they predicted it would (in the vision).

Essentially, the leader's vision acts as a *road map for resource mobilization*. However, the vision and the leader's actions are also energizing for the followers who actively contribute to the concretization of the vision. Why? If the vision implicates the self-concept of followers (i.e., how they see themselves, who they want to be), then it is in the interest of followers to help make the vision happen (Shamir et al., 1993). Followers become committed to the vision because if the vision occurs, it will reinforce their ideal.

In more specific terms, the way in which followers become committed to the vision can be explained in a three-step, but not necessarily sequential, process (Conger & Kanungo, 1998; see also Sashkin, 1988, 2004), which include transformational, instrumental, and transactional leadership:

(1) *Leaders set the stage.* They assess the status quo, assess changes in the external environment, determine the needs of the followers, evaluate organizational and human capital resources (all instrumental leader processes), and arouse follower interest by articulating a compelling and realistic argument for change (i.e., they use metaphor, symbolic actions, impression management, all elements of transformational leader behavior).

(2) *Leaders cascade the vision.* Like prophets, leaders communicate the vision and call the followers to action (transformational leadership). The communication flows both ways as the leader takes in the feedback and ensures that the vision becomes meaningful for all parts of the organization. This dialogue around the vision starts to create follower commitment because the followers start to see and feel how the vision will affect them and what contribution they can and are expected to make. That is, the followers can now see how the vision embodies a future state of affairs that is valued by them (transformational leadership). Leaders in this stage need to convey an aura of confidence and competence by demonstrating conviction that the mission is achievable (transformational leadership), carve the vision into strategic and tactical plans (instrumental leadership), provide technical expertise (instrumental leadership) and socio-emotional support (transformational leadership).

(3) *Leaders assess the impact of the cascading process.* Leaders first need to assess whether they are leading by example (transformational leadership) and then whether the different parts and groups of the organization have reached agreed-upon milestones (transactional leadership).

Below we have further detailed this vision cascading and commitment generating process in terms that are more practical.

SETTING THE STAGE FOR VISION CREATION

In this phase, the top leadership team formulates the vision for the company as well as the broad implementation parameters. Depending on the complexity of the company and its environment, the leadership team seeks advance inputs from relevant internal and external experts as well as relevant stakeholders to guide it in the formulation of its vision. These inputs could include information about GDP (gross domestic product) developments in a particular region of the world, competitor actions, customer and consumer demands, human resource trends, innovation pressures, currency exchange concerns, and other threats and opportunities on both the supply and demand side of the business and both external and internal to the organization.

The analyses will result in various possible images of the future of the company. The views of the future at this point, however, represent cognitive, rational pictures. Successful cascading of a vision requires that the top management team does much more than cognitive, "logical" analyses. In addition to the logical analyses, the top management team needs to identify which image of the future they feel most passionate about and then find a way to communicate this vision in easy-to-understand terms. They need to use analogies, metaphor, stories, or any other mechanisms that will make the vision into a "picture" that the followers can see and feel and which will implicate follower action (Den Hartog & Verburg, 1997).

Why this Vision?

In order to find out which view of the future they find exciting, the members of the team need to hold conversations about what they want the organization to look, feel, and act like. It involves conversations about how customers, shareholders, employees, suppliers, distributors, and others would look at the leadership of the company. It involves conversations about which markets, products, and customer segments they find exciting. In other words, these conversations help the members of the team decide about which view of the future they feel most passionate. This bottom-up approach is useful; however, leaders should also play an active role in transforming follower needs and making them aware of important issues (Bass, 1985). Thus, leaders must reflect the collective aspirations of their constituencies (followers) – whether these aspirations are follower or leader induced – in order to influence them toward a common ideal while instituting veritable social change.

If the members do not have these conversations, they run the risk of generating vision statements that really do not stand for more than strategies or even targets – they will get reflect slogans that can be stuck on the wall. For example, a company may state that in three years time it wants to grow to $1 billion, from $600 million today, with an EBITDA (earnings before interest, taxes, depreciation, and amortization) of 16%, having exited the UK market because the company cannot be competitive there. Whereas these goals do give a glimpse of the desired future, they beg the question as to why the team chose these goals, what they allow the company to do, and what the team finds exciting about them.

Vision Implementation Strategies

Besides the rational analyses and the identification of the most appealing future, the team also needs to identify the key challenges that need to be tackled to arrive at the desired future. This is what Killing and Malnight

(2005) refer to as the "must win battles." One can see that this can evoke heavy and emotional discussions because this is when the immediate consequences for the team members will become apparent. For example, if a chemical company decides that its future lies in specialty rather than commodity chemicals, those on the team responsible for the commodity part of the business will start to wonder about their role in the future of the company. One of the key challenges the company then faces may involve the selling off of the commodity parts of the business.

Whereas Senge (1990) argues that a vision should inspire people and provide creative tension for action, one can see that a significant proportion of the chemical company mentioned before will be anything but inspired. In general, all parts of the setting-the-stage phase can generate conflict among the members of the top management team.

Top Management Commitment

For a top management team to have a vision of the future that can successfully cascade throughout the organization, all members will need to give their emotional commitment to this vision. It is necessary that the other members of the organization see a united management team, if the process is to succeed. A united management team sends the message that the formulated vision and its associated key strategies will indeed drive the actions of the company over the next three to five years.

In discussions about trends in the markets and world, sharp disagreements might arise over which analyses are correct and/or relevant. Sharp disagreements may also arise as well as to which view of the future members of the top management team feel most passionate about. Finally, sharp disagreements may arise over the key strategies that need to be executed to achieve the vision. One can imagine that at this stage some members of the management team may find it difficult to fully commit themselves to the vision.

Given the importance of having a unified management team behind the vision, it is essential that this commitment be obtained. It is clear that we cannot force people to genuinely commit. However, we can hope that they see the process of arriving at the vision as sufficiently fair, so that they too feel some ownership of the vision. It is important that they identify with the vision and become better as a result of the vision having been reified. As this commitment is essential, one cannot sit back and hope it happens. This is the time to convince team members why the vision is important and to identify key strategic initiatives necessary to make it happen. Of course, there might be individuals who simply will not buy into the vision; however, their resistance might well be overcome once the vision has gained momentum (i.e., many others have already bought into the vision). Alternatively, and realistically, some key players simply might choose to voluntarily leave the organization. It is important that resistance be handled in the open and in a dignified manner, lest individuals who do not accept the vision actively work against it. Thus, leaders need to ask each member of the team whether or not he or she can commit to the vision. Once this process has been completed and the members have given their commitment, the management team can move to the next step of the cascading process.

CASCADING THE VISION AND KEY STRATEGIES

Sharing the vision in its broad sense represents only a small part of the cascading process. The CEO and other members of the team can hold presentations for the various parts of the organization, posters can be created and distributed, mugs with the vision statement can be distributed, and screen savers can be put on the computers by the IT department. Again, these visions must render a vivid picture of the mission and sense of purpose of the organization. They are not simply catchphrases and slogans that adorn the company's walls. Whereas these activities can positively contribute to the awareness of the vision, they tend not to have a strong positive impact on making the vision come alive in the organization. For that to happen, other channels of communication need to be identified and used. Here we highlight a few.

Dialogue with the Next Level of Management

Rather than mere speeches and posters, it is essential that the next level of management has the opportunity to ask questions and, where relevant, to contribute to the strategic formulation and implementation processes. Whereas they may have been asked in the earlier phases of the process to provide key information about their departments and perhaps even broader trends, they are unlikely to have a complete picture of the vision, the key strategic initiatives, and the rationales and passion behind them.

They will be curious as to why the management chose this vision and what the implications are for them and their departments. An open, honest, and non-defensive dialogue can do much to get the next level of management to buy into the vision. Such an open and honest dialogue may make the managers in the commodity part of the business realize that their job over the coming years is to optimize their cash flow to both fund the growth of the specialty part of the business and to make the commodity part of the business attractive to potential buyers.

Whereas this message may not be easy to swallow for the managers in the commodity part of the business, the messages for the specialty part of the business are not necessarily easy either. One of the key strategic initiatives may be to double the rate of internal growth in the next three years. Another key strategic initiative may be to double the hiring of outside talent in the specialty chemicals area.

Clearly, one would prefer to have everyone feel excited about the vision; however, real dialogue about the contributions of people in all parts of the organization to the vision needs to be held. As the above examples indicate, the company vision will have different implications for the different parts of the company, and people need an opportunity to assess the vision, come to terms with it, and become committed to what it means to them.

In order for all parts of the company to become involved with and committed to the vision, the vision needs to have some moral overtones. Any economic activity has normative implications that affect a variety of stakeholders (e.g., customers, owners, greater society, environment, etc.). To the extent that visions that can really capture the contribution the organization will make to these stakeholders, and can excite followers about making those economic and non-economic goals, the greater the commitment to the vision will be.

The commitment of the leadership, however, needs to be expressed in more than inspiring visions. The translation of the vision into medium and long-term objectives is also important. One way the importance of these objectives is conveyed is by expressing them in measurable terms.

Setting Measurable Objectives

The expressed commitment to the vision will need to be expressed in terms of measurable objectives or key performance indicators. This is necessary both to translate the commitment into concrete actions and to provide an opportunity to assess progress toward the vision. This is also the part in the process where serious discussions need to take place about what behaviors people will start doing, continue doing, and stop doing. This concerns not just behaviors but also projects, services, activities, as well as necessary resources to make the vision happen (i.e., work facilitation tasks). In other words, this is where the vision is translated into concrete actions, where plans are created, and milestones are set. These milestones provide the cornerstone for the next stage.

ASSESSING THE IMPACT OF THE CASCADING PROCESSES

Whereas the first two stages of the cascading process are essential, people will know you are really serious when you hold reviews and assess them against stated objectives. This means that the leadership has to review and, where necessary, adjust and adapt the HR systems, processes, and structures. Specifically, the leadership will need to review existing bonus schemes, appraisal systems, promotion processes, the criteria for identifying talent, board composition and responsibilities, and so on.

Some of the milestones will be assessed at short-term intervals, whereas others will have a longer time span (one year out or more). At the one-year review, the assessment not only focuses on whether the key performance indicators have been met, but also whether the vision and key strategies are still valid in light of the existing business environment. While a revision of the vision itself is unlikely, some of the key strategic initiatives may need to be adjusted. These adjustments of key strategic initiatives can be related to the departure or arrival of key people, the discovery of a unique product or service, regulatory changes, a currency crisis, the outbreak of contagious disease, the opportunity to acquire an interesting company, or the possibility that another company wants to buy you.

CONCLUSION

A cascading process done well will lead to an emotionally and intellectually engaged and focused organization. It will result in an organizational culture where people face reality, hold open and honest dialogue, take ownership of key initiatives, support each other, and both hold each other accountable and expect to be held accountable for results. The following chapters by Malnight and Keys and by Verburgh and Lane show how this cascading process worked in practice at Carlsberg Breweries and at Wellant College respectively.

NOTE

1. when we speak of the "leader" or of "leadership" we are not specifically referring to the CEO but to the CEO and his or her top management team.

REFERENCES

Antonakis, J., & Atwater, L. (2002). Leader distance: A review and a proposed theory. *The Leadership Quarterly, 13*, 673–704.

Antonakis, J., & Autio, E. (2006). Entrepreneurial leadership. In: J. R. Baum, M. Frese & R. A. Baron (Eds), *The psychology of entrepreneurship* (pp. 189–208). SIOP Organizational frontiers series. Mahwah: Lawrence Erlbaum.

Antonakis, J., & House, R. J. (2002). An analysis of the full-range leadership theory: The way forward. In: B. J. Avolio & F. J. Yammarino (Eds), *Transformational and charismatic leadership: The road ahead* (pp. 3–34). Amsterdam: JAI Press.

Antonakis, J., & House, R. J. (2004). On instrumental leadership: Beyond transactions and transformations. Paper presented at the Gallup Leadership Institute conference. University of Nebraska.

Argyris, C. (1957). *Personality and organization: The conflict between system and individual.* New York: Harper & Row.

Baer, M., Oldham, G. R., & Cummings, A. (2003). Rewarding creativity: When does it really matter?. *Leadership Quarterly, 14*, 569–586.

Bass, B. M. (1985). *Leadership and performance beyond expectations.* New York: The Free Press.

Burns, J. M. (1978). *Leadership.* New York: Harper & Row.

Cianciolo, A. T., Antonakis, J., & Sternberg, R. J. (2004). Practical intelligence and leadership: Using experience as a "mentor". In: D. V. Day, S. J Zaccaro & S. M. Halpin (Eds), *Leader development for transforming organizations* (pp. 211–236). Mahwah: Lawrence Erlbaum.

Conger, J. A., & Kanungo, R. N. (1998). *Charismatic leadership in organizations.* Thousand Oaks, CA: Sage Publications.

Deci, E. L., Koestner, R., & Ryan, R. M. (1990). A meta-analytic review of experiments examining the effects of extrinsic rewards on intrinsic motivation. *Psychological Bulletin, 125*, 627–668.

Den Hartog, D., & Verburg, R. M. (1997). Charisma and rhetoric: Communication techniques of international business leaders. *Leadership Quarterly, 8*, 355–391.

Downton, J. V. (1973). *Rebel leadership: Commitment and charisma in the revolutionary process.* New York: The Free Press.

Gneezy, U., & Rustichini, A. (2000). Pay enough or don't pay at all. *Quarterly Journal of Economics, 115*, 791–810.

Hambrick, D. C., & Mason, P. A. (1984). Upper echelons: The organization as a reflection of its top managers. *Academy of Management Review, 9*, 193–206.

Hill, C. W. L., & Jones, G. R. (1998). *Strategic management: An integrated approach.* Boston, MA: Houghton Mifflin.

Hooijberg, R., Hunt, J. G., & Dodge, G. E. (1997). Leadership complexity and development of the Leaderplex model. *Journal of Management, 23*, 375–408.

Hunt, J. G. (1991). *Leadership: A new synthesis.* Newbury Park, CA: Sage Publications.

Jenkins, G. D., Mitra, A., Gupta, N., & Shaw, J. D. (1998). Are financial incentives related to performance? A meta-analytic review of empirical research. *Journal of Applied Psychology, 83*, 777–787.

Katz, D., & Kahn, R. L. (1978). *The social psychology of organizations.* New York: John Wiley & Sons.

Killing, P., & Malnight, T. (2005). *Must-win battles: Creating the focus you need to achieve your key business goals.* London: Financial Times Prentice Hall.

Lowe, K. B., Kroeck, K. G., & Sivasubramaniam, N. (1996). Effectiveness correlates of transformational and transactional leadership: A meta-analytic review of the literature. *The Leadership Quarterly, 7*, 385–425.

Miller, D., Kets de Vries, M. F., & Toulouse, J. M. (1982). Top executive locus of control and its relationship to strategy-making, structure, and environment. *Academy of Management Journal, 25*, 237–253.

Mio, J. S., Riggio, R. E., Levin, S., & Reese, R. (2005). Presidential leadership and charisma: The effects of metaphor. *Leadership Quarterly, 16*, 287–294.

Peterson, R. S., Smith, D. B., Martorana, P. V., & Owens, P. D. (2003). The impact of chief executive officer personality on top management team dynamics: One mechanism by which leadership affects organizational performance. *Journal of Applied Psychology, 88*, 795–808.

Sashkin, M. (1988). The visionary leader. In: J. A. Conger & R. N. Kanungo (Eds), *Charismatic leadership: The elusive factor in organizational effectiveness* (pp. 122–160). San Francisco, CA: Jossey-Bass Publishers.

Sashkin, M. (2004). Transformational leadership approaches. In: J. Antonakis, A. T. Cianciolo & R. J. Sternberg (Eds), *The nature of leadership* (pp. 171–196). Thousand Oaks: Sage Publications.

Senge, P. M. (1990). *The fifth discipline: The art and practice of the learning organization.* New York: Doubleday/Currency.

Shamir, B. (1995). Social distance and charisma: Theoretical notes and an exploratory study. *Leadership Quarterly, 6*, 19–47.

Shamir, B., House, R. J., & Arthur, M. B. (1993). The motivational effects of charismatic leadership: A self-concept based theory. *Organization Science, 4*, 577–594.

Weber, M. (1947). *The theory of social and economic organization (T. Parsons, Trans.).* New York: The Free Press (Original work published 1924).

Willner, A. R. (1984). *The spellbinders: Charismatic political leadership.* New Haven: Yale University Press.

Zaccaro, S. J., Kemp, C., & Bader, P. (2004). Leader traits and attributes. In: J. Antonakis, A. T. Cianciolo & R. J. Sternberg (Eds), *The nature of leadership* (pp. 101–124). Thousand Oaks: Sage Publications.

Zaccaro, S. J. (2001). *The nature of executive leadership.* Washington, DC: American Psychological Association.

CHAPTER 14

CASCADING MUST-WIN BATTLES AT CARLSBERG

Thomas Malnight and Tracey Keys

ABSTRACT

In 2001, Carlsberg became the fourth largest brewer in the world – but that world was increasingly competitive. This chapter explores how Carlsberg's top management team translated its vision into a few critical priorities, their must-win battles – and then cascaded these throughout the organization to create the alignment, energy, and motivation to realize its goals. At the core, its approach was creating not only shared priorities intellectually, but also a strong culture of cooperation. Five key factors underpin Carlsberg's significant improvements in market position and financial returns: (1) walking the talk, (2) communicating constantly on many levels, (3) maintaining a solid grip on reality, (4) embedding the agenda in the core processes of the organization, and (5) the personal commitment and ownership of the CEO.

Forged in 2001 from the merger of Carlsberg and Orkla's brewing operations, Carlsberg Breweries counted itself as the fourth largest brewer in the world after Anheuser-Busch, Heineken, and Interbrew. By joining forces, these companies had achieved the critical mass that both needed in terms of broadening their distribution base and their brand portfolio.

Being There Even When You Are Not: Leading Through Strategy, Structures, and Systems
Monographs in Leadership and Management, Volume 4, 245–254
Copyright © 2007 by Elsevier Ltd.
All rights of reproduction in any form reserved
ISSN: 1479-3571/doi:10.1016/S1479-3571(07)04013-8

Their combined strengths offered a strong platform for international growth from their Nordic base, particularly for the global Carlsberg brand.

Two years later, Carlsberg Breweries (CB) had been successful in outperforming the brewing industry in volume and profitability growth, as well as share price development. But the competitive landscape was becoming increasingly challenging – CB would have to fight hard to stay ahead.

SETTING THE STAGE: CREATING THE VISION AND MUST-WIN BATTLES

In November 2002, the top management team of CB met to discuss how the company would tackle the challenges ahead. They agreed that company's strategic priorities, created after the merger, still broadly applied, as shown in Fig. 1.

What they needed now though was to establish focus and energy around the critical battles they needed to win to achieve their objectives: their must-win battles. The must-win battle (MWB) approach is based on the premise that defining strategic priorities is just part of the equation. The MWB approach focuses not only on building the strategy, but also on aligning the leadership team and the organization to follow through and

---

- Focus on beer

- Participate in the consolidation of the industry

- Achieve market leadership

- Concentrate on Western Europe, Eastern Europe, and Asia

- Increase ownership in core breweries

- Branding:

    o   Make Carlsberg the leading international brand

    o   Build regional and national brands

Fig. 1. The Strategic Direction for the Group after the Merger.

implement the strategy. As Killing, Malnight, and Keys (2006, p. xi) say:

> Priorities only become real when people, across the organization, give them full support. A great strategy with no commitment will go nowhere. But a great team without a clear sense of direction will do no better. And without strong, authentic leadership at many levels of the organization, even both together are not sufficient.

A top team of 15 people drawn from across the CB business spent several days off-site debating not only the intellectual issues of what should be the strategic priorities, but also the emotional dimensions of what had got in the way of working together in the past as well as what it would take to succeed working together in going forward. Taboo subjects such as directly confronting underperformance were tackled, behaviors were debated – what we should and should not do as a leadership team – and a vision for the future for which each individual on the team could feel ownership was created. Some of the debates along the way addressed the sometimes-difficult relationship between the headquarters and the national affiliates or the challenges in promoting alignment across the traditionally strong national affiliates – such as "you don't understand, my market is different." By the end of the workshop, the team had forged agreement around six global MWBs, as shown in Fig. 2., as well as to the team behaviors that it would take to lead them effectively to implementation in the marketplace.

But this was not enough. It was clear that to succeed they would need to engage a much broader cadre of leadership across an organization that was still far from fully integrated. The decision was made to launch a major initiative called *The Way Ahead*, to define further the shape and direction of

---

- Develop a group culture

- Grow the Carlsberg brand

- Develop operational excellence

- Optimize the value proposition

- Develop people capabilities

- Optimize our investments with JV partners

Fig. 2. Global Must-Win Battles.

the company. This initiative also addressed how the global MWBs would align and shape the priorities and leadership teams of the different regions.

The objectives of *The Way Ahead* were to

- define the mission and vision of the organization globally;
- agree on a number of MWBs globally and per region, i.e., specific and actionable topics necessary to achieve the Carlsberg Breweries' global vision and strategy;
- advance the development of a Carlsberg Breweries' common culture and values necessary to achieve the objectives through focusing on desirable and undesirable behaviors;
- build leadership team accountability and ownership of the execution process.

The Way Ahead represented a major effort to cascade the global MWB agenda throughout the organization. It would be the primary vehicle for building the organizational ownership and support of a shared vision and priorities – without this, the top team's work would be relegated to just one more "nice event" that went nowhere.

CASCADING THE VISION AND GLOBAL MWBS

The Way Ahead was launched swiftly after the top team meeting, in January 2003, along with a monthly newsletter for the top 100 managers in CB. This candid newsletter, called *ahead*, always began with a message from the CEO, Nils Andersen, and would soon become an institution for sharing ideas, successes, progress on MWBs, and learnings from what was not working.

Between the end of January and the start of May, four off-site workshops were held for the three regional groups in CB and the corporate support team. This was the first step in the cascading process. Over four days, each team not only defined MWBs for their regions that would support the global MWBs but also, more importantly, how they would work together to achieve this. The bold goals set out in the global MWBs could only be achieved with increased trust and cooperation across countries, facilities, and functions.

The workshops built on the same model as the top-team event: The regional teams debated how the changing industry environment would affect the business, what their priorities should be to tackle these challenges, what their vision and business model should be, and how this would help the broader company. They also focused on how they should work together, for example, in integrating the four Nordic companies, across consumers, customers, and operations – and what this would mean for the individuals on the Nordic team. The conversations were far from easy at times, given the previous autonomy of the countries:

> I think a lot of us had expected a nice talk about vision, values, and key actions, as well as a good time with colleagues from the other countries. This was also the case, but I guess we were surprised about how fast we were discussing a Nordic business model. This led to interesting discussions but also some frustration: 'what is the implication for me, for my function?' Once this was over, we started moving forward. And in the end, it was widely accepted that working closely together across borders is the way ahead. I think we are a much better team now – I can sit down at any Swedish, Norwegian, or Finnish table and feel that I am part of the Group.

> A lot of us were probably expecting a global strategy to be presented in the beginning solving our problems ... As it had not appeared after the first two days, it seemed like we took charge of the situation ourselves and started working together, defining common agendas and discussing where we could benefit from each other.

A key objective of the workshops was to build a spirit of cooperation for mutual benefit – creating a foundation for a company culture that involved working and competing more effectively as a group. The process was extremely important in building this culture as Nils Andersen explained:

> Putting our mission, vision and values on a piece of paper and hanging it on the wall does not create company culture. Culture is made by the people living in it, working together. The more we work together as a group, the stronger our group culture will be ... We will have to understand the same basic rules of the game, define the same challenges and work towards the same goals. We will probably never get to the point where we can claim to have 100% uniform company culture across the Group, but we will be able to measure significant progress already at the conference in Interlaken in May after the completion of all regional workshops.

This approach was reinforced at all of the workshops, as some of the executives attending commented in *ahead*:

> We have created a community and found some 'free friends.' We have all left the workshop with a better understanding of each other's challenges, a network of contacts with whom to share ideas, and a commitment to participate in the way ahead.

> Before coming to the workshop, I feared we were too different to act like a region, and that it would be difficult to form a team. It was therefore satisfying to see that we quickly agreed on a common vision, and quickly developed a team spirit, based on a common understanding of challenges and growth possibilities.

> In the end we are all trying to crack the same nuts. It encourages me that we can now work like a region. It changes the whole management outlook.

A conference for senior management (around 100 people) was scheduled for May 2003 in Interlaken to discuss how the company would drive its growth agenda forward. Here, the team endorsed the vision, the mission, and the core values of the Group to which they had all now had inputs. The six global MWBs were also confirmed as critical to moving CB forward – and it was now the main task to secure progress against these.

Specific projects and targets had been defined for each battle, but Andersen and the team recognized that success would require full-time efforts from the MWB teams – and that these should be cross-organizational, with each team comprising people from across the countries and HQ functions. The management committee – the Executive Board, plus the country and the functional heads – would directly monitor the progress on a regular basis against the targets and milestones for each battle.

However, as the workshops were being completed, the business situation was becoming tougher. Ahead of the conference, Nils Andersen had announced in the *ahead* that Q1 2003 results were disappointing and below market expectations. The global MWBs would remain the essential pillars of the Group's strategy in the coming years, but needed to be complemented by focusing on market performance and cost effectiveness at the same time. Nils Andersen reinforced the importance of the shared energy and excitement that *The Way Ahead* was building:

> I hope you all returned from Interlaken full of energy and excited about pursuing the vision of becoming probably the best beer company in the world. We need the energy because time and urgency is of the essence if we really want to get ahead of the competition.

The operational excellence MWB was one of the most important initiatives to improve cost effectiveness. Two teams, one focusing on productivity improvement and the other on optimizing administrative functions, were starting to make good progress. By the May conference, pilot plants and companies had been identified to start implementing the improvement initiatives – which would make a substantial impact on the company's bottom line. The project teams drew on both central and local resources, establishing virtual networks of expertise across the Group, along with centers of excellence to ensure continuous sharing of ideas and best practices.

At the same time as operations and administrative functions were being improved, the Group was also very active on the structural front. It closed some plants, which served noncore businesses such as private label and soft drinks. In the Nordic region, some country functions were combined.

In Asia, CB increased its shareholding in two breweries in Vietnam to ensure control, while canceling cooperation with a partner to allow it full control in a high-potential market.

By August, results were showing significant improvement and many of the 20 global and supporting regional MWBs were showing good progress. But not all. Early disappointment with the "develop people capabilities" MWB had already been addressed, but it was clear that the commercial MWBs that focused on consumers/portfolio and customers/channels needed better coordination and greater resources. It was decided that these MWBs (the global "optimize value proposition" and supporting regional MWBs) would be brought together and be subject to deeper research, so that the company could focus on them whole-heartedly and effectively in the coming year. To underline the importance of the MWB, a new MWB leader was hired to drive the effort, becoming part of the top management team.

ASSESSING THE IMPACT OF THE CASCADING PROCESSES

CB experienced a turbulent year in 2003. But by the end of the year, significant progress in revenues and profits was evident – far outperforming the competition. The Carlsberg brand was now the fastest growing international beer brand in the world according to independent industry research. Significant savings were being generated through productivity and administrative improvements. However, country results were mixed and there were still major challenges ahead to address not only these challenges, but also the tough economic and industry conditions that were expected to continue. Carlsberg's MWBs and *The Way Ahead* process had laid a good foundation for 2004, but continued energy and commitment would be needed to sustain the momentum to make further progress.

In reviewing the cascading process that Carlsberg undertook, five key factors contributed to its success in taking goals and translating them into action and shared energy across the Group:

(1) walking the talk;
(2) communicating constantly on many levels;
(3) maintaining a solid grip on reality;
(4) embedding the MWB agenda in the core processes of the organization;
(5) the personal commitment and ownership of the CEO

First, top management *walked the talk*: The top team was clearly committed, active, and vocally supportive of the new direction and vision for the company. They put the process and the battles front and center in their regular meetings – the MWBs were the critical pillars for the future. The team also actively removed roadblocks, aligned resources with the efforts, and constantly communicated with the broader organization. For example, they drew on their best people – always a controversial decision – to lead critical MWB projects.

Communications can be distinguished as a second success factor, operating on several levels. The monthly newsletter was not a one-off. Averaging six to eight pages, it offered a rich and candid source of information on results to date, current activities, and future challenges, as well as feedback from many different leaders across the organization. It was not simply the CEO's message, but rather a way of building a shared focus on reality and what was possible in the future, based on the ideas and learnings it contained. The importance became such that circulation soon extended beyond the top layers of the management (it was initially for the top 100 executives).

Another critical part of Carlsberg's communications was the annual meeting, like the one at Interlaken. Here, the top 120 or so managers shared progress on the MWB agendas, identifying and focusing the organization on the challenges ahead. The interactive sessions allowed everyone to be involved in the discussion of key issues. In addition to celebrating the successes of the past 12 months, the events provided renewed energy and shared commitment to the future.

Two-way conversations were also important on a more informal basis: The senior leaders became the visible "face" of the agenda. For example, executives visiting different parts of the company's worldwide operations talked about the changes underway, and what they meant for that part of the organization. These small-group conversations were more informal and the messages more specific, focused on the expected role of the individual units and the local executives. Such personal touches helped to build motivation and demonstrate to the team on the ground that the senior leaders really were focused on the new agenda.

A third major driver of Carlsberg's ability to cascade the new agenda quickly and effectively was their ability to maintain a *solid grip on reality*: To paraphrase Jack Welsh, "Reality as it is, not as we wish it were." Yes, success was celebrated and learnings were shared generously and quickly, but challenges and disappointments were not avoided. The beer industry is tough worldwide and Carlsberg did not shy away from addressing the need to improve continuously to stay ahead. This honesty and sense that the ambitious targets could be realized as a team served as a great motivator – the same messages were communicated consistently by each member of the leadership team across the organization.

The sense of reality extended to how the new agenda would be, and was, implemented. Balancing the short-term demands of delivering results to shareholders in a difficult market with the longer-term realization of growth through the MWB agenda was far from easy. As the year went on, it became clear that Carlsberg not only did not have enough coordination on the commercial MWBs, but more importantly, it also did not have enough resources or leadership time and depth to pursue the MWB simultaneously with the others. It therefore delayed full-scale efforts on this MWB until it had these critical components in place in 2004.

These actions sent important messages to the organization. The first was clear: We will not hide failure, but learn from it to reshape and reaccelerate the battles or projects that are not on track. The second was more intangible, but equally important: Ambitious does not mean impossible. The top management knew that driving forward on the commercial MWBs without a clear coordination and required resources could end in burned-out managers and acrimonious failure, destroying the progress on operating as "one" organization and culture that they had achieved so far. However, they did not shelve the ambition; in fact, they reiterated it. But they made sure they could do it.

The fourth driver of success in cascading the new agenda came from focus on an often-overlooked part of the process: *Embedding the MWB agenda in the core processes* of the organization. The "develop people capabilities" MWB had defined new processes for managing and building talent internally – the critical next generation of leaders. Part of this involved a new appraisal system for managers and an employee survey that was rolled out across the company. They also increasingly aligned rewards and incentives with the new direction of the company, both strategic and in terms of behaviors and culture. IT platforms were aligned initially across regions, and subsequently across the company, allowing teams to have access to shared information and best practices. The corporate center workshop also served to redefine the roles and focus of the central functions, both in terms of providing the required governance oversight, and also in developing processes and initiatives to support implementation of the MWBs and new agenda across the organization.

Finally, *Nils Andersen's deep personal commitment* to and ownership of the journey was critical. He embodied all the success factors above: Leading by example he walked the talk, listened and discussed the challenges with everyone he met across the organization, ensured a clear grip on reality, and engaged the whole organization, including the center. It was not always easy; it required energy, tenacity, and at times courage, but personal accountability for Carlsberg's vision and battles was simply part of how he lived and worked. He strongly believed in the future the team had created and consistently demonstrated this, motivating the organization to join together in realizing it.

CONCLUSION

Looking back on its success, the January 2006 issue of *ahead* highlights the success in transforming the company from a position of stagnation five years earlier. The culture is stronger with good communication and cooperation, the Carlsberg brand was the fastest growing international beer brand in the world between 2002 and 2004, significant operational improvements have been realized, leadership capabilities have improved, and structural complexity is reduced. Overall EBITDA (earnings before interest, taxes, depreciation, and amortization) has increased around 50%, while margins are up significantly in spite of increased marketing spending.

Now Carlsberg is setting its sights on taking performance to the next level. Launching its new strategy and MWBs at the start of 2006, Carlsberg's overall ambition is to be the leader in beer and beverages in the markets where it operates. The strategy is aggressive and ambitious. The MWBs are clearly linked to those defined in 2003, but are more focused around customers, consumers, and growth. As Nils Andersen says:

> We have taken Carlsberg very far over the last five years. We now face a number of challenges. It is the Carlsberg leadership team's firm belief that this is the time to take the next step in our strategic journey.

REFERENCE

Killing, P., Malnight, T., & Keys, T. (2006). *Must-win battles: How to win them, again and again.* New Jersey: Wharton School Publishing (by Pearson Education Inc.).

CHAPTER 15

A JOURNEY FROM A TRADITIONAL TO A NEW LEARNING MODEL USING CASCADING LEADERSHIP

Luc Verburgh and Nancy Lane

ABSTRACT

We follow Dr. Luc Verburgh through his first two years as CEO of Wellant College. He arrived there in the middle of a major strategic change and his mandate was to implement a change away from a traditional learning model to a new one. His first task was to define, with the executive team, the college's overall vision and strategy. Once that was accomplished, he turned his attention to the task of cascading both the vision and the strategy down throughout the organization and quickly implementing them. He achieved this by focusing on four areas: (1) making sure that the right people were on the team; (2) changing Wellant College's organizational structures and processes to promote communication and to manage performance; (3) communicating clearly and transparently throughout the entire process to all of the stakeholders about the changes taking place and the evolution of the strategy, seeking their views when appropriate; and (4) gradually changing from a top-down approach to one that had clearer guidelines and regulations, as well as allowing, even encouraging, more local ownership.

Being There Even When You Are Not: Leading Through Strategy, Structures, and Systems
Monographs in Leadership and Management, Volume 4, 255–270
Copyright © 2007 by Elsevier Ltd.
All rights of reproduction in any form reserved
ISSN: 1479-3571/doi:10.1016/S1479-3571(07)04014-X

How does an outsider, arriving in the middle of a major strategic change, motivate employees to increasingly commit to an entirely new learning philosophy and get them to adopt the work habits necessary to support this philosophy? How does he not only bring about such a change through the organization itself but also convince its key external stakeholders, such as parents and industry, to become much more actively involved in the education process? These were the challenges Dr. Luc Verburgh took on when he became the CEO of the Board of Wellant College in December 2004. In this chapter, we describe how he rolled out the new learning philosophy.

BACKGROUND ON WELLANT COLLEGE

The secondary school system in The Netherlands offers targeted training to students opting to pursue nonacademic subjects. It consists of both preparatory vocational education and vocational education, which students undertake after their primary education. The secondary education students range in age from 12 to 22 years. The Netherlands secondary education system has almost 700 schools serving the needs of approximately 900,000 students. One option for secondary students is to attend an agricultural college. One such college is Wellant College.

In August 2001, four agricultural colleges merged to form Wellant College. These colleges all specialized in providing agricultural-related secondary and advanced vocational training. The specialties offered included: floristry and interior decoration; animal care, commerce; land, water, and environment; contract work and mechanization; environmental control; horse care; recreation; garden, park, and landscape; horticulture; and animal husbandry and countryside renewal.

After the 2001 merger, Wellant College was the largest agricultural school in The Netherlands and was responsible for the education of around 15,000 students – approximately 25% of the agricultural students in the Dutch secondary school system. The students were spread out among 28 different campuses. Even though its share of the agricultural education market was high, it only had about 1.6% of all secondary school students in The Netherlands, which was a reflection of the fact that the Dutch agricultural industry was small. In 2003, the agriculture industry accounted for about 3% of the Dutch GDP, down from about 3.3% in 1998 (IMD World Competitiveness Online, 2004).

The Wellant College executive team is responsible for the executive management of the college and its members are appointed by the Wellant

College board of directors. When Luc arrived as CEO, he became a member of the executive team. The executive team had three members, Luc and two other board members. Luc had the same responsibilities and votes as the other two members.

MOVING WELLANT COLLEGE TOWARD A "NATURAL LEARNING MODEL"

The Dutch agricultural industry was highly productive and innovative; it had to be because, of the industrialized countries, it had one of the lowest ratios of square meters per capita dedicated to agriculture (IMD World Competitiveness Online, 2004). Often, industry used the most modern and up-to-date equipment well before the research centers at the Dutch Agricultural University in Wageningen had access to it. Therefore, it made sense to try to involve the agriculture industry earlier in the education of its future employees – the students of the newly formed Wellant College. Thus, the previous CEO of the board developed a strategy that changed its students' educational experience from a traditional learning model to a new natural learning model, which was based on the learning theory of social constructivism.

Traditionally, students "received" the expertise that teachers decided to "teach" them in classroom lectures and exercises. Teachers alone decided what content to use in the lectures and exercises. In contrast, under the natural learning model, the school would act more as a content provider. Students would have many more options and could choose what they wanted to learn. Wellant College would then provide the content and the practical applications for them. In addition, Wellant College would collaborate with the agricultural industry to provide the practical applications because the students would ultimately be working for that industry.

Luc described the change to a natural learning model as moving from an educational model that was characterized by an inside-out orientation to a model with an outside-in orientation. The inside-out orientation, or traditional teaching method, focused on teaching students inside the school and then sending them outside only when their education had been completed. The outside-in orientation involved inviting industry to take part in the education of the students and hence involving the outside world in the day-to-day lives of the students. In addition, the new learning model gave students more direct control over their education and was dramatically different from the traditional model. In fact, it was a new paradigm. It not only required new behavior on the part of the teachers, but also changes in organizational structures, task descriptions, and even new or remodeled buildings.

Although the former CEO of the board had a vision of the new learning model, he did not have a clear strategy for moving Wellant College toward that model. Consequently, when the former CEO left to pursue a next step in his career, the board decided to search for an external CEO capable of implementing fundamental changes in a traditional educational organization.

WELLANT COLLEGE'S EVOLVING VISION

When Luc first arrived, he sought to discover the unifying vision of Wellant College. He asked many key people what they thought the Wellant College vision was and he heard many different answers. Although, at a high level in the college, there seemed to be a single vision, every person had different notions of just what it meant. For example, some believed that the new system meant teachers were to withdraw from the learning process altogether. As a result, they started creating small offices for the teachers that were away from the students. Others believed, conversely, that the teachers should be in an open space all the time with their students, interacting intensively. Imagine what these extremes would imply for building designs and educational processes!

Luc concluded that Wellant College did not have a unified vision. Therefore, among his first tasks were the following: Specify a vision, lead the merged organization to a shared understanding of that vision, develop ways of reinforcing key values, and implement the strategy. He spent his first two months at Wellant College meeting with the middle management team and school directors, discussing and clarifying its evolving vision.

Together they defined a three-part vision. The first part was the educational vision, that is, the change to the natural learning model – a strategy that had already been defined and was being implemented. For this vision, they continued to push through the redefined role of educators from the traditional role of passive learning to the natural learning role where teachers are the coaches/mentors and the students could decide what was best for them. The school would then act to facilitate the interaction between the students, their teachers, and the industry in which they chose to study.

The second part of the vision they defined was how the educational programs related to one another. In the traditional preparatory vocational education and vocational education programs, students followed core subjects. For example, they would study dairy only. The new vision would have what Luc called "Agriculture Plus." This would require that students take a core subject, for example, dairy, and complement their core topic with "plus" subjects, such as recreational agriculture or commercial agriculture. Students, as in the first part of the vision, would choose the "plus" topics based on their own career interests. Additionally, new product-market combinations were developed to increase Wellant College's market share in the agricultural secondary education market (e.g., select programs and even an associate degree).

The executive team's third strategy involved defining how to position the school itself in the Dutch educational system. Although Wellant College represented 25% of the Dutch agricultural education market, the fact remained, as mentioned above, that the agriculture sector itself only represented around 3% of The Netherlands's GDP and this was probably a declining market. The executive team pondered what strategies and/or partnerships should be adopted to maintain a good position or even to grow in the overall system – not just in agricultural education.

MAKING CHANGES AT WELLANT COLLEGE

Management Structure

The Wellant College middle management team comprised three regional directors and the director of shared services. The regional directors were responsible for the 28 directors of the individual schools in their regions. The director of shared services was responsible for the back-office operations of Wellant College: information technologies, human resources, finance and administration, and janitorial services. Until December 2004, the three regional directors and director of shared services were reporting to different members of the executive team as shown in Fig. 1.

One of the first changes Luc made was to the reporting structure of the executive team. He convinced his colleagues that it was essential to have the three regional directors report to him, as shown in Fig. 2. He firmly believed this would be the best way to cascade the vision and strategy quickly to the rest of the organization because it would allow him to maximize the effects of his communication. The new structure allowed him to influence 1,400 of the 1,500 employees at Wellant College. It was not, however, solely a matter of communication; Luc also wanted to bring focus to the organization and to change the culture to one that was more performance based. The regional directors, in turn, would cascade the vision and strategy to their teams and

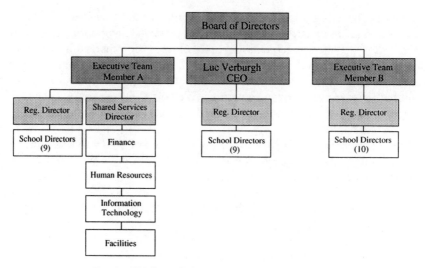

Fig. 1. Wellant College Board, December 2004.

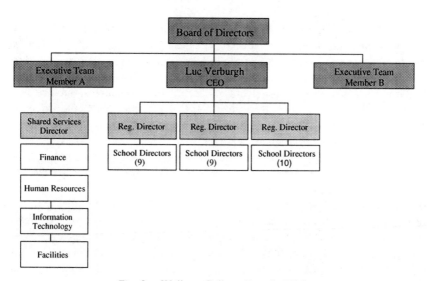

Fig. 2. Wellant College Board, 2005.

thereafter throughout the organization. Once the regional directors had been focused on their line-management roles, they quickly had an impact on the quality of the local directors by using performance management.

Course Offerings

In order to implement the "Agriculture Plus" vision, the executive team needed to focus on its scope and how they could create the necessary building blocks. Some of the basic questions they needed to answer included: At what level should "Agriculture Plus" be offered – advanced education only or both advanced and basic? Where should the courses be located – on every Wellant College campus or in specially created centers of excellence?

By mid-March 2005, the executive team had decided that "Agriculture Plus" would be offered to every student taking advanced agricultural courses. This would allow them to pursue careers that were not necessarily related to traditional agricultural vocations. On top of this, an additional certificate program for only the best students, called MBO Select, would be developed jointly with the best-in-class agricultural businesses. A task force, comprising the three regional directors, six local school directors, and staff, developed a more detailed strategy focused on the segmentation of their market. Their strategy was then presented to and approved by the board of directors in late 2005.

ROLLING OUT THE STRATEGY

School Directors Take Ownership

Early on, Luc and the executive team realized that they had a strategy for a new educational process – that is moving from the traditional to the natural learning environment. By October 2005, this part of the strategy was well on its way: 20 out of the 28 schools had already started implementing the new model, and employees had started to take ownership of the model. Furthermore, school directors were talking amongst themselves to find out what worked and what did not work. They asked the middle management team to provide more help in implementing the strategy. They were mainly interested in having (1) more clarity on how to change to the new learning model, (2) more clarity about how to choose what to do or what not to do, and (3) more ways for schools that were implementing the changes to share their experiences.

In addition, the implementation team, which included the regional directors, a communication expert, and the manager of the natural learning program, took steps to make the new learning model strategy more concrete. They defined eight concrete components for schools to implement, each component consisting of four or five levels, so that now it was clear where the schools were in their implementation. The more concrete steps toward implementation grew out of the regional directors' wish for formalization and would probably not have happened if they had been given the mandate to "develop a formal implementation plan." The already successful implementations, the increased communication, and the clarity of how to implement the strategy motivated people to become involved.

Throughout 2005, Wellant College advanced on the "Agricultural Plus" initiative. The strategy had been rolled out in three schools, which also created momentum and enthusiasm and increased the sense of ownership. Despite the fact that Wellant College was still on a steep learning curve for the 2005 implementation, they planned five to six further rollouts for Fall 2006 where they would take advantage of the key insights from 2005.

Adjusting the Executive Management Structure to Reflect Progress

Now that Wellant College had moved rapidly from vision development to implementation and had increased the quality of its local directors, it was time to flatten the organization by removing the layer of regional directors. To manage the span of control, the number of board members was increased to five, effective August 2006. This, in turn, decreased the total number of executive and middle managers supervising the 28 local school directors from 6 (3 in the board and 3 regional directors) to 5 as shown in Fig. 3. On top of this, the strategic staff (3 people in total) was merged with the shared service center. At the beginning of the merger, everyone kept his or her job, and a performance management system was put into place. However,

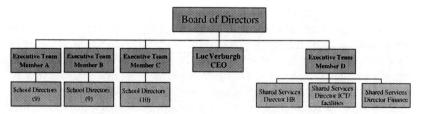

Fig. 3.   Wellant College Board, as of August 2006.

changes took place over time: The director was replaced, people evolved into different roles, and others left – either voluntarily or not. The process was laborious and took more time than expected, but by Fall 2006, the changes were starting to take hold. All of these actions reflected the change from the conceptual/vision phase to implementation and execution.

KEY TECHNIQUES LUC USED IN CASCADING THE VISION AND STRATEGY

Communication

Luc believed personal, face-to-face communication to be a key strategy tool and in his first few months at Wellant College he focused on talking to both the executive and middle management teams. In these meetings, it became clear that henceforth they would be expected to perform at a higher level. Luc also emphasized that he would coach the managers and do all he could to help them meet their goals, but he would not do their work for them. During these meetings, he encouraged the middle management team to get to know its own groups better and to work more directly with them rather than spending a lot of time being involved in policy-making or related activities on either a Wellant College level or even on a national educational level. Operational performance and managing change clearly was the major objective for the whole management team.

The following anecdote reveals the impact that the individual meetings, coaching, and emphasis on communication had on the culture at Wellant College. During one of his initial meetings with a regional director, Luc recommended Jim Collins' book, *Good to Great* (Collins, 2001). Without any prompting, the manager later returned with a detailed list of which managers should be "on the bus." Of course, having his boss recommend a book had sent a strong signal that Luc thought that this was an important book and, therefore, acted as an impetus for this manager to consider the book's ideas seriously. Someone else might have directed his or her management team to read the book and then implement a particular strategy. Instead, Luc let the manager reach the conclusion himself that the ideas in the book were, as in Luc's opinion, valid and worth implementing.

Luc did not restrict his direct communication and coaching efforts to only the middle management team; he made a point of also visiting the schools. He regularly attended classes, discussed issues with both the school directors and the students, and spoke directly to the school directors about his vision and the values he wanted to instill at Wellant College. He also used indirect communication. One message he wanted to communicate was that natural learning was the way of the future. To emphasize this, he deliberately attended a substantial number of sessions in the natural learning environment while visiting only a few classes in the traditional learning environment. He visited the traditional classrooms so that he could understand for himself the problems inherent in that model. When visiting the natural learning environments, he deliberately spent time with the people who were actively working on the change and asked the students, teachers, and school directors many questions including what they thought of the new paradigm, what new materials they developed, and what pitfalls they had experienced. Additionally, in October 2005, Luc taught for four days to emphasize his commitment to the new model.

Because communication was a key strategy, Luc made sure it had a clearly defined structure, which allowed him to share his vision with the middle management team, who would then cascade this vision throughout the organization. However, the communication was not only about the vision and strategy. It was also about making sure that managers knew that having a leadership role also meant having responsibility. Clarity in the communication structure also opened a way to link performance evaluations to results. Furthermore, by separating the weekly, quarterly, and yearly performance targets from the program change targets, Luc was able to effect deeper changes in the organization and to highlight when the program change targets were in conflict with performance targets. Raising these issues caused the management team to ask the right questions about strategy and what it meant for the organization.

Picking the Right Team

Luc felt it was imperative to pick the right team. This was something he would communicate on more than one occasion and in more than one way to the middle management team and school directors.

When Luc started, one manager was not performing and had not been for some time. In the past, the manager's lack of performance had been ignored by management. Luc, in contrast, confronted the issue head-on. He was forthright and told the manager that he would not be part of the team and that he would be let go. This involved costs and was not pleasant for anyone involved. However, since Luc addressed the issue so quickly after starting at Wellant College, it served to underline his message to the team: If you are not right for the job, he would not keep you on board, and he would tell you honestly. It also sent a message to the team, early in his tenure, that its performance mattered.

Save Energy to be Able to Effect the Change

During his career, managing thousands of people, Luc had learned the importance of setting boundaries so that he could focus on getting his job done. So, he made it clear to the middle management team and school directors that he did not want to be the one solving their problems. He was open to contact from them but did not encourage an open door policy per se. He wanted to build and nurture a culture such that when managers were facing a challenge they would use the following steps: Try to tackle the problem themselves; if they could not solve it, ask their team members for help; if the team was unable to solve the problem, ask regional peers for help; then, ask their managers; and finally, if no one else could help ask Luc. He told the managers during his meetings to use this model.

Prioritizing Initiatives

Another important task that Luc concentrated on at the beginning of his tenure was prioritizing the multiple initiatives that already existed. He called this "Focus on Initiatives." In typical fashion, he did not "direct" his team members to prioritize their initiatives and pick the most important one that they would like to see implemented. Rather, he used his ongoing conversations with the management team as coaching sessions and would plant seeds for further thought. He would ask the team, such as:

- Why are you pursuing this initiative?
- What are you doing?
- How does the initiative fit into Wellant College's overall vision and strategy?
- If you had to pick an initiative again, would you choose the same one?

REMAINING CHALLENGES

Luc's vision of the Wellant College future depended on which process was being discussed, and whether it was about the short or long term. In the short term, he wanted to continue the implementation of the educational process change from the traditional learning model toward the natural learning model. In this area, substantial progress had been made and a more solid implementation strategy had been developed. He also wanted more clarity on the educational programs offered and the overall Wellant College product and service portfolio. The new offerings had resulted in an 8% growth in the number of vocational students, which was the first increase following more than five years of declining enrollments. Clearly, the new educational programs, together with the gradual implementation of new (educational) product offerings, had started having an impact on the bottom line.

In the long term, which is in about five years, Luc wanted to move toward a freer market at Wellant College. He envisaged that each individual student would be allocated an educational budget so that, in effect, the students would really be the clients. The students/clients would have a wide portfolio of topics from which to choose to study. In addition to choosing the subjects they would like to study, they would also be able to choose the campus where they would like to study.

In fact, Wellant College had already begun taking steps in this direction. The board of directors had approved an acquisition that would provide them with more market-oriented capabilities (product development, account management, and sales). These additional capabilities would allow them to operate in an even more liberalized market; that is, an educational system that would allow for vouchers and/or permit students to move easily from one institution to another; hence, the market would be more competitive. The acquisition would be finalized by January 2007. They also had formed a strategic alliance with three non-agricultural educational institutions, each approximately the same size as Wellant College. The purpose of the alliance was threefold: (1) to improve their position in the regular educational market, (2) to enable the internal mobility of personnel, and (3) to create a corporate academy to develop employees. The alliance would be announced in Spring 2007 and would be organized in as flat a structure as possible in order to increase flexibility. The executive management teams of all involved organizations were aware of the plans and had started working on four joint strategic projects in Fall 2006.

Luc's long run vision would have huge consequences for the Wellant College teachers, counselors, and administrators. It would mean moving from a system that provided education to students to one designed more to support the students in making the best choices for their education and helping them obtain that education. The administrators and counselors would manage support. And the teachers – either by themselves or through the school's network – would provide the education. The meaning of "delivering" education could change to the extent that Wellant College would buy the services to be offered to its students from outside the educational system. Luc was already gradually introducing these strategies by having schools in the same region, both agriculture and non-agriculture schools, see if they could form alliances to serve the students' learning needs by offering the choice to take courses from other campuses. For example, they could offer "Agriculture-Plus-Plants." Luc would tell the director not to build the plant expertise at Wellant, but rather explore the possibility of working with another institution to offer this expertise. The obvious next step would be for him to tell the schools to then go and find a partner where the "plus" part of the package is the least expensive.

MANAGERIAL PHILOSOPHY

Luc felt especially strongly that structures affect processes. Earlier, we described how he changed the reporting structure so that all of the regional directors reported to him in order to effectively cascade his vision and strategy on educational and cultural change throughout the organization and to ensure that his message was being clearly communicated. He felt so strongly about how structures affect processes and the way people interact that he chose to intervene in one department's planned reorganization.

Normally, he would allow managers latitude when making changes, even if he did not entirely agree. However, this situation was different: The director planned a reorganization that would have allowed external consultants, who had been brought in to help in changing the organizational culture, to be allocated to four middle managers on a permanent basis. Luc thought that this structure might allow the consultants to take over the middle managers' roles thereby letting the middle managers move away from their own responsibilities. He preferred a structure in which responsibility was clearly linked to the managers, not the consultants. He also thought that the proposed structure would allow the consultants to develop "process" rather than "content" expertise. Luc did not want that, as there was a high potential for bureaucracy to creep in: Managers would ask the consultants for advice, the consultants would then send the answer back, and they would go back-and-forth and the consultants would act as the intermediaries. Finally, he wanted to make sure that the structure was really aligned with what he wanted to achieve. He wanted all structures within Wellant College to have clear communication lines, with clear responsibilities and full accountability.

OBSTACLES TO STRATEGY IMPLEMENTATION

External Risks

There were significant external risks to the Wellant College strategy. First and foremost was that the market – the agricultural industry and parents choosing schools for their children – would reject its educational process strategy. Understandably, during the natural learning pilot classes, not all of the parents were enthusiastic about having their children make decisions about what they wanted to learn. The parents felt that deciding what the students learned was the teachers' responsibility, and they also felt that they should know what to expect in the process.

Some of their concerns were due to the fact that there were no report cards for the "subjects" studied by their children. Wellant College solved this problem by increasing its communication about natural learning and incorporating one or two parts of the traditional program into the course of study. For example, students started to receive quarterly progress reports on what they were learning. Parents were also allowed to look at their children's portfolio, which was a digitized record of what children were working on with their teachers, peers, third parties, and industry. During these portfolio meetings, with the parents and children, Wellant College was able to manage the parents' expectations and at the same time allow them to see their children's progress. Another way Luc planned to address this in the future was to both get parents more involved in their children's education and send the message that the Wellant College executive team took their views seriously. Luc signaled this by regularly attending their meetings.

A second external market risk was the fact that the Dutch agricultural market was small and had a high chance of declining. Wellant College had already addressed this by starting to diversify its offerings, changing from offering only agriculture to offering "Agriculture Plus," as discussed above, for the advanced students. Luc wanted to pursue this change more aggressively in the future.

Internal Challenges

One internal challenge that he faced was that his own pace was different from that of the rest of the organization. Luc, his colleagues on the executive team, and the board of directors had the same sense of urgency regarding reform. However, the rest of the organization did not. He had to be aware of this fact and carefully manage it using various methods. For example, Luc asked his colleagues on the executive team to pay special attention to this issue; he regularly discussed it with the middle managers, and in 2006 he explicitly addressed the issue by discussing the tension between the pace of change and Wellant College's ability to absorb the changes in a meeting with all school directors. Luc also discussed this theme with the teachers when visiting individual schools – some of the teachers indicated their preference for a faster pace and felt that they had to wait for management to catch up! He also needed to make sure that the unions, which were strong but also cooperative, agreed with the changes.

Another major concern was aligning the organization to the vision, once that vision had been clarified. This meant that Wellant College must have the required management capabilities in place. The executive team also had to ensure that the structures, coaching, and education needs of the teachers were met in order to support them through the change. One internal challenge or obstacle to successfully aligning the organization was time: Employees could be simply too busy and not have the necessary energy to change.

The internal obstacles he faced were failures in communications, not getting the right structures in place, and not getting everyone involved in the process. In addition, there was some resistance because previous change efforts had not been well managed and/or prepared. Finally, there was the operational day-to-day pressure that made it difficult for teachers to become involved in the change process. This led to some solutions being developed in isolation from the intended users and hence more resistance due to the "not-invented-here" syndrome.

CONCLUSION

Luc came to Wellant College in the middle of a strategic change. His first task was to define, with the executive team, the college's overall vision and strategy. Once defined, he turned his attention to the task of cascading both the vision and strategy down throughout the organization and quickly implementing them. He accomplished this by focusing on four areas. First, he made sure that the right people were on the team. Second, he changed Wellant College's organizational structures and processes to promote communication and to manage performance. Third, he communicated clearly and transparently throughout the entire process to all of the stakeholders about the changes taking place and the evolution of the strategy, seeking their views when appropriate. Finally, he gradually changed from a top-down approach to one which had both clearer guidelines and regulations apply as well as allow for, indeed encourage, more local ownership.

The four key steps discussed above were not the only ones Luc effectively used to cascade the new vision and strategy throughout his organization. He also extensively coached managers and quickly moved from the vision to the implementation. This was possible because he made the line management and employees part of the solution, not only in the implementation phase, but also in the design phase of the new processes and work routines: Luc firmly believes that communication is a two-way street and that this enhances employee involvement and ownership.

REFERENCES

Collins, J. (2001). *Good to great: Why some companies make the leap ... and others do not.* New York: HarperBusiness.
IMD World Competitiveness Online. (2004). http://www.imd.ch/research/centers/wcc/index.cfm

PART VI: LEADERSHIP IN COMPLEX ENVIRONMENTS

This part aims to push thinking on strategic leadership one step further. In all of the previous parts we follow quite a hierarchical model, in which leaders at the top outline the vision, the strategy, and the key implementation tools. Here, Russ Marion and Mary Uhl-Bien challenge the validity of this view of strategic leadership. They argue that strategic leadership is about interacting effectively within a complex interplay of environmental and organizational forces to enable fit environments and adaptive organizations. For them this means that strategic leaders need to pay significant attention to the interdependence between their organizations and both competitors and other relevant organizations in the niches in which they operate. It also means that they need to develop adaptive leadership capacity far down in the organization and show a willingness to follow those leaders at the lower levels. Marion and Uhl-Bien then argue both that strategic leaders have a more interdependent view of organizations and that they have a greater willingness to act as followers than we see in any of the leadership and/or strategy literature. As this approach to strategic leadership is quite new, we do not have application chapters here.

CHAPTER 16

COMPLEXITY AND STRATEGIC LEADERSHIP

Russ Marion and Mary Uhl-Bien

ABSTRACT

The current strategic leadership literature tends to advocate a leader-centric (upper-echelon) approach to strategy, one in which the leader positions the organization competitively within an environment. Based on complexity theory, we argue that strategic leadership in a fast-paced environment works to organize both the environment and the organization in ways that enhance the firm's adaptability, innovativeness, and fitness. We propose a two-pronged strategy: Foster cooperative relationships with the organization's environment, and enable adaptive organizations that are "partners" in the strategic leadership function.

In the 1990s, Capital One was a relatively small organization trying to survive in a highly volatile, competitive environment (Bonabeau & Meyer, 2001). The company initially exploited credit card customers who ran up big debts but eventually paid them off; their strategy was to offer low teaser rates and pay-offs. Larger companies soon caught on and began to edge Capital One out of this market, causing it to move to other markets such as selling cellular phones. Capital One's 1995 annual report summarized its strategy: "Many of our business opportunities are short-lived. We have

Being There Even When You Are Not: Leading Through Strategy, Structures, and Systems
Monographs in Leadership and Management, Volume 4, 273–287
Copyright © 2007 by Elsevier Ltd.
All rights of reproduction in any form reserved
ISSN: 1479-3571/doi:10.1016/S1479-3571(07)04015-1

to move fast to exploit them and move on when they fade" (Bonabeau & Meyer, 2001, p. 113).

Capital One's story is clearly a story of strategic leadership, but what is the nature of that leadership? One might assume that intelligent executives made creative, informed choices, but this doesn't quite fit the evidence. Capital One doesn't appear to have chosen its market-hopping strategy; rather, the strategy seems to have been imposed on it by environmental imperatives. Its 1995 strategy statement may have reflected emergent reality more than intelligent choice. What, then, is strategic leadership? Is it something that informed executives choreograph, or is it more? And if it is more, then what are the implications for leaders and for the leadership function?

We argue that, while much of the existing literature has viewed strategic leadership as top-down, vision-led, and centralized (Canella & Monroe, 1997), the reality of strategic contexts, particularly in the highly dynamic world of the knowledge era, is much too complex to be managed in a traditional sense (Ireland & Hitt, 1999). We propose, instead, that strategic leadership is about *interacting effectively within a complex interplay of environmental and organizational forces to enable fit environments and adaptive organizations*. Further, we propose that strategic leadership is not about survival of the fittest but rather about "survival of the cooperative" – the forming of interdependent relationships with other organizations and industries that foster the health and fitness of an environmental network (or organizational niche) in ways that support the viability of the firm. We argue that effective strategy includes the fostering of adaptive organizations, and that strategic leadership operates within these organizations to enable the firm's functionality, innovation, learning, and capacity to strategically adapt to the environment.

We look to the science of complexity theory to help us understand strategic leadership in this different light. Complexity theory departs significantly from views that focus narrowly on leaders at the top of a hierarchy, manipulating their organizations in ways that give them advantage in their environment. Instead, complexity describes networked, interactive behaviors among actors in an organization and in an environment, and suggests that strategic leadership must act within the context of those dynamics. Below we briefly describe current perspectives of strategic leadership. We then develop a view of strategic leadership that is grounded in the interactive principles of complexity theory. We propose two general functions of strategic leadership: that of fostering an environmental niche within which the organization can thrive, and that of enabling the organization to function effectively and adaptively within that niche.

CURRENT PERSPECTIVES OF STRATEGY

Most writers perceive strategy as what CEOs do to position their firms relative to the competition. By that definition, GM and Ford are struggling unsuccessfully to strategically place themselves and are losing millions of dollars yearly. Chrysler, by contrast, has done quite well with its market strategy – a success that is attributed to the strategic acumen (such as re-introducing the Dodge Charger muscle car) of the CEO, Dieter Zetsche.

This is a leader-centric interpretation of Chrysler's success. Canella and Monroe (1997) describe strategic leadership relative to five such leader-centric perspectives – positive agency theory, strategic leadership theory, personality theory, transformational leadership, and visionary leadership. All are focused on the man or woman at the top – e.g., their relationships with shareholders and how their actions shape strategy (e.g., positive agency); the characteristics (values, cognitions, personalities, and demographic characteristics) and the choices of individuals at the top (e.g., strategic leadership); the psychological makeup of the CEO (e.g., personality theory); the top leader's ability to lead change and transform followers (e.g., transformational theory); and/or the CEO's ability to identify and align organizational members with a vision (e.g., visionary leadership).

More recently, theorists have begun to look at strategic leadership in a hyperturbulent, globalized economy. Ireland and Hitt (1999), for example, argue that the competitive landscape of today makes it difficult to institute activity-limiting, top-down control, and propose instead that leaders institute controls that "facilitate flexib[le], innovative employee behaviors" (p. 52). Leaders must provide group members with sufficient flexibility to "take advantage of competitive opportunities that develop rapidly in the new competitive landscape" (p. 52). They argue that strategic leadership, "should be executed through interactions that are based on a sharing of insights, knowledge, and responsibilities for achieving outcomes" (p. 47), and cite John Browne, the CEO of British Petroleum Company, who "believes that top management must stimulate the organization rather than control it" (p. 48). This is a significant departure from traditional perspectives: It suggests that strategic leaders need the help of flexible, interactive organizations (Heckscher, 1994) to deal effectively in turbulent environments. Strategic leaders must look both "inward" and "outward," and strategy involves more than a "general moving [of] troops and supplies," it involves troops who are themselves capable of creating strategy (Rowe, 2001).

Boal (2004) reinforces this view by proposing that firms in fast-paced environments need to be learning organizations, and that strategic leadership's role is to enable that capacity. Strategic leaders accomplish this by creating contexts for learning (e.g., capacity and desire), by brokering internal *and* external networks of interaction, by fostering organizational storytelling about the firm's historical creativity (which serves a role similar to that of Schein's [1985] notion of myths), by managing dialog about priorities, infrastructure, and identity, and by supporting innovative behavior. He proposes leadership that assumes a less leader-centric role in this process. That is, leaders serve as enablers of context, interaction, dialog, and innovation rather than as architects who single-handedly shape the firm's future.

Ireland and Hitt, and Boal (and others) provide two important ideas upon which we will expand. First, Boal acknowledges the importance of interactions among agents in a niche – the contexts within which strategic leadership operates. Complexity theory suggests that niches comprise competitive but interdependent organizations which struggle against one another for resources, but whose struggles are, ironically, framed by cooperation; that is, competition and cooperation are synchronously related. Second, both Ireland and Hitt, and Boal argue that part of the strategic leader's responsibility is to enable firms that can adapt to fast-paced contexts. Complexity theory proposes that internal flexibility is critical to the system's capacity to deal effectively with rapidly changing environments. Complexity theory proposes that both the nature of dynamic relationships with other organizations and the nature of interactive dynamics *within* an organization are key to effective organizational fitness and organizational adaptability – and, consequently, to organizational strategy. Complexity theory provides comprehensive understanding of the dynamics and implications of these notions, which we discuss below.

A COMPLEXITY THEORY PERSPECTIVE OF STRATEGY

Complexity theory focuses on patterns of interaction among the members (or "agents") of a *complex adaptive system* and how these interactions generate adaptability and new (emergent) ideas and structures. Complex adaptive systems (CAS) are networks of interactive agents who are motivated by internal and external tension and dependent on one another for fitness. Complexity theory describes how the sheer dynamics of interaction among interdependent agents within a CAS, each of which is seeking to survive and thrive, lead to elaboration of both the individual and the group as a whole – indeed the fitness of both agent and group (CAS) are intimately intertwined. It is the potency of the interactive dynamic – as much as (or even more than) the leader or the plan or preferences of any given individual – that decides the nature of organizational and CAS structure and behavior.

Complexity theory is related to natural selection in that both describe the evolution of structure. There are important differences, however. Like natural selection, complexity is a science of motivating forces; unlike selection, however, it finds that those forces are not only competitive in nature but also emanate from the dynamics of interaction and cooperation. Further, while natural selection sees little role for leadership (Pfeffer, 1997), complexity theory envisions leadership as an activity that interacts with, and supports, complex dynamics.

External Dynamics: Cooperation within the "Niche"

Complexity theory envisions the organizational environment as a niche. By "niche" we mean a broad, complex adaptive system of species that interact and compete, but which are ultimately dependent upon one another for their individual fitness. In this chapter, we examine "organizational species," defined as different firms and different technologies. We illustrate the concepts that follow by considering the organizations that comprise the niche of the automobile industry. Chrysler's niche, for example, includes other auto producers (competitors such as Ford, GM, and Toyota), an extensive auto repair industry, parts suppliers, fuel processors, fuel distributors, rubber and tire industries, after-market producers, auto insurance companies, road pavers, and traffic control technologies.

In a niche, the patterns of interaction are determined by two broad characteristics of adaptive networks (Kauffman, 1993): the number of organizations and the degree to which each organization can alter the fitness of other organizations (i.e., interdependency). If either (or both) of these characteristics is high, system dynamics will be chaotic (excessively dynamic) and the capacity of organizations to enhance their fitness will be compromised. Any given change dramatically alters the fitness of participating organizational species, because the intense level of interaction and interdependency creates disruption across the network. Without some level of stability, fitness advances are offset as soon as they occur. Neither individual organizations nor the collective of organizations benefits from this situation, for such systems typically freeze at relatively low levels of overall fitness in order to control disruptive change. Kauffman (1993) called this the Stalinist limit, referring to the centralized, hence, highly interdependent nature of the USSR under Stalin. Alternatively, when the number of participants and degree of interdependency are low, there is little incentive for organizations to change or enhance fitness. Nor is there opportunity to create relationships that would enable cooperative initiatives or the migration of ideas and innovations (Weick, 1976).

Only in situations where the number of competitors and degree of inter-dependency are effectively balanced between these extremes will fitness searches be productive. A fitness search is merely the elaboration or im-provement of the fitness strategy selected by a given organization. It could include, among other things, improvements or diversification in products, changes in relationships with other industries in the niche, or improvements in the adaptability of the organization. Kauffman (1993) observed, based on a series of simulations of biological niches, that interactive dynamics and natural selection tend to "move" networks to moderate levels of interde-pendency and to winnow the number of niche competitors to an *almost* manageable number. That is, networked systems of adaptive agents tend to settle into semi-stable, vibrantly interdependent states in which there is sufficient tension (explained below) to pressure species to elaborate their fitness strategies. If there is too much interdependency, the niche is over-whelmed by so many conflicting strategies that fitness improvements could become prohibitively difficult to achieve; too little interdependency, and there is insufficient incentive to elaborate. Langston (1986) calls this vibrant, moderately interdependent state *the edge of chaos*.

A vibrant balance not only enables organizations to increase their fitness but also produces diversity that further benefits the system and the agents within it. In complex networks, diversity creates competing needs, also called conflicting constraints, and the pressure to work through these constraints creates tension, or pressure to elaborate. This tension prompts the network to work to resolve the conflict by changing – often in ways that create novel solutions or new approaches. For example, when one organization needs to access a given resource while another organization is compelled to protect or limit access to that resource, the resulting tensions pressure agents within the system to elaborate their respective strategies. The auto industry, for in-stance, adopted computer technologies to help it deal with pollution – a need born of tension between advocates of limiting fossil fuel emissions and auto producers' desire to generate profits. This tension pressured the competing industries (environmentalist and automotive) to find a new technology that ultimately improved the fitness of both. And in so doing, the complex dynamic created new diversity (the computer technology industry) thus propagating the tension/fitness elaborating cycle.

Species in a given niche, then, coevolve (Kauffman, 1993). This is an interactive process in which diverse species struggle with one another to enhance their individual fitness (defined generically as capacity to survive) and, in the process, enhance the fitness of each other and of the niche. Species coadapt and co-elaborate in dynamic relationship with one another. In struggling over conflicting preferences, they not only elaborate their respective strategies but also grow to depend upon each other. Each provides some function that directly or indirectly serves the needs of others in the niche. They move from being simply competitors to being interdependent competitors.

Interactive dynamics move beyond even this: They pressure the niche toward a state that is dominantly defined by cooperation rather than competition (for excellent discussion, see Nowak, May, & Sigmund, 1995). Complex systems quickly learn that significant advantages derive from cooperation – it is what might be called, twisting Spencer's famous phrase, "survival of the cooperative." Thus ants cooperate with aphids and honeybees cooperate with flowers. In human societies, organizations themselves are cooperative assemblages, as are niches such as that of the automobile industry described above. The paving industry depends almost exclusively on its cooperation with the needs of automotives, and automobiles would be seriously hampered if the paving industry failed to thrive. Chevrolet may compete with Chrysler, but both automobiles improve and define themselves and their niche in part because of their relationships within a common niche.

To further appreciate the potency of this elaboration and cooperation "formula," imagine the difficulties and disruption that would be unleashed if governments were to order the dismantling of the gas-driven auto industry within a short span of time (to be replaced by non-polluting technologies). The network is far too extensive, fit, and viable for that to occur easily (for a more extensive discussion, see Marion, 1999).

Implications for Strategic Leadership: Cooperation

For strategic leadership, complexity theory suggests actions that enhance organizational fitness by stimulating growth and diversity in their industry's network or niche. Strategic leaders should think of their environments not only in terms of competition but also in terms of the health of the niche:

Strategic leadership thus comes to be about positioning the organization cooperatively within the niche as opposed to positioning it in a competitive environment. Chrysler is intimately dependent upon the health of its environmental network – the automobile would be virtually useless without such things as a distribution system for providing fuel and a repair network for maintaining automobiles. It also benefits from its competitors, who create tension that helps drive Chrysler to innovate and adapt. That is, the interdependent interaction of network constituencies creates fitness for Chrysler and for the network, and creates a vibrancy that stimulates growth in Chrysler and in its network.

Effective niche networks are the product of (among other things) efforts by organizations to seek out alliances with useful spin-off technologies, to advocate for the welfare of niche allies (when they are threatened by unfair competition, for example), or by sharing technology that helps niche allies to be more productive. Effective organizations should even weigh carefully the ramifications of destroying competition, for competition provides pressure that stimulates fitness elaboration.

Failure to nurture a niche can be self-destructive. Marion and Bacon (1999), for example, relate the story of a non-profit organization that was viable and dynamic before it was taken over by a leader who systematically dismantled its environmental network. That network was extensive before this person became the director and was the source of its strength. The new administrator drew back from the network – terminating relationships with other NGOs, alienating supporting organizations, overturning the board, and firing and replacing most of the seasoned (and connected) employees. Non-profits are intimately dependent upon their network of support and relationships, and that infrastructure for this particular non-profit collapsed. There was little foundation on which fundraising or other forms of support could be built; there was a limited network of supporting volunteers and agencies, and little historical knowledge of strategies that worked and people who could support the operations. These actions depleted the cooperative network and the organization wound up filing for bankruptcy.

The environments with which strategic leaders must deal are exceedingly complex; however, the very characteristics that lend the system fitness and viability (elaboration, diversity, and network interactions and interdependency) also make them difficult to manage using traditional top-down approaches. Ireland and Hitt (2005, p. 69), for example, observed that businesses in the 21st century – businesses today – are faced with "unstable market conditions resulting from innovations, diversity of competitors, and an array of revolutionary technological changes..." They also note:

"Changes happen swiftly, are constant, even relentless in their frequency, and affect virtually all parts of an organization simultaneously" (p. 64). Strategic leaders cannot navigate this complexity alone, for the complexities of modern business environments create challenges that quickly overwhelm the capacity of a small cadre of executives to process and deal with. Consequently, strategic leaders must foster organizations that themselves interact with the environment to enhance the firm's functionality, innovation, capacity to learn, and adaptability. We address this issue in the next section.

Internal Interactive Dynamics: Organizational Fitness as Strategy

In the opening paragraphs of this chapter we discussed the flexibility of Capital One in its infant years of the 1990s. We now discuss the network dynamics that likely contributed to the adaptability, creativity, and learning it exhibited during those years. We propose that complex adaptive learning organizations contribute to an organization's strategic need to effectively respond to environmental exigencies, and that they are particularly important when the environment is highly complex.

Network dynamics are similar to the dynamics described earlier for the relationship between an organization and its environment, but there are some differences in emphasis. The adaptive dynamics that occur within an organization (as within an environment) are functions of interaction, interdependency, and tension. The informal interactions that go on within organizations are described by complexity theorists in terms of neural-like networks of interaction and interdependency. Interdependency inevitably produces conflicting constraints and tension, which stimulates change and elaboration.

Tension, however, is also imposed by external factors, a notion that was not an issue in the earlier discussion of external dynamics. This tension can arise from external events, as when another organization exerts influence over the focal organization – that is, external interdependencies, which were discussed in the last section, can influence the internal dynamics of an organization. Tension is also created by the actions of the formal hierarchy in an organization, as when Jack Welch told his GE production units to be No. 1 or 2 or be terminated (Slater, 2001).

The less obvious issue involves how one fosters flexibility – what Lorange (2000) calls the bottom-up organization. Lorange argues that bottom-up organizations are quick to recognize opportunities and are willing to experiment with new ideas. Uhl-Bien, Marion, and McKelvey (in press) have developed a model of leadership that is focused on encouraging such bottom-up flexibility. Their model proposes three leadership roles: administrative, adaptive, and enabling.

Administrative Leadership
This occurs in the formal managerial role and involves:

> ... the actions of individuals who plan and coordinate organizational activities. Administrative leadership (among other things) structures tasks, engages in planning, builds vision, allocates resources to achieve goals, manages crises (Mumford, Bedell-Avers, & Hunter, in press) and conflicts, and manages organizational strategy (Uhl-Bien et al., in press).

The administrative role is typically associated with upper and middle echelon personnel. This administrative role is significant, for it provides the structure within which complex dynamics can occur and the glue which holds them together. Administrative leadership plans a trajectory and articulates a mission for creative initiatives (Jaussi & Dionne, 2003).

Several caveats are pertinent, however, all of which relate to the informal nature of dynamics in complex systems. First, administrative leadership involves the direction of a long-term, evolutionary system or dynamic process. Administrative leadership supports, protects, and (broadly) guides that system's evolution (see Mumford et al., in press); it does not, as a general rule, coordinate the specific direction of that dynamic or the mechanisms by which it operates.

Second, administrative leadership actions vary according to the evolutionary stage at which the creative process operates at any given time. The key dynamics that complexity leadership focuses on are creativity and innovation. Briefly, creativity is the creation of new ideas, and innovation is the unfolding of those ideas. There are three points at which administrative leadership is involved: the creative process itself, the transition to an innovative process, and the innovative process. The creativity process must be unfettered, thus administrative leadership actions are generally restricted to such things as providing appropriate resources and protecting the process from political assaults (Mumford et al., in press). Once new ideas are generated, the administrative leader helps decide which of them are marketable and consistent with the competencies, or thematic focus (Mumford et al., in press), of the firm (the transition period). During the subsequent innovation phase, the administrative leader is somewhat more directive, but still a lot of creativity is involved in innovation and the roles defined above for the creative phase apply as appropriate.

Third, administrative leadership shapes vision and mission in a manner that enables the creative and innovative functions without hampering them. Overly specific missions – for example, "take the hill by bombing it into oblivion;" or "develop procedures for making a pill for this chemical model" – can distort or even obviate the creative process. Vision and mission should be shaped as a guide for the long-term dynamic rather than as an outcome for an event.

Enabling Leadership

By engaging in activities that foster the emergence of flexible behaviors, enabling leadership creates the conditions necessary for effective learning and adaptability.

> Enabling leaders ... foster [flexibility] by (1) fostering interaction and interdependency; (2) enabling the conditions necessary to produce a fabric of *internal* tensions; and (3) injecting *external* tensions to help motivate and coordinate the interactive dynamic (Uhl-Bien et al., in press).

Enabling leadership also serves to help move creativity into innovation and to disseminate innovative products of adaptive leadership upward and through the formal managerial system. Enabling leadership is most often the function of middle management, which has direct, day-to-day access to complex adaptive behaviors.

Adaptive Leadership

This type of leadership is a distributed form of informal behavior that emerges in interactive events and can occur anywhere within an organization. According to Uhl-Bien et al. (in press):

> Adaptive leadership is a dynamic rather than a person (although people are, importantly, involved); we label it leadership because it is a (and, arguably, the) proximal source of change in an organization.

Adaptive leadership, then, refers to behaviors of complex adaptive systems that lead to emergent learning, creativity, adaptation, and change, which in turn result in movement toward organizational vision and mission. This perspective dramatically reconceptualizes leadership as the actions of a group rather than an individual. It focuses on a collective dynamic rather than an act or a series of planned events. Importantly, this collective behavior is organically dynamic and responds efficiently and creatively to complex, dynamic environments; such adaptability is a crucial strategic tool for the organization.

The key to effective, adaptive leadership lies in the nature of the interactive, complex network which spawns it. Complex networks are not fixed structures, rather they are organized to flex and change with a changing environment. They enable ideas, innovations, and adaptations to interact in a milieu of interdependency and tension, such that they combine, diverge, and foster even newer, higher level ideas, innovations, and adaptations.

At Nordstrom, the key rule for employees – what Nordstrom calls rule No. 1 – is, "use your good judgment in all situations. There will be no additional rules" (Pfeffer, 2005, p. 99). The company explains:

> We also encourage you to present your own ideas. Your buyers have a great deal of autonomy, and are encouraged to seek out and promote new fashion directions at all times...and we encourage you to share your concerns, suggestions and ideas (p. 99).

Pfeffer continues:

> The fundamental change [at Nordstrom] involves moving away from a system of hierarchical control and coordination of activities to one in which low-level employees, who may have more and better information, are permitted to do things to enhance performance (p. 99).

Thus, Nordstrom fosters a culture in which employees can respond creatively to environmental changes. Although complexity science would suggest that it does more to deliberately foster complex networks, its appreciation of individual initiative is, at least, a step in the direction advocated in this chapter.

Adaptive leadership is an important adjunct to the strategic functions normally assigned to administrative leadership. Strategic leaders seek to position their organizations to respond flexibly to environmental exigencies. They can help accomplish this by fostering adaptive internal structures, which can themselves change in response to organizational changes. Such adaptability depends on social and organizational networks that allow ideas to dynamically emerge and interact with one another and with the environment (as was the case at Nordstrom). Such networks are pressured to innovate when network members experience tension that requires them to adapt. Strategic leaders enhance these processes by being willing to shift decisions and initiatives to all levels of the system.

Summary

Taken together, administrative, enabling, and adaptive leadership are intertwined with and influence one another in a manner that we can describe as being *entangled*. Administrative leadership creates the mission and structure within which the others operate. Enabling leadership fosters conditions that are conducive to adaptive action and helps move the products of the adaptive into the mainstream of the bureaucracy. Adaptive leadership defines both the potentialities and the limitations with which the organization has to operate. Nordstrom apparently realized this when it enabled the judgment of its workers.

CONCLUSION

We began with an example of dynamic adaptability from Capital One, and asked whether strategic leadership is something that informed executives choreograph or something more; and if it is more, what the implications are for leaders. In this chapter, we answered this question by suggesting that strategic leadership is not only about leadership *of* an organization's systems, structures, and processes, but also about the leadership *of* the leadership *in* the organization. That is, administrative and enabling leadership set the stage for adaptive leadership to occur and contribute. Moreover, it is not only about competing but also about cooperating with one's environment.

We suggest that the contexts facing organizations today are too complex to be limited to the few brains at the top. Instead, "strategy is best developed through a social process of discussion that uses the full intelligence of all" (Heckscher 1994, p. 21). As noted by Dess and Picken (2000):

> As the strategic emphasis shifts from the efficient management of mass markets and tangible assets to innovation and the effective utilization of knowledge and human capital resources, organizations and their leaders must also change. More capable leadership at the top – smarter managers – is not necessarily the answer. Rather, to compete in the information age, firms must increasingly rely on the knowledge, skills, experience, and judgment of *all* their people. The entire organization, collectively, must create and assimilate new knowledge, encourage innovation, and learn to compete in new ways in an ever-changing competitive environment (p. 18).

We agree with Heckscher (1994) that flexibility and adaptability are best enabled in the context of an "interactive organization" (Heckscher, 1994), in which strategic leadership effectively balances top-down and bottom-up forces (Lorange, 2000). In such organizations, the role of "enabling leaders" is to foster effective interactive dynamics (e.g., interaction, interdependency, and tension) in order to foster "adaptive leadership" (Uhl-Bien et al., in press). Adaptive leadership accomplishes the recommendations of Dess and

Picken (2000) by capitalizing on the intellectual capabilities of agents and groups of agents throughout the organization.

In conclusion, we propose a perspective of strategic leadership that differs rather radically from the traditional view of a select cadre of leaders navigating their organizations through hostile, competitive waters. Our perspective, grounded in complexity theory, proposes that leaders approach the challenges faced by their firms with a two-pronged strategy. First, strategic leaders nurture an extensive network of collaborators and even competitors – they develop a niche that is itself healthy in order to support the health and vibrancy of the firm. We call this survival of the cooperative, arguing along with Lorange and Contractor (2004) that competition and cooperation are synchronous paths to fitness and that cooperation is an important element of successful business strategy.

Second, strategic leaders enable firms to be powerfully adaptive and to change flexibly in the volatile environment of the knowledge era. In this way, they can create firms that are, in a sense, "partners" in strategy, firms that are able to respond to environmental pressures that are too complex for a small group of leaders to anticipate or process.

REFERENCES

Boal, K. B. (2004). Strategic leadership, organizational learning and network ties. Paper presented at the conference on strategic leadership on both sides of the Atlantic, IMD – International Institute for Management Development, Lausanne, Switzerland, August 17–19.

Bonabeau, E., & Meyer, C. (2001). Swarm intelligence: A whole new way to think about business. *Harvard Business Review, 79*(5), 107–114.

Canella, A. A., & Monroe, M. J. (1997). Contrasting perspectives on strategic leaders: Toward a more realistic view of top managers. *Journal of Management, 23*(3), 213–230.

Dess, G. G., & Picken, J. C. (2000). Changing roles: Leadership in the 21st century. *Organizational Dynamics, 28*(3), 18–34.

Heckscher, C. (1994). Defining the post-bureaucratic type. In: C. Heckscher & A. Donnellon (Eds), *The post-bureaucratic organization: New perspectives on organizational change* (pp. 14–62). Thousand Oaks, CA: Sage.

Ireland, R. D., & Hitt, M. A. (1999). Achieving and maintaining strategic competitiveness in the 21st century: The role of strategic leadership. *Academy of Management Executive, 13*(1), 43–57.

Ireland, R. D., & Hitt, M. A. (2005). Achieving and maintaining strategic competitiveness in the 21st century: The role of strategic leadership. *The Academy of Management Executive, 19*(4), 63–77.

Jaussi, K. S., & Dionne, S. D. (2003). Leading for creativity: The role of unconventional leadership behavior. *The Leadership Quarterly, 14*, 475–498.

Kauffman, S. A. (1993). *The origins of order*. New York, NY: Oxford University Press.

Langston, C. G. (1986). Studying artificial life with cellular automata. *Physica, 22D*, 120–149.

Lorange, P. (2000). Balancing bottom-up with top-down. In: P. Strebel (Ed.), *Focused energy: Mastering bottom-up organization* (pp. 119–131). Chichester, UK: Wiley.

Lorange, P., & Contractor, F. J. (2004). Why should firms cooperate? The strategy and economic basis for cooperative ventures. In: J. J. Reuer (Ed.), *Strategic alliances: Theory and evidence* (pp. 19–47). Oxford: Oxford University Press.

Marion, R. (1999). *The edge of organization: Chaos and complexity theories of formal social organizations*. Newbury Park, CA: Sage.

Marion, R., & Bacon, J. (1999). Organizational extinction and complex systems. *Emergence: A Journal of Complexity Issues in Organizations and Management, 1*(4), 71–96.

Mumford, M., Bedell-Avers, K. E., & Hunter, S. T. (Eds). (in press). Planning for innovation: A multi-level perspective. In: *Research in multi-level issues*. Oxford, GB: Elsevier.

Nowak, M. A., May, R. M., & Sigmund, K. (1995). The arithmetics of mutual help. *Scientific American, 272*, 76–81.

Pfeffer, J. (1997). *New directions for organization theory: Problems and prospects*. New York, NY: Oxford University Press.

Pfeffer, J. (2005). Producing sustainable competitive advantage through the effective management of people. *The Academy of Management Executive, 19*(4), 95–108.

Rowe, W. G. (2001). Creating wealth in organizations: The role of strategic leadership. *The Academy of Management Executive, 15*(1), 81–94.

Schein, E. H. (1985). *Organizational culture and leadership*. San Francisco, CA: Jossey-Bass.

Slater, R. (2001). *Get better or get beaten* (2nd ed.). New York, NY: McGraw-Hill.

Uhl-Bien, M., Marion, R., & McKelvey, B. (in press). Complexity leadership theory: Shifting leadership from the industrial age to the knowledge era. *The Leadership Quarterly*.

Weick, K. E. (1976). Educational organizations as loosely coupled systems. *Administrative Science Quarterly, 21*, 1–19.

CHAPTER 17

LEADING THROUGH STRATEGY, STRUCTURES AND SYSTEMS: CONCLUDING THOUGHTS

Robert Hooijberg, James G. (Jerry) Hunt,
John Antonakis and Kimberley B. Boal

When we think about "being there even when you are not," we think about ways in which executives can shape their organizations to reflect their vision, strategy, and philosophy. Thus, we have organizations that not only deliver the products and services they find important but also deliver them in the way they want them delivered. Executives in larger companies face the challenge of engaging their people in both the "whats" and the "hows" of their vision when they cannot personally, through direct leadership, motivate and align all of their employees. Whereas most leadership researchers have paid attention to the more direct form of leadership, few have paid attention to more indirect forms of leadership. As mentioned previously, Dubin (1979) referred to this distinction between direct and indirect leadership when he discussed leadership *in* and leadership *of* organizations. We refer to the leadership *of* organizations when we talk about leading through strategy, structures, and systems. The higher up one moves in organizations, the more leaders' impact will come through their indirect rather than their direct leadership approach.

In our book we have touched on only a small subset of topics where leaders want and need to exercise such indirect leadership. However, we

Being There Even When You Are Not: Leading Through Strategy, Structures, and Systems
Monographs in Leadership and Management, Volume 4, 289–300
Copyright © 2007 by Elsevier Ltd.
ISSN: 1479-3571/doi:10.1016/S1479-3571(07)04016-3
All rights of reproduction in any form reserved

venture to suggest that most senior leaders would place the topics we have discussed – leadership development, knowledge management, management of meaning, leader discretion, cascading leadership, and leading in complex environments – high on a list of important leadership topics. We have also, in the application chapters, touched on only a small subset of tools at leaders' disposal to lead through strategy, structures, and systems in these important areas. Below we briefly review what we have learned from these theoretical and application chapters. We then move on to future directions that leadership should take.

LESSONS LEARNED

Developing Leadership Capacity

A key question with which many senior executives struggle concerns the development of future generations of leaders throughout their organizations. Because these senior leaders realize that they cannot personally groom these next generations of leaders, they have started to explore what conditions will make the leaders of the future "emerge." They face the challenge of creating conditions that simultaneously provide opportunities for people to demonstrate their leadership potential and that keep the current business running well. Day, in Chapter 2 of Part 1 of the book, proposed the social architecture most conducive to such leader development. His social architecture has three main pillars: low power distance, psychological safety, and a learning orientation. The two application chapters in this part of the book presented two ways of building such a social architecture for leader development.

In Chapter 3, Van Velsor and O'Connor showed how a large US service organization created such conditions by combining leadership training with important real-life projects executed by cross-functional teams with accountability and exposure to senior executives. In Chapter 4, Broeckx and Hooijberg showed how Nestlé created such conditions with its Nestlé on the Move program. The program shaped conditions that increase the chances that people throughout the organization will contribute more insight and initiative to the organization. Nestlé on the Move, in a sense, forces managers to rely more on the insight and initiative of their people. It does so by removing layers from the organization so that managers face an increasing span of control. As their span of control increases, their opportunities to micromanage decrease and, therefore, they have to rely more on the insights and initiatives of the people who report to them.

Knowledge Management

Ideas and knowledge increasingly represent the key assets of companies. Even companies that operate in asset-intensive industries in the more traditional sense of the word, are more inclined to see new ideas and knowledge as the key to competitive advantage and success. In his theoretical introduction to Part 2 of the book Boal, in Chapter 5, described various strategies that leaders can employ to obtain new ideas and to create shared knowledge. He especially stressed the use of organizational networks for both learning and dissemination of knowledge. Ichijo in Chapter 6 showed how Sharp's focus on LCD panels both captured the benefits of Boal's approach and had some limitations. The limitations of the network approach became clear in the sense that creating opportunities for knowledge creation and dissemination through networks can also result in key knowledge leaking to competitors. Because using organizational networks may simultaneously present opportunities and threats, we need to answer the question of how to get the benefits without the drawbacks. Part of Sharp's answer came in the form of co-locating R&D with manufacturing.

Managing Meaning

One of the most difficult tasks senior leaders face involves creating a common understanding of the environment in which the organization operates and what actions matter most. In Chapter 7, the theoretical introduction to Part 3, Shamir addressed the strategic leader's role of making meaning of the environmental context, performance, goals, means, and efficacy. In so doing, leaders enact a system of shared meanings that provides a basis for organized action. He further argued that the meaning-making role of the leader is probably the most important one in contexts in which assessment is difficult, members' involvement is segmented and incomplete, and technology or the connections between actions and results are ambiguous. Under such conditions of ambiguity, meanings are less "given" or agreed upon, and leaders' input to the construction of reality is likely to be especially important and consequential. He further suggested that the importance of management of meaning activities under such conditions stems from their real consequences for the motivation and mobilization of support, the diversion or satisfaction of stakeholders' demands, and the implementation of change in the organization.

The two application chapters in this part explored this meaning-making role of the strategic leader in two diverse contexts. In Chapter 8, Bruch,

Shamir, and Eilam-Shamir explored how the CEO used weekly e-mail letters to manage the meaning of his company's environmental context, performance, goals, means, and efficacy. Their analysis of his e-mail letters showed that the CEO moved from first brutally laying out the stark facts, and an image of a company near death, to showing improved performance and finally an image of a company on the rebound.

Using a Positive Organizational Scholarship lens, Spreitzer, Coleman, and Gruber, in Chapter 9 illustrated how University of Michigan President Mary Sue Coleman handled an affirmative action lawsuit filed against the university's undergraduate and law school admissions policies. They showed how having a purpose in mind, appreciating divergent views and having a willingness and even a desire to be a beacon for the future can bring a divergent group of stakeholders together. In doing so, President Coleman showed she understood that she represented the face of the university and that she had to focus on what the university needed most. In the end, the affirmative action lawsuits and President Coleman's handling of them resulted in a clear image of the University of Michigan for all stakeholders as a public institution that values diversity.

Leadership Discretion

In most of our work we seem to operate on the assumption that leaders will act in the best interests of the organization. We of course know that not all leaders do this. In Chapter 10, the theoretical introduction to Part 4, Kaiser and Hogan explored how to give senior leaders maximum opportunity to contribute to the success of their organizations while at the same time finding ways to prevent personality variables from having a negative impact. They showed many examples of how personality variables can have a negative impact on organizational performance and ended with suggestions for how organizations can prevent, or at least minimize, such negative influences.

In the two application chapters, we saw examples of both the dark and the bright sides of leader discretion. On one hand, Santalainen and Baliga, in Chapter 11, illustrated how a leader with a great amount of discretion used that discretion primarily to enhance and sustain his own leadership status and associated privileges. They showed, furthermore, that external monitors did not intervene because the organization performed well financially. Santalainen and Baliga apply the label "healthy-sick organization" in such instances. Their chapter enhanced our ability to spot the dark side before it brings down the organization.

Billington and Barnett Berg, on the other hand, in Chapter 12, showed the bright side of leader discretion. They illustrated how leaders, when given an organization in deep trouble, can use their discretion to build a strategy with supporting structures and systems that engage employees.

The two application chapters highlighted the importance of Kaiser and Hogan's recommendation to pay serious attention to the personality of senior leaders in selection and succession issues.

Cascading Vision for Real Commitment

In Part 5 we addressed the key overall theme of the book. In the theoretical introduction, Chapter 13, Antonakis and Hooijberg presented a model for how senior leaders can get the leaders of all parts of the organization engaged in the organization's vision and strategy and their implementation. Essential parts of the model are dialogue around the key issues the organization needs to resolve in order to attain the vision; top management commitment to these issues; and serious follow-up on their execution.

The application chapters described how this model works in two very different environments. In Chapter 14, Malnight and Keys told how CEO Andersen at Carlsberg formulated and then rolled out his vision. They showed how Andersen used multiple serious dialogue sessions with the regional leaders to develop their must-win battles. This involvement of the regional leaders created important ownership of the must-win battles, which Andersen then supported with resources, extensive communication, and key performance indicators.

In Chapter 15, Verburgh and Lane followed Luc Verburgh through his first two years as CEO of Wellant College in the Netherlands. They showed how Verburgh used extensive dialogue with his regional directors as well as certain structural changes to introduce and implement a new learning philosophy. As the new learning philosophy placed more responsibility for learning on the students, so the supporting philosophy had to place more responsibility on the local directors and teachers. The CEO and the regional directors then had to find ways to enable these local directors and teachers to create and support such an active learning environment.

Leadership in Complex Environments

In Chapter 16, Marion and Uhl-Bien challenged the more traditional leader-centric view of leadership in general and especially the view that leaders at the top need to set the vision and strategy for the organization. Instead they argued for the creation of adaptive organizations where strategy can come from the bottom of the organization and where organizations form cooperative relationships with other organizations in their industry. They maintained that organizations that foster this type of cooperation and adaptiveness have a greater chance of success in the long run than organizations that solely seek to outdo their competitors.

UNLEASHING HUMAN POTENTIAL

In our introduction we defined leadership as getting performance beyond expectations through people. In order to get performance beyond expectations, one needs to really unleash all of the available human potential. Senior leaders will not achieve grand visions and strategies if they cannot engage the hearts and minds of (most of) their organizations' members. Only when they do so, can they hope to harness all of the available knowledge, experience, insight, ideas, and effort and bring it to bear on realizing said vision and strategy. All of the chapters explored ways in which senior leaders can unleash this human potential through strategy, structures, and systems.

While leadership researchers have focused on variables such as charisma, intellectual stimulation, inspirational motivation, idealized influence, and individualized consideration (i.e., the "full-range" leadership model, e.g., Bass & Avolio, 1994), we find that such approaches are limited when it comes to understanding how senior leaders can gain commitment from people in large organizations. To reach and gain commitment from people in large, international organizations, leaders need to use strategy, structures, and systems in addition to the direct influence approaches such as those of the full-range leadership model.

This book has made a start toward better understanding how leaders create the conditions that stimulate others to contribute meaningfully to the overarching goals of the organization. Throughout the book we have seen examples of how leaders at the top have created such conditions. When we talk about "creating conditions" we are really referring to the strategic leader's role as architect of the organization. We have explored how strategic leaders – in this role as architect – create organizations where leaders develop, knowledge is created and disseminated, meaning is shaped and shared, discretionary power gets (mis)managed, and vision gets cascaded – and throughout it all the organizations remain adaptive to the complex environments in which they operate. In this way, these strategic leaders engaged and aligned far more people than they could have ever reached by themselves through a direct leadership approach.

FUTURE DIRECTIONS

Whereas researchers such as Dubin (1979) and Katz and Kahn (1978) referred to the importance of indirect leadership or the leadership *of* organizations, leadership researchers have focused primarily on direct leadership or leadership *in* organizations. Leadership researchers now need to address this imbalance. One cannot run global organizations with direct leadership alone. Indirect forms of leadership need to be used to engage those who cannot be touched personally. As we mentioned in Chapter 1, research on leadership-at-a-distance, strategic and instrumental leadership and related constructs (e.g., Antonakis & Atwater, 2002; Antonakis & House, 2004; Boal & Hooijberg, 2000; Hunt, 1991; Napier & Ferris, 1993; Waldman & Yammarino, 1999; Yammarino, 1994) have started to move the leadership field in the direction of exploring indirect forms of leadership. We now need to look deeper at issues around the topics discussed in this book, as well as topics such as empowerment, compensation, information systems, succession planning, and training and development. We briefly elaborate what kind of research we would like to see in these areas.

Empowerment

Empowerment has received quite a bit of attention from leadership researchers. Within this topic, some academics and practitioners have explored the role they believe organizational structures, policies, and practices play in bringing about high levels of empowerment (e.g., Bennis & Nanus, 1985; Blanchard, Carlos, & Randolph, 1999; Block, 1987). Drawing on extensive experience with a set of organizations implementing an empowerment strategy, Blanchard and his colleagues (Blanchard et al., 1999; Randolph, 1995) identified three key organizational practices associated with empowerment: information sharing, autonomy through boundaries, and team accountability. One of the few empirical articles on the topic comes from Spreitzer (1996). She explored and found positive relationships between social structural characteristics at the level of the work unit (perceptions of role ambiguity, span of control, socio-political support, access to information and resources, and work unit climate) and feelings of empowerment. A recent paper by Seibert, Silver, and Randolph (2004) further explored the role of organizational climate on feelings of empowerment. Another aspect that should also be considered is the personality profile of individuals who can be empowered (or given autonomy, Barrick & Mount, 1993); indeed, empowerment does not work for everyone and is moderated by personality factors such as extraversion (extraverts do better when empowered). However, we have found little additional empirical evidence in this area.

Compensation

While management researchers have explored the relationship between executive pay and company performance, relatively few have explored the impact of pay differentials between executives and other staff on overall motivation. Some exceptions come from the work by Jaques (1996), and Chen and his colleagues (Chen, Choi, & Chi, 2002; Choi & Chen, 2004) who did look at justice perceptions associated with pay differences between locals and expatriates. Gardner, Van Dyne, and Pierce (2004) found a relationship between pay levels and organization-based self-esteem and then between organization-based self-esteem and performance. This suggests that pay levels have an indirect effect on employee motivation and performance. Other interesting work takes place outside of the management area in such domains as labor law and political economy. For example, Lazear (1989), in the *Journal of Political Economy*, explored the relationship between compressed salary structures and morale and cooperative behavior. It seems time for management researchers to seriously explore the relationship between compensation schemes and such variables as morale, involvement, initiative, and commitment.

Information Systems

Few researchers have explored the relationship between information systems and employee motivation and performance, even though researchers in areas such as empowerment and commitment mention the importance of good information management systems. The work of Marchand, Kettinger, and Rollins (2002) is an exception. In an extensive empirical study they found strong relationships between information orientation (consisting of information behavior and values, information management practices, and IT practices) and business performance. Most practitioners and researchers have looked at information systems only as systems for storing and sharing information. We would encourage researchers to explore the potential of information systems as leadership tools. A small example might shed light on what we mean. The CEO of a French-speaking bank recently decided that the main sites of the bank's intranet would have all the text in English. This decision made many people angry. However, the CEO insisted, saying, "If our strategy says that we want to become a meaningful international player we need to conduct business in English." He realized that setting the language of the bank's main intranet sites to English sent a powerful message in support of that strategy.

Succession Planning

Whereas family business researchers have paid significant attention to succession planning, management researchers have given it more limited attention and, when they have done so, have primarily focused on CEO succession planning (e.g., Biggs, 2004; Davidson, Nemec, & Worrell, 2001; Shen & Cannella, 2003). Shen and Cannella (2003), for example, present interesting results regarding the relationship between relay succession planning and shareholder reactions and Davidson et al. (2001) explored the relationship between succession planning and shareholder wealth. We believe that succession planning throughout an organization – not just for the office of the CEO – will serve as a powerful leadership tool for both engaging people and enhancing the organization's performance. Rothwell (2005), for example, gives an extensive overview of succession planning systems and links such succession planning to building talent. Building talent can take place because senior executives will need to clarify what competencies, experiences, and assignments matter. This type of clarification will both increase the number of people with the right qualifications and energize people as they can clearly see the path to progression in the company.

Training and Development

Companies and individuals spend a considerable amount of money on management and leadership training; however, researchers have not found a clear correlation between training and performance beyond that which is explained by the cognitive ability of the trainee (Schmidt & Hunter, 1998). Inroads are being made and researchers are exploring how other individual-level variables affect training success. For example, Kozlowski et al. (2001) examined the effects of training goals and goal orientation traits on multi-dimensional training outcomes and performance adaptability. Alvarez, Salas, and Garofano (2004) and Wang and Wilcox (2006) conducted reviews of training effectiveness research and report several variables that relate positively to post-training effectiveness, such as pre-training self-efficacy, experience, post-training mastery orientation, learning principles, and post-training interventions. We would like to see this research go even further and look at the organizational structures and systems that influence effective and successful transfer to the organization of knowledge and skills acquired during training programs.

From our own experience in executive education, we know that participants do not always feel that the organization offers them important opportunities to apply new knowledge and skills. This lack of application then results in frustration and even departures from the organization! This type of research then would focus on what companies can do to ensure that the learning from the training finds useful outlets. For example, organizations might link training to new job challenges, job rotation, more responsibility, and so on.

CONCLUSION

It is our hope that this book broadens the thinking of academics and practitioners alike around getting performance beyond expectations through people. We hope it broadens readers' thinking about strategic leadership to include both direct and indirect leadership, and leadership *of* and *in* organizations. We also hope that the juxtaposition of theoretical thinking with practical application provides the reader with rich insights into the practical and theoretical benefits that can be had in this field. Like pilots, leaders must be able to switch on the organizational autopilot for most of the flight because they cannot constantly and continuously steer the organization toward its destination. Leaders need to be there and intervene when there is turbulence, when they are charting a new course, taking off, or landing. In all other instances, the plane should be able to get to the destination with a minimum of intervention from the leader. The better the navigating equipment, the better the plane, and the better the team, the more pilots are able to trust that the plane will fly in the right direction even when they are not there.

REFERENCES

Alvarez, K., Salas, E., & Garofano, C. M. (2004). An integrated model of training evaluation and effectiveness. *Human Resource Development Review, 3*(4), 385–416.

Antonakis, J., & Atwater, L. (2002). Leader distance: A review and a proposed theory. *The Leadership Quarterly, 13*, 673–704.

Antonakis, J., & House, R. J. (2004). On instrumental leadership: Beyond transactions and transformations. Paper presented at the Gallup Leadership Institute conference, University of Nebraska.

Barrick, M. R., & Mount, M. K. (1993). Autonomy as a moderator of the relationships between the Big Five personality dimensions and job performance. *Journal of Applied Psychology, 78*, 111–118.

Bass, B. M., & Avolio, B. J. (Eds) (1994). *Improving organizational effectiveness through transformational leadership*. Thousand Oaks, CA: Sage.

Bennis, W., & Nanus, B. (1985). *Leaders*. New York, NY: Harper & Row.

Biggs, E. L. (2004). CEO succession planning: An emerging challenge for boards of directors. *Academy of Management Executive, 18*(1), 105–107.

Blanchard, K. H., Carlos, J. P., & Randolph, W. A. (1999). *The 3 keys to empowerment*. San Francisco, CA: Berrett-Koehler Publishers.

Block, P. (1987). *The empowered manager: Positive political skills at work*. San Francisco, CA: Jossey-Bass.

Boal, K. B., & Hooijberg, R. (2000). Strategic leadership research: Moving on. *The Leadership Quarterly, 11*, 515–550.

Chen, C. C., Choi, J., & Chi, S.-C. (2002). Making justice sense of local-expatriate compensation disparity: Mitigation by local referents, ideological explanations, and interpersonal sensitivity in China – foreign joint ventures. *Academy of Management Journal, 45*(4), 807–817.

Choi, J., & Chen, C. C. (2004). Event and entity justice perceptions: Distributive justice and compensation system fairness in international joint ventures. *Academy of Management Proceedings*, F1–F6.

Davidson, W. N., Nemec, C., & Worrell, D. L. (2001). Succession planning vs. agency theory: A test of Harris and Helfat's interpretation of plurality announcement market returns. *Strategic Management Journal, 22*(2), 179–184.

Dubin, R. (1979). Metaphors of leadership: An overview. In: J. G. Hunt & L. L. Larson (Eds), *Crosscurrents in leadership* (pp. 225–238). Carbondale, IL: Southern Illinois University Press.

Gardner, D. G., Van Dyne, L., & Pierce, J. L. (2004). The effects of pay level on organization-based self-esteem and performance: A field study. *Journal of Occupational and Organizational Psychology, 77*, 307–322.

Hunt, J. G. (1991). *Leadership: A new synthesis*. Newbury Park, CA: Sage.

Jaques, E. (1996). *Requisite organization: A total system for effective managerial organization and managerial leadership for the 21st century*. Arlington, VA: Cason Hall & Co. Publishers.

Katz, D., & Kahn, R. L. (1978). *The social psychology of organizations* (2nd ed.). New York: Wiley.

Kozlowski, S. W. J., Gully, S. M., Brown, K. M., Salas, E., Smith, E. M., & Nason, E. R. (2001). Effects of training goals and goal orientation traits on multidimensional training outcomes and performance adaptability. *Organizational Behavior and Human Decision Processes, 85*(1), 1–23.

Lazear, E. (1989). Pay equality and industrial politics. *Journal of Political Economy, 3*(June), 561–580.

300   ROBERT HOOIJBERG ET AL.

Marchand, D. A., Kettinger, W. J., & Rollins, J. D. (2002). *Information orientation: The link to business performance*. Oxford, UK: Oxford University Press.

Napier, B. J., & Ferris, G. R. (1993). Distance in organizations. *Human Resource Management Review, 3*, 321–357.

Randolph, W. A. (1995). Navigating the journey to empowerment. *Organizational Dynamics, 24*(4), 19–32.

Rothwell, W. J. (2005). *Effective succession planning*. New York, NY: AMACOM.

Schmidt, F. L., & Hunter, J. E. (1998). The validity and utility of selection methods in personnel psychology: Practical and theoretical implications of 85 years of research findings. *Psychological Bulletin, 124*, 262–274.

Seibert, S. E., Silver, S. R., & Randolph, W. A. (2004). Taking empowerment to the next level: A multiple-level model of empowerment, performance and satisfaction. *Academy of Management Journal, 47*(3), 332–349.

Shen, W., & Cannella, A. A. (2003). Will succession planning increase shareholder wealth? Evidence from investor reactions to relay CEO successions. *Strategic Management Journal, 24*(2), 191–198.

Spreitzer, G. M. (1996). Social structural characteristics of psychological empowerment. *Academy of Management Journal, 39*(2), 483–504.

Waldman, D. A., & Yammarino, F. J. (1999). CEO charismatic leadership: Levels-of-management and levels-of-analysis effects. *Academy of Management Review, 24*(2), 266–285.

Wang, G. G., & Wilcox, D. (2006). Training and evaluation: Knowing more than is practiced. *Advances in Developing Human Resources, 8*(4), 528–539.

Yammarino, F. J. (1994). Indirect leadership: Transformational leadership at a distance. In: B. M. Bass & B. J. Avolio (Eds), *Improving organizational effectiveness through transformational leadership* (pp. 26–47). Thousand Oaks, CA: Sage.

ABOUT THE AUTHORS

John Antonakis (PhD, Walden University) is professor of Organizational Behavior at the Faculty of Management and Economics of the University of Lausanne, Switzerland. His research is centered on individual-difference antecedents of effective leadership, the measurement of leadership, and the links between context and leadership as applied to neocharismatic and transformational leadership models, and the development of leadership.

B.R. Baliga (DBA, Kent State University) is the John B. McKinnon Professor of Management at the Babcock Graduate School of Management, Wake Forest University. He earned his BE from the University of Madras and a PGDBA from the Indian Institute of Management, Ahmedabad. Ram's teaching and research interests are in the areas of strategic management, strategic transformation, international marketing, and international management. His research has been published in many of the major academic journals in management and he is the co-author of three books: *Emerging Leadership Vistas, Tables are Turning: German and Japanese Multinational Companies in the United States* and *Quest for Survival and Growth.*

Michèle Barnett Berg (BA in psychology, University of California at Santa Cruz) has worked with IMD, in Lausanne, Switzerland, as a consultant since 2004. There, she assists MBAs as a career strategy coach and works with professors on research and writing projects that focus on innovation and leadership. Prior to IMD, Michèle spent 12 years in executive recruiting and consulting. She worked for a large international executive search firm where she completed a variety of senior level searches for the advanced technology and venture capital practices. While in consulting she worked with private and public sector clients on organizational design issues, human capital optimization, and restructuring.

Corey Billington (PhD, Stanford University) is professor of Procurement and Operations Management at IMD in Lausanne, Switzerland. Prior to this Corey, a pioneer and leader in supply chain innovation and procurement practices, was vice president of supply chain services at Hewlett-Packard (HP) where he managed procurement and central engineering. Among his previous roles, Corey was executive director of strategic planning and modeling, serving as a key pioneer of HP's approach to supply chain management. In addition, Corey managed a design company with clients in consumer goods, high-tech, and services. He was also a consulting associate professor at Stanford University's school of engineering in the department of management and engineering. Corey's focus on supply chain stems from a desire and ability to constantly innovate new processes, products, and business methods. He has written numerous articles and case studies on the subject.

Kimberly B. Boal (PhD, University of Wisconsin) is the Rawls Professor of Management at Texas Tech University. Kim was co-editor-in-chief of the *Journal of Management Inquiry* from 1997 to 2006. He served on the Board of Governors of the Academy of Management from 2001 to 2004, and as president of the Western Academy of Management in 2000. He was twice awarded the Joan G. Dahl Presidential Award by the Western Academy of Management. His work has appeared in the *Academy of Management Review*, *Administrative Science Quarterly*, the *Journal of Management*, *Leadership Quarterly*, and the *Strategic Management Journal* as well as in other journals and as book chapters.

Paul Broeckx (PhD, University of Louvain, Belgium) is director of Nestlé's Corporate Human Resources division. He rejoined Nestlé headquarters in 1999 after serving as corporate human resources director and executive vice-president North America at SGS. Before that, Paul held various positions at Nestlé.

Heike Bruch (PhD, University of Hanover, Germany) is Professor of Leadership and Director of the Institute for Leadership and Human Resources Management of the University of St. Gallen, Switzerland. Her primary research focus is on leadership and organizational energy. She is Academic Director of the Organizational Energy Program (OEP).

Mary Sue Coleman (PhD, University of North Carolina) has led the University of Michigan since being appointed its 13th president in August 2002. As president, she has unveiled several major initiatives that will have an impact on future generations of students, the intellectual life of the campus, and society at large. These include campus initiatives that will examine student residential life, the interdisciplinary richness of the U-M, ethics in our society, and issues related to health care. For 19 years she was a member of the biochemistry faculty at the University of Kentucky. Her work in the sciences led her to administrative appointments at the University of North Carolina at Chapel Hill and the University of New Mexico, where she served as provost and vice president for academic affairs. From 1995 to 2002, she was president of the University of Iowa.

David V. Day (PhD, University of Akron) is professor of Organizational Behavior in the Lee Kong Chian School of Business, Singapore Management University. Prior to joining SMU, he was a professor of Industrial-Organizational Psychology and director of Graduate Training at The Pennsylvania State University, University Park, PA. He has published more than 50 journal articles and book chapters, many pertaining to the core topics of leadership and leadership development. He serves on the editorial boards of *Human Performance*, *Journal of Applied Psychology*, *Journal of Management*, and *Personnel Psychology*; and also serves as an associate editor of *Leadership Quarterly* and *Human Resource Management Review*. David is the lead editor on a recently published book, *Leader Development for Transforming Organizations: Growing Leaders for Tomorrow* (Lawrence Erlbaum Associates, 2004). He is a Fellow of the American Psychological Association.

Galit Eilam-Shamir (PhD, Hebrew University of Jerusalem) is senior lecturer and head of the Organizational Management MBA specialization at Ono College, Israel. Her main research focus is on organizational change.

Daniel A. Gruber (MILR/MBA, Cornell University) is a doctoral candidate in the Management and Organizations department at the University of Michigan's Stephen M. Ross School of Business. Dan is a graduate of Washington University in St. Louis, where he earned his undergraduate degree in business administration, and Cornell University, where he completed a Master's degree in business administration and a Master's degree in industrial and labor relations. Dan's research interests include organizational resilience, high reliability organizations, and the fusion of sensemaking and decision making.

Robert Hogan (PhD, University of California, Berkeley) is president of Hogan Assessment Systems and an international authority on personality assessment, leadership, and organizational effectiveness. He was McFarlin Professor and Chair of the Department of Psychology at the University of Tulsa for 14 years. Prior to that, he was Professor of Psychology and Social Relations at The Johns Hopkins University. He has received a number of research and teaching awards, and is the editor of the *Handbook of Personality Psychology* and author of the Hogan Personality Inventory. Robert is the author of more than 300 journal articles, chapters, and books. He is widely credited with demonstrating how careful attention to personality factors can influence organizational effectiveness in a variety of areas – ranging from organizational climate and leadership to selection and effective team performance. He is a fellow of the American Psychological Association and the Society for Industrial/Organizational Psychology.

Robert Hooijberg (PhD, University of Michigan) is professor of Organizational Behavior at IMD in Lausanne, Switzerland. His research, teaching, and consulting focus on leadership and 360-degree feedback, negotiations, team building, and organizational culture. His research has appeared in journals such as *Leadership Quarterly*, the *Journal of Management, Human Relations, Organization Science, Human Resource Management, Hospital and Health Services Administration, Journal of Applied Social Psychology*, the *Journal of Management Education, Administration and Society*, the *International Journal of Organizational Analysis*, and the *Journal of Organizational Behavior*. He received his BA and MA from the University of Nijmegen, The Netherlands.

James G. (Jerry) Hunt (PhD, University of Illinois) is Paul Whitfield Horn, professor of Management and Director Emeritus of the Institute for Leadership Research at Texas Tech University. He is a Fellow of the Academy of Management and Southern Management Association and has authored, co-authored, edited or co-edited more than 20 books and monographs and nearly 200 articles, book chapters, and related materials. His current interests are dynamic approaches to organizational behavior and leadership and the sociology of science of management.

Kazuo Ichijo (PhD, University of Michigan) is Professor of Organizational Behavior and Management at IMD in Lausanne, Switzerland. He also is at the Graduate School of International Corporate Strategy at Hitotsubashi University in Tokyo. He has written two books: *Enabling Knowledge Creation: How to Unlock the Mystery of Tacit Knowledge and Release* *the Power of Innovation* (2000) and *Knowledge Creation and Management: New Challenges for Managers* (2006), both published by Oxford University Press.

Robert B. Kaiser (MS in organizational psychology, Illinois State University) is a partner with Kaplan DeVries Inc. He began his career at the Center for Creative Leadership, studying how executives are hired. He joined Kaplan DeVries in 1997 to expand the firm's research and development capabilities. Rob also has a coaching practice; his specialty is helping high potentials prepare for the executive suite. And he provides unique research-based services like developing custom leadership models and talent management tools for organizations such as Motorola and Unilever. He edited the book *Filling the Leadership Pipeline* (Center for Creative Leadership, 2005) and is the co-author, with Bob Kaplan, of *The Versatile Leader: Make the Most of Your Strengths – Without Overdoing It* (Pfeifer/Wiley, 2006). He lives in North Carolina with Molly and their kids, Claire and Ben.

Tracey Keys (MBA, The Wharton School) has 20 years of consulting and management experience, focused on complex international strategy and organizational issues. Previously, she held senior roles at the BBC and Booz Allen Hamilton, as well as advising several successful start-ups. With Peter Killing and Tom Malnight, Tracey is co-author of the book *Must-Win Battles*, and contributor and co-editor with Professor Paul Strebel of *Mastering Executive Education: How to Combine Content with Context and Emotion, The IMD Guide* (FT Prentice Hall, 2005). She has also co-authored several articles and case studies. Tracey is a Fulbright Scholar and was distinguished as a Palmer Scholar at Wharton.

Nancy Lane (MSc, London School of Economics) is a researcher at IMD in Lausanne, Switzerland, whose work focuses on coaching effectiveness and leadership. Before joining IMD she worked in the financial services industry. She earned her BA in Economics from the University of California at Berkeley.

Tom Malnight (DBA, Harvard Business School) is a professor of Strategy at IMD in Lausanne, Switzerland, whose work focuses on complex strategic and organizational challenges. He has worked extensively with management teams across a range of organizations, including Unilever, A. P. Moller-Maersk Group, Carlsberg, and Masterfoods, among others, who are creating winning strategies using the must-win battle concepts. At IMD, Tom directs the Managing Corporate Resources program, as well as numerous company-specific programs. Over the past 20 years, he has written books, including *Must-Win Battles, Creating the Focus You Need to Achieve Your Key Business Goals* (with Peter Killing and Tracey Keys, FT Prentice Hall, 2005), as well as many articles on strategy, change, and leadership. Tom previously taught at The Wharton School after working for Mitsubishi International Corporation for 10 years.

Russ Marion (PhD, North Carolina at Chapel Hill) is Professor of Educational Leadership at Clemson University. He is the author of *The Edge of Organization* (1999), *Leadership in Education* (2001), and "Leadership in Complex Organizations" (*The Leadership Quarterly*). He is currently co-editor of a special edition on Complexity Leadership for *The Leadership Quarterly*, and is co-editor of a volume of *Leadership Horizons: The Series*. He co-organized workshops on complexity leadership at the Center for Creative Leadership and at George Washington University. Russ has presented on complexity leadership at the India Institute of Technology, IMD in Lausanne, Switzerland, and in workshops on destructing complex movements at the US Department of Defense.

Patricia M.G. O'Connor (MBA) serves as research director, Emerging Leadership Practices at the Center for Creative Leadership (Singapore campus). Since joining CCL in 1994, she has served in both management and senior faculty roles. Her current work examines the development of interdependent leadership practices and beliefs in complex contexts. Patricia is also a specialist in action learning leadership methodology. She has applied the methodology in a variety of settings, producing both developmental changes in leadership practices and innovation outcomes of tangible benefit to her client organizations.

Timo J. Santalainen (Dr. Sc. (Econ.) and Lic. Pol. Sc.) has a career approach that implies three perspectives: academia (A), practical business (B), and consulting (C). He currently works as President of STRATNET, a Geneva-based network of strategy advisors, and Adjunct Professor of Strategy and International Management at Helsinki School of Economics. His previous academic positions include professorships at Thunderbird Graduate School of International Management, Texas Tech University, and Management Centre Europe. He has held senior executive positions in banking and retailing in Finland, and senior consultant positions at MANNET (Geneva) and S.A.M.I. (Finland). Timo's most recent field of interest is strategic management and thinking in transformational and parastatal organizations such as telecommunications, energy, sports, public and professional services, and research. He has been an advisor on strategy and a board member for many of these organizations throughout the world. He is also a founding member of the Strategic Management Society and a Senior Member of the Academy of Management. He is the author or co-author of eight books, numerous chapters in books, and articles in leading international publications.

Boas Shamir (PhD, London School of Economics and Political Sciences) is the Dean of Social Sciences, Hebrew University of Jerusalem, Israel. His main research focus is on leadership in organizations.

Gretchen M. Spreitzer (PhD, University of Michigan) is professor of Management and Organizations at the Stephen M. Ross School of Business at the University of Michigan. Her research has focused on employee empowerment and leadership development, particularly during times of change. At Michigan, she is part of the Center for Positive Organizational Scholarship, where her recent research is on enabling employee thriving at work.

Mary Uhl-Bien (PhD, University of Cincinnati) is the Howard Hawks Chair in Business Ethics and Leadership and the associate director of the Gallup Leadership Institute at the University of Nebraska-Lincoln. She has published articles on leadership (e.g., relational leadership theory, leader-member exchange, social exchange, and complexity leadership) in leading national and international journals, including *Academy of Management Journal, Journal of Applied Psychology, Journal of Management, Human Relations*, and *The Leadership Quarterly*. She is senior editor of the Leadership Horizons Series published by Information Age Publishing, and serves on the editorial boards of *The Leadership Quarterly* and the *Academy of Management Journal*. She has consulted with organizations, including State Farm Insurance, Walt Disney World, the US Fish & Wildlife Service, British Petroleum, and the General Accounting Office.

Ellen Van Velsor (PhD, University of Florida) is a senior fellow and group director at the Center for Creative Leadership in Greensboro, NC. She has expertise in the use and impact of feedback-intensive programs and 360-degree feedback, gender differences in leader development, how managers learn from experience, and the dynamics of executive derailment. Her current research focuses on leadership practices and processes related to successful execution of sustainability/social responsibility strategies, and on how Asian leaders learn, grow, and change as a result of their experiences. Ellen is an editor of the Center for Creative Leadership's *Handbook of Leadership Development* (1998, 2003), and co-author of *Breaking the Glass Ceiling: Can Women Reach the Top of America's Largest Corporations?* (1987, 1991).

Luc Verburgh (PhD, Nijmegen University, the Netherlands) is currently chairman of the executive team of a vocational educational institution with over 1,500 employees. Prior to that, he was responsible for various businesses and business units both nationally and internationally. Part of this was in the call center industry, where he was responsible for activities in various European countries. Before this, he worked in the airline industry and ran the Dutch national super-computer center. After graduation, he started his career at Accenture, where he worked on projects in the area of strategy and change management. Luc currently resides in the Netherlands.

AUTHOR INDEX

SUBJECT INDEX

Printed in the United Kingdom
by Lightning Source UK Ltd.
125201UK00002B/46-78/A